Apple pie to Waterzooi

THE AMERICAN WOMEN'S CLUB OF BRUSSELS

The American Women's Club of Brussels (AWCB)) was established to create a center for social,
cultural and philanthropic activities for its members,
to foster fellowship among American women resident in Brussels and environs and to engage in cultural
and welfare activities which contribute to closer Belgo-American understanding.
The AWCB is a non-profit "association sans but lucratif" (asbl).

All rights reserved.
No part of this publication may be reproduced in any form or by any means without the prior permission of
the American Women's Club of Brussels.

Additional copies of this book may be obtained by contacting:
The American Women's Club of Brussels
Avenue des Erables 1
1640 Rhode St. Genèse, Belgium
Telephone (+32.2) 358.47.53
Fax (+32.2) 358.47.44

Cover and Illustrations: Judy Clifford

Graphic Design: Amy Morgan at Designer Ink, Brussels
(+32.2)770.63.83

Printing and Binding: Imprimerie Poot, Brussels
(+32.2)467.30.30

Reprinted 1997, 2002

Text copyright © 1996 by The American Women's Club of Brussels
Illustrations copyright © 1996 by Judy Clifford
D/2002/7764/1

ISBN 90-806582-2-7

*T*he idea to publish a cookery book began in the spring of 1994. It had been over 15 years since the American Women's Club of Brussels (AWCB) published a cookbook, and while that book had its place in history, we wanted our new publication to reflect the energy, sophistication, vitality and vision of today's AWCB.

Americans living in Belgium have had the opportunity to discover and experience Belgian culture through the Belgian's love of fine dining and conviviality. As our lives here have evolved, we have gradually adopted many of the customs of our Belgian friends, feeling richly blessed and forever changed. This book reflects the special relationship between Americans and their home abroad as we share some of our favorite recipes and fondly embrace the regional dishes of Belgium that we have grown to love.

Hundreds of AWCB members gave their time and talents to produce this book. Our testing committee tested thousands of recipes, and selected over 300 of the best. Careful attention was paid by our Recipe Chairmen to create a

> **The purpose of a cookery book… can be no other than to increase the happiness of mankind.**
> Joseph Conrad

perfect balance and representation from both culinary traditions. Our research group searched for products and information helpful to expatriates and Belgians. In her soft-toned illustrations of the sights and tastes of Belgium, our artist captured the essence of life and the quiet beauty of this gentle country.

We hope "Apple Pie to Waterzooi" will delight you with its lovely art work, help you with food product selection and tantalize your taste buds with its delicious recipes. Here's to your happiness - Bon Appétit!

The Cookbook Committee

Cookbook Committee

Chairmen
Lisa Fischer
Louise Symmes

Editor and Writer
Kris Loeber

Recipe Chairmen
Beth Eley
Nancy Savage

Artist
Judy Clifford

Graphic Designer
Amy Morgan

Typing Production
Sandy Anhorn-Phillips

Finance
Carrie Doyle

Marketing
Linda Tesauro

Table of Contents

Appetizers	7
Soups	45
Salads	67
Seafood	103
Poultry, Game and Meat	139
Pasta, Rice and Vegetables	187
Bread and Brunch	229
Desserts	273
Acknowledgments	329
Equivalents and Measurements	332
Oven Temperatures	333
Abbreviations	333
Index	335

*A*ppetizers

Appetizers

Artichoke Dip	41
Asparagus Wrapped in Prosciutto	19
Asperges à la Flamande	20
Brie with Sun-Dried Tomatoes	36
Bruschetta	27
Caviar Pie	44
Chutney Cheese Spread	41
Crab Squares	29
Croquettes aux Crevettes Grises	24
Curry Dip	42
Egg Spread	19
Eggplant and Roasted Pepper Terrine with Parsley Sauce	16
Endive Boats with Marinated Smoked Salmon	27
Foie Gras Poêlé au Vinaigre Balsamique	22
Garlic Shrimp	17
Gâteau de Crêpes à la Florentine	11
Gâteau de Langoustines au Parfum de Curry Léger	13
Ginger Prawn Tarts	25
Green Goddess Dip	42
Herbed Tomato Tart	28
Langoustines au Curry	18
Mousse de Foie de Volaille	40
Mousseline Sauce	21
Mushroom Croustades	33
Petite Tarte aux Herbes Potagères	14
Petites Gougères	30
Phyllo Flowers	35
Poached Ray with Brunoise of Potatoes and Tomatoes	10
Roquefort Tartlets	37
Shrimp Spread	39
Smoked Chicken and Gorgonzola in Endive Spears	26
Smoked Salmon and Chèvre Canapés	31
Smoked Trout Pâté	38
Spanakopeta	34
Super Guacamole	43
Tapenade of Sun-Dried Tomatoes	44
Terrine de Poissons Fumés	9
Warm Chèvre with Red Bell Pepper Sauce	12
Wild Mushrooms on Croutons	23

SPECIAL TOPICS

Asparagus/Asperges	21
Aspic/Gelée	40
Brie en Croûte	36
Celery Root (Celeriac)	22
Dining "Chez Vous"	15
Last Minute Appetizers	32
Miniature Quiches	37
Parsley	16

Terrine de Poissons Fumés
(Smoked Fish Terrine)

Soak the gelatin sheets in cold water to cover, allowing it to become pliable. Drain the gelatin sheets, squeezing out excess water, and dissolve the gelatin in the hot, not boiling, water.

5 sheets/10 g unflavored gelatin*
1 cup + 1 tbsp/250 ml hot water
7 oz/200 g smoked trout
7 oz/200 g smoked salmon
white pepper
1 cup + 1 tbsp/250 ml heavy cream
1 (2 oz/50 g) jar red caviar

Sauce:
4 tbsp mayonnaise
2 tbsp lemon juice
7 oz/200 ml heavy cream
2 tbsp chopped fresh lemon balm, parsley or chives
salt
freshly ground pepper

Garnish:
tomato roses
salade de blé

Yield: 6 - 8 servings

In a food processor, separately purée each fish, beginning with the trout. Place the puréed fish in separate bowls and mix half of the gelatin and pepper to taste into each. Put the bowls in the refrigerator for 10 to 15 minutes to firm up, but do not let the gelatin set.

Lemon balm is called citronelle in Belgium. Whichever herb you choose, chop with a knife, not a food processor, for the prettiest presentation.

Whip the cream until stiff and fold half into each of the fish mixtures.

Oil the inside of a 1 quart/liter mold. Spoon the salmon mixture evenly on the bottom of the mold; thinly spread the caviar on top. Spread the smoked trout mixture on top of the caviar. Refrigerate at least 4 hours.

To make the sauce, mix together the mayonnaise and lemon juice. Add the remaining ingredients and stir.

Before serving, dip the mold in hot water for a few seconds and invert to unmold. Cut into generous slices. Ladle a pool of sauce on individual plates and top each with a slice of terrine. Garnish with tomato roses and salade de blé.

Variation: Substitute cooked puréed spinach for one of the fish.
* or 1 envelope powdered gelatin (see index)

Poached Ray with Brunoise of Potatoes and Tomatoes
Patrick Devos Restaurant, Bruges - Patrick Devos, Chef

To make the vinaigrette, sauté shallots in a little of the olive oil. Add the sherry vinegar, salt and pepper to taste, and the remaining olive oil. Whisk together and set aside.

2 - 3 medium potatoes
2 tbsp olive oil
4 tomatoes
salt
1 shallot, minced
splash of white wine vinegar
4 ray fillets (17 oz/500 g)
1½ tsp small capers

Peel and dice the potatoes; fry in 2 tablespoons olive oil until cooked and well browned. Peel, seed and dice the tomatoes (see index). Add to potatoes and mix with vinaigrette to taste.

To make the sauce, combine the fish stock, thyme and shallots in a pan. Add white wine and reduce. Thicken with a beurre manié (see note) made from the butter and flour. Whisk in the cream. Pour through a sieve and add the chives.

Vinaigrette:
1 shallot, chopped
3½ oz/100 ml olive oil
2 tbsp sherry vinegar
salt
freshly ground pepper

Bring a large frying pan of water to a gentle simmer. Add salt, the shallot and white wine vinegar and gently poach the ray fillets for approximately 10 minutes. Remove the fish with a slotted spoon.

To serve, make a bed of the tomato and potato mixture. Place the fish on top and sprinkle with capers. Pour sauce over the fish and garnish.

Sauce:
¼ cup/60 ml fish stock
1 tsp fresh thyme or rosemary
3 shallots, minced
3½ oz/100 ml white wine
1 tbsp/15 g butter, softened
1 tbsp flour
4 tbsp heavy cream
2 tbsp chopped fresh chives

A beurre manié is a paste made of equal proportions of softened butter and flour. Whisk it into a sauce and bring the sauce to a boil until it thickens.

Garnish:
chervil or parsley, chopped

Yield: 4 servings

Gâteau de Crêpes à la Florentine

Mornay Sauce: Melt butter and add flour. Add milk and whisk until smooth. Add cream and cook, stirring, until moderately thick. Stir in cheeses and cook until melted. Add salt and pepper to taste.

18 7"/18cm CRÊPES

Cheese Filling: Mix together all ingredients (adding milk if it seems too thick).

Mornay Sauce:
3 tbsp butter
4 tbsp flour
1½ cups/350 ml milk
½ cup/120 ml heavy cream
½ cup/120 ml grated Swiss cheese
½ cup/120 ml grated Parmesan
salt
freshly ground pepper

Spinach Filling: Cook the spinach, place in a colander and press out all the moisture. Sauté the onion in butter. Stir all filling ingredients together, reserving extra Mornay Sauce.

If you have extra spinach and cheese fillings, do not try to use it all or the layers will slide when they are heated.

To form the gâteau, evenly spread a thin layer of spinach filling on a crêpe to within ½"/1¼cm of the edge. Place the crêpe in a lightly buttered 10"/24cm shallow round baking dish. Spread another crêpe with a small amount of cheese filling. Place on top of previous layer. Continue alternating layers, ending with a spinach layer and then a plain crêpe. Cover and refrigerate.

Cheese Filling:
8 oz/225 g whipped cream cheese
4 oz/115 g whipped chive cream cheese
1 egg
1 tbsp milk (optional)

When ready to bake, heat reserved Mornay Sauce and pour over the top of the gâteau, covering completely. Bake in a preheated oven for 25 to 30 minutes. Sprinkle the additional grated cheese on top and broil until the top is flecked with brown. Let set a few minutes before cutting into wedges.

Spinach Filling:
20 oz/560 g frozen chopped spinach
1 small onion, chopped
1 tbsp butter
salt
freshly ground pepper
⅔ cup/160 ml Mornay Sauce

additional grated Swiss and Parmesan

> *An educated palate is like any of the social graces - it has to be earned.*
> Elisabeth Luard

Oven Temp: 350°F/175°C
Yield: 6 - 8 servings

Warm Chèvre with Red Bell Pepper Sauce

This beautiful first course may be prepared early in the day and cooked just before serving.

3 small red bell peppers
10 small garlic cloves
salt
freshly ground black pepper
10 oz/280 g log of mild chèvre
¾ cup/175 ml dry bread crumbs
1 tbsp minced fresh parsley
⅓ cup/80 ml freshly grated Parmesan
2 large eggs, beaten lightly

Oven Temp: 450°F/230°C
Yield: 4 servings

Roast, peel and seed the bell peppers (see index). In a food processor, purée the peppers, garlic, salt and pepper until smooth. Transfer the mixture to a small saucepan, cover and heat gently.

Cut the chèvre into rounds approximately 1"/2½cm thick, and flatten them slightly between sheets of wax paper or plastic wrap. Combine bread crumbs, parsley, and Parmesan. Dip the cheese rounds in the eggs, letting the excess drip off. Coat them in the crumb mixture and place on a baking sheet. Bake in the middle of a preheated oven for 5 minutes or until they are pale gold. Divide the sauce among 4 small plates and put the cheese rounds on top. Serve warm.

Gâteau de Langoustines au Parfum de Curry Léger
La SaliCorne - Stéphane Charlier, Chef

16 langoustines
1 tsp liquid honey (acacia)
3 tbsp/45 g butter
¼ Granny Smith apple, peeled
curry powder
chives, chopped

Cake:
8½ oz/250 ml crème fraîche
17 oz/500 ml langoustine stock
3 large eggs
salt
freshly ground pepper

Sauce:
8½ oz/250 ml langoustine stock
3½ oz/100 ml crème fraîche

Oven Temp: 325°F/165°C
Yield: 4 servings

Clean and shell the langoustines, separating the tails from the bodies, reserving heads and claws for garnish. Prepare the langoustine stock (see note).

Cake: Mix together crème fraîche, stock and eggs. Season with salt and pepper. Preheat the oven. Pour mixture into 4 oven-proof ramekins and cook in a bain marie (see index) for approximately 25 to 30 minutes.

Sauce: Pour langoustine stock into a saucepan and reduce by half. Add the crème fraîche and reduce again. Season to taste.

Dip the langoustine tails in honey and quickly fry in sizzling butter until firm, no more than 3 minutes. Keep warm.

Cut apple into fine julienne.

Unmold the langoustine cakes onto warm serving plates. Cover each with sauce. Put 4 langoustine tails on each of the cakes. Top with the apple and dust with curry powder. Decoratively arrange the reserved langoustine heads with claws around the cakes and sprinkle with chopped chives.

For langoustine stock, heat 1 quart/liter homemade or purchased good quality fish stock. Fry bodies and meat from head (reserving shell of head with tiny claws attached) in very hot olive oil, pounding the shells to crush and extract all the juice. Add 2 chopped carrots, 1 chopped onion and 2 chopped celery stalks and continue cooking for 5 minutes. Add 2 tablespoons tomato paste, a sprig of thyme and a bay leaf. Pour shell mixture into stock and simmer, uncovered for ½ hour. Strain through a very fine sieve (chinois). Measure and add water, if necessary, to make a generous 3 cups/750 ml. If time does not permit, purchase a fine quality prepared lobster stock.

Petite Tarte aux Herbes Potagères

7 oz/200 g Pâte Brisée or pâte feuilletée
2 tbsp/30 g butter
5 small leeks, minced (see note)
2 large green onions, minced
4 spinach leaves, sliced
4 sorrel leaves, sliced
4 tbsp chopped chives
salt
freshly ground pepper
6 tbsp heavy cream

Oven Temp: 400°F/200°C
Yield: 4 servings

Roll out the pastry and cut into 4 (5"/13cm) circles. Put on a cookie sheet and prick the pastry with a fork. Cover the pastry with aluminum foil and weight with beans or pie weights to keep the pastry from rising. Cook for 20 minutes in a preheated oven.

Melt 1 tablespoon of the butter and sweat the leeks and green onions. Cover and cook slowly without browning. Season with salt and pepper.

In a nonreactive saucepan, melt remaining butter and cook the sorrel and spinach over low heat until limp. Add this and the chives to the onion mixture. Continue to cook slowly for 5 minutes. Add 2 tablespoons of cream and reduce the mixture. Adjust the seasoning and spread the mixture on the cooked pastry circles.

Whip the remaining 4 tablespoons of cream. Spread on top of the tarts and broil until the top begins to brown. Serve immediately.

Variation: You may replace the chives with another herb such as chervil or tarragon.

Leeks are quite sandy so it is necessary to clean them well. Trim the root end and cut off the green top. (Reserve the tender, lighter green trimmings for stock.) If using the leeks whole, cut an X in the root ends and soak them for 30 minutes in 10 cups/2¼ liters of water mixed with 1 tablespoon of vinegar. Rinse thoroughly under cold running water. If using the leeks halved or chopped, cut the leeks in half lengthwise. Run under cold running water, fanning out the leaves and allowing the water to run in between. For chopped or sliced leeks, you may prefer to cut them up first, cover them with cold water and swish them around. Lift out of the water, drain thoroughly and dry on a towel or in a salad spinner. Two pounds of leeks, or about 1 kilo, will yield around 4 cups/950 ml of chopped leeks.

DINING "CHEZ VOUS"

Although American and Belgian food is equally enjoyable, the approach to serving the meal can be quite different. When invited to an American home for dinner, guests begin with "pass around" appetizers and drinks. These appetizers might include warm finger foods, dips, spreads or even cheese and crackers. Once this "cocktail hour" is over, diners advance to the table for a large meal of meat, vegetables and potato or other starch, followed by dessert with coffee.

When invited to dinner at a Belgian home, it is customary to send flowers in advance or bring fine Belgian chocolates/pralines. Wine, a traditional "thank you" gift in America, is only appropriate for very good friends. Guests in a Belgian home are usually offered pretzels, nuts or chips with drinks before moving À TABLE. Belgians typically serve more courses in smaller portions than Americans. The first course is called L'ENTRÉE (not to be confused with the American entrée which is the main course) and is likely to be a soup, light vegetable or fish dish, pâté or composed salad. This is followed by LE PLAT (the main course) consisting of a meat or fish with one or two vegetables. The next course might be LA SALADE (a simple green salad tossed with a light vinaigrette) and/or LE FROMAGE. (If both a salad and cheese are being served, they will be served on separate plates.) All these courses are served with baguettes or rolls. LE DESSERT is followed by the final course, LE CAFÉ, (taken in the living room) - pass the chocolates please!

A very formal Belgian dinner might begin with an AMUSE-GUEULE (tiny, tasty morsels served on very small plates) and include two PLATS - a PREMIER PLAT of fish and a SECOND PLAT of meat or poultry. Belgians are fortunate to have wonderful traiteurs (catering shops) in every town. If the entire meal is not catered, Belgians take advantage of traiteurs for a course or two in a multi-course meal and a fabulous dessert often comes from a local pâtisserie. Regardless of how many courses are served, Belgian mealtime is a leisurely opportunity for conviviality and conversation. Bon Appétit!

Eggplant and Roasted Pepper Terrine with Parsley Sauce

2 large eggplants
⅓ cup/80 ml olive oil
salt
¼ cup/60 ml black olive paste
3 red bell peppers
7 oz/200 g soft mild chèvre

Parsley Sauce:
1 cup/240 ml chopped Italian parsley
2 small garlic cloves, sliced
3 tbsp balsamic vinegar
4 tbsp water
¾ cup/175 ml extra virgin olive oil
salt
freshly ground pepper

Garnish:
parsley sprigs

Yield: 8 servings

Cut the eggplants lengthwise into ½"/1 ¼cm thick slices and arrange them in one layer on baking sheets. Brush both sides of the eggplant with the oil, and sprinkle with salt. Broil the eggplant in batches about 4"/10cm from the heat for 4 to 5 minutes on each side, or until golden and tender. Transfer to paper towels to drain. Roast, peel and seed the bell peppers (see index). Cut lengthwise into 3 sections.

Tapenade or olivada are bottled olive pastes found in specialty stores.

Line a loaf pan with plastic wrap, leaving a substantial overhang. Arrange the eggplant, olive paste, bell peppers, and chèvre in several layers, beginning and ending with eggplant. Cover with the plastic overhang, weight the terrine with a 4 lb/1 ¾ kg weight (such as a loaf pan filled with canned goods), and chill it for 24 hours or up to 3 days.

To make the sauce, purée all the sauce ingredients in a blender or food processor until very smooth. Strain through a fine sieve, pressing hard on the solids.

When ready to serve, invert the terrine and remove the plastic wrap. Cut into 1"/2 ½cm slices. Pour 2 tablespoons of sauce onto the center of each of 8 plates, tilting the plate to spread the sauce. Top with a slice of terrine and garnish each serving with parsley.

PARSLEY
- Flat-leaf or Italian parsley has a robust flavor for recipes where parsley is an assertive taste.
- Curly-leaf parsley is much more decorative and is frequently used as a garnish.
- Cilantro, also known as fresh coriander or Chinese parsley, has a more pungent taste and is frequently found in Asian and Latin American cooking.

Garlic Shrimp

Although excellent as an appetizer, this may also be served for a light supper.

1 lb/450 g uncooked large shrimp
2 tsp coarse salt
½ cup/120 ml water
2 small red chili peppers
½ cup/120 ml olive oil
2 tbsp chopped garlic
2 small bay leaves
2 tbsp minced fresh parsley

Yield: 4 servings

Peel and devein the shrimp (see note) and put them in a bowl with the salt and water. Let stand for 15 minutes.

Seed and chop chili peppers. Heat oil in a medium sauté pan over high heat. Add garlic, bay leaves and peppers and stir 1 minute. Add shrimp mixture and stir until just cooked through, about 3 minutes. Transfer to a serving dish and sprinkle with parsley. Serve with crusty French bread.

Always purchase fresh shrimp from someone you trust and do not be afraid to ask to smell one. It should have the pleasant aroma of the sea, not a fishy or ammonia smell. Keep shrimp chilled and use them as soon as possible. Before preparing, rinse the shrimp in cold water. If the heads are on, cut them off and then remove the shell. Using a sharp knife, devein the shrimp by cutting a shallow slit down the back along the length of the shrimp. Remove the black intestinal track.

> *I, on the other hand, consider the smell of garlic - raw, sautéed, roasted or stewed - to be always a promise of good food and at times practically an aphrodisiac.*
> Barbara Kafka

Langoustines au Curry
Scholteshof - Roger Souvereyns, Chef

Put the ingredients for the sauce in a small saucepan. Mix well with a whisk and reduce it slowly over medium heat until the sauce is well bound, stirring often. Cool the cream sauce over ice. Cut apple into matchsticks and fold into the sauce. Set aside.

1 tart apple, peeled
20 langoustines
2 oz/55 g bread crumbs
1 tbsp mild curry powder
1 tsp hot curry powder
½ tsp freshly ground coriander seed
4 leaves curly leaf lettuce
2 tbsp olive oil

Sauce:
3½ oz/100 ml heavy cream
3 drops of lemon juice
1 tsp beef stock
pinch of freshly grated nutmeg
salt
freshly ground pepper

Yield: 4 servings

Wash the langoustines in cold water; peel, dry and devein. Roll them in a mixture of bread crumbs, curry powders and coriander.

Arrange a leaf of lettuce, with the curly edge to the outside, on each of 4 serving plates. Spoon the apples and cream sauce next to the lettuce.

Over moderate heat, sauté the langoustines in olive oil until firm, about 2 minutes. Arrange the langoustines over the lettuce and drizzle with remaining warm olive oil from the pan.

A langoustine is a miniature variety of lobster primarily found in European waters. Most of the meat is in the tail. If you cannot find langoustine, you may substitute large shrimp (prawns).

Asparagus Wrapped in Prosciutto

It's little additional effort to make extra egg spread for tea sandwiches or stuffed eggs.

12 green asparagus spears
4 large thin slices prosciutto
1 recipe EGG SPREAD

Garnish:
hard boiled egg whites
chopped parsley
sprouts
hard boiled egg slices
sour cornichons
quartered tomatoes

Yield: 4 rolls

Spread:
2 eggs
1 tbsp mayonnaise
1 tsp Dijon mustard
1 tbsp chopped fresh parsley
1 tbsp chopped fresh chives
½ tbsp chopped fresh tarragon
salt
white pepper

Yield: ¼ cup/60 ml

Wash and trim the asparagus to even lengths. Cook in salted, boiling water until tender. Drain on paper towel and allow to cool.

Spread each slice of prosciutto with a little EGG SPREAD, place 3 asparagus tips on each slice and roll the ham around them.

Arrange on individual serving plates garnished with chopped hard boiled egg whites mixed with chopped parsley, cornichons, sprouts, slices of hard boiled eggs and quartered tomatoes.

Egg Spread

Hard boil the eggs and immediately plunge in cold water. Shell when cool. Remove the yolks and combine them with the mayonnaise, mustard and herbs to make a paste. Add salt and pepper to taste.

Prosciutto, the Italian word for ham, is a salty, flavorful ham sold in transparently thin slices. The hams are seasoned, salt-cured, air-dried and pressed. Parma ham is made from an excellent strain of pigs which are fed on the whey left over from making Parmesan cheese. San Danielle prosciutto, a pale pink, very tender and delicate ham, comes from a small town in the north of Italy where the pigs feed on acorns. Prosciutto comes in different price ranges and qualities. Use the very finest, delicately flavored prosciutto to wrap around melon or serve with fresh figs. Less delicate prosciutto is perfectly acceptable in pasta sauces and vegetable dishes.

Asperges à la Flamande

Asparagus announces the arrival of spring on every menu in Belgium. Don't be afraid to pick up the spears - two fingers only - and dip them in the sauce.

1 lb/450 g white asparagus*
8 hard boiled eggs
⅓ cup/80 ml chopped parsley
½ cup/115 g butter, melted
salt
freshly ground pepper

Yield: 4 servings

Peel the asparagus and snap off the tough base. Cook just until tender, 15 to 20 minutes, and drain well. Mash the eggs with a fork and combine with the parsley and butter.

On another occasion, try asparagus spears served warm with MOUSSELINE SAUCE or at room temperature with a mild vinaigrette.

Arrange the asparagus on 4 serving plates. Spoon the egg mixture across the middle of the spears. Sprinkle with salt and pepper and a little additional chopped parsley.

* If white asparagus is not available, fat green asparagus may be substituted.

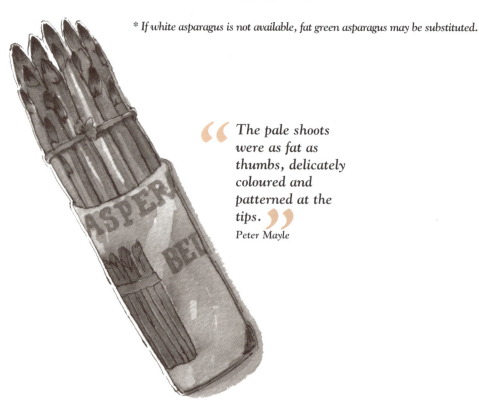

> *The pale shoots were as fat as thumbs, delicately coloured and patterned at the tips.*
> Peter Mayle

Mousseline Sauce

3 egg yolks
2 tsp water
1 - 2 tsp lemon juice
salt
freshly ground pepper
⅞ cup/200 g butter, softened

Yield: 4 servings

In a bowl set over barely simmering water, whisk together the egg yolks, water, lemon juice, salt and pepper until just warm and thickened. Do not let the water touch the bottom of the bowl or get too hot. Remove the bowl from the heat and slowly whisk in bits of the butter until all of it has been absorbed and the mixture is thick and fluffy (move on and off the heat if necessary). Keep sauce over barely warm water until ready to serve, whisking frequently.

ASPARAGUS/ASPERGE

White, violet and familiar green asparagus are in season from March to the end of June. White asparagus are particularly prized for their tender texture and mild taste. Select firm, smooth, shiny asparagus with closed tips; plump stalks are equally as tender as slim ones. Purple veining is desirable, but not present in all variations of white asparagus. To prepare white asparagus, peel from the base of the tip to within an inch or two of the bottom. Snap off the base of the stalk (it will separate at the point where the tender stalk begins). Clean, tender green asparagus does not need to be peeled.

Foie Gras Poêlé au Vinaigre Balsamique
Bistrot Du Mail - Pascal Devalkeneer, Chef

4 slices of raw foie gras (¾"/2cm thick)
1 small celeriac
2 Golden Delicious apples, peeled
salt
freshly ground pepper
1½ oz/50 ml light balsamic vinegar
3½ oz/100 ml red port wine
4 tbsp/55 g butter

Oven Temp: 400°F/200°C
Yield: 4 servings

Peel the celeriac and cut in thin slices; cut slices into triangles or diamonds. Quickly boil the celeriac for several seconds and rinse under cold running water. Thinly slice raw apples and cut into diamonds. Melt butter in a pan and sauté the celeriac slices until slightly browned. Add the apples, sauté briefly and season with salt and pepper.

Heat another sauté pan on high until it starts smoking. Season the foie gras slices with salt and pepper and quickly sear on both sides until they are crisp and browned. Finish cooking the foie gras in a preheated oven for approximately 2 minutes (the insides should remain pink). Add the vinegar to the hot sauté pan; then add the red port wine. Reduce liquid by a third. Remove from heat and whisk in butter.

Foie gras refers to the liver of a goose or a duck that has been purposely fattened. Serve foie gras as a first course, with toast or a slice of brioche and a glass of fine sauterne.

Warm 4 individual serving plates. Arrange the celeriac and apple mixture on one side of each plate and the foie gras slices on the other. Pour the sauce around the foie gras and serve immediately.

CELERY ROOT (CELERIAC)

Although celeriac, also called celery root and céleri-rave, has the mild taste of celery, it is a completely different plant. This knobby brown vegetable is firm and dense. Choose small ones since the larger roots can be woody and tough. To make the flavor more delicate and the flesh white for use in salad, peel and blanch for 2 minutes in acidulated water. Julienne into fine matchsticks and combine with mayonnaise well seasoned with mustard (Céleri-rave Rémoulade). Celeriac may also be boiled, braised, roasted or puréed. It combines well with other cooked vegetables, particularly potatoes.

Wild Mushrooms on Croutons

⅓ lb/150 g fresh wild mushrooms
9 thin slices of firm white bread
10 tbsp/140 g butter, melted
2 tbsp olive oil
½ tsp minced garlic

Garnish:
4 - 5 sprigs Italian parsley

Oven Temp: 350°F/175°C
Yield: 6 servings

This tasty, easy to prepare first course also makes a wonderful hors d'oeuvre - simply cut the bread into smaller pieces.

Remove bread crusts and cut in half diagonally. Lightly brush both sides with 8 tablespoons/115 grams of the melted butter. Bake the bread slices in a preheated oven until the croutons are golden brown, about 10 minutes.

Carefully clean and trim mushrooms. Cut them into ¼"/½cm slices. Heat the olive oil, the remaining butter, and garlic in a pan. Add the mushrooms and sauté over moderately low heat until tender, but not limp.

Put 3 croutons on each of 6 warm plates. Arrange the mushrooms on the croutons and garnish with parsley.

The secret to this recipe is the fresh wild mushrooms. Do not substitute dried. A mixture, such as boletus, chanterelles and morels, is more interesting than using just one variety.

> " Their forms and hues some solace yield, in wood, or wild, or humid field... "
> James Woodhouse

Appetizers

Croquettes aux Crevettes Grises
Les Brasseries Georges - Jean-Claude Demurger, Chef

Remove heads and shells from the shrimp and reserve them. Clean and devein shrimp (see index) and refrigerate.

Soak gelatin leaves in cold water; set aside. Over high heat, quickly fry shells and heads with a pinch of cayenne pepper; crush with spatula or pestle. Pour on cognac and flambé. When the flames have died, add milk and heat. Infuse for 10 minutes without boiling. Pour into food processor and process until fine. Strain through a fine strainer, pressing on solids.

Prepare a white sauce by melting the butter and adding the flour. Cook on low temperature for approximately 5 minutes, being careful not to let it brown. Pour in the strained liquid, whisking constantly. Drain the water from the gelatin. Add the gelatin and let melt into the sauce. Add the grated Emmentaler, mix well and fold in the shrimp. Season with salt and pepper. Pour into an oiled rectangular pan and cover with plastic wrap. Cool in the refrigerator for 12 hours.

Shape the croquettes by cutting the mixture into cubes or rolling into quenelles with your hands. Mix together the milk, eggs, salt, pepper and oil. Roll the croquettes in flour, then the egg mixture, then the bread crumbs. Heat oil in a deep fryer to 350°F/180°C and fry the croquettes for 4 to 6 minutes depending on their size. Serve with fried parsley.

Ingredients:
- 2⅕ lb/1 kg grey shrimp, with shell
- 4 gelatin leaves (see index)
- cayenne pepper
- ⅓ cup/80 ml cognac
- 1 quart/liter milk
- 6 tbsp/80 g butter
- ½ cup/70 g flour
- 3½ oz/100 g grated Emmentaler
- salt
- freshly ground pepper

- 1 cup/240 ml milk
- 4 eggs
- salt
- freshly ground pepper
- 1 tbsp peanut oil
- flour
- dry bread crumbs

- oil (for deep frying)

Garnish:
fried parsley

Yield: 6 servings

To make fried parsley, immerse washed and very well dried parsley tops in hot oil for 15 seconds. Scoop out with a slotted spoon and drain well.

Ginger Prawn Tarts

A lovely first course or serve with a salad for lunch. The filling is also wonderful in CRÊPES.

Pastry:
1 cup/130 g flour
6 tbsp/85 g butter
1 egg yolk
1 tbsp lemon juice

Filling:
2 tbsp/30 g butter
1 tbsp oil
1 tbsp peeled, grated fresh ginger
1 garlic clove, minced
1 small red chili, minced
2 tbsp flour
1¾ lb/750 g uncooked prawns, shelled
1 tbsp honey
½ cup/120 ml dry white wine
½ cup/120 ml heavy cream
2 tbsp chopped fresh chives

Garnish:
shredded coconut, toasted (optional)
additional chopped chives

Oven Temp: 400°F/200°C
Yield: 6 servings

Pastry: Sift flour into a medium bowl and rub in butter. Add egg yolk and enough lemon juice to make ingredients cling together. Knead gently on a lightly floured surface until smooth. Cover and refrigerate 30 minutes.

Divide pastry into 6 portions and roll out to line 3"/8cm tart tins. Gently ease pastry circles into tins and trim edge, leaving a little extra to allow for shrinkage. Place tins on a baking sheet. Line each pastry with foil, fill with weights and bake in a preheated oven for 7 minutes. Remove weights and foil and bake for another 7 minutes or until lightly browned. Cool to room temperature.

Filling: Heat butter and oil in a large frying pan. Add ginger, garlic and chili, stirring over medium heat for 2 minutes. Stir in the flour and cook over medium heat for 1 minute. Add prawns, honey, wine and cream. Stir over high heat until sauce boils and thickens and prawns are tender. Stir in the chives.

Pour filling into pastry cases (and sprinkle with toasted shredded coconut). Sprinkle additional chives around the tart. Serve immediately.

Pastry cases may be made a day ahead and kept in an airtight container, but the filling must be made just before serving.

Smoked Chicken and Gorgonzola in Endive Spears

This fantastic blend of flavors also looks elegant.

2 oz/55 g green beans
8 oz/225 g smoked chicken, diced
½ red bell pepper, diced
⅓ cup/80 ml chopped watercress leaves
1 large shallot, minced
1 tbsp chopped fresh tarragon
¼ cup/60 ml walnut oil
2 tbsp white wine vinegar
3 oz/85 g Gorgonzola, crumbled
3 tbsp chopped toasted walnuts
salt
freshly ground pepper
4 Belgian endives

Garnish:
watercress

Yield: 30 spears

Cook green beans in boiling water just until tender, about 4 minutes. Refresh with cold water and drain. Cut into thin crosswise slices. Combine with chicken, red pepper, watercress, shallot and tarragon. Cover and chill. (May be prepared 1 day ahead.)

Combine oil and vinegar in a small saucepan. Bring mixture just to a simmer, swirling pan occasionally. Stir in Gorgonzola. Pour over salad mixture and toss to coat. Stir in toasted walnuts. Season to taste with salt and pepper. Cover and refrigerate at least 30 minutes or up to 8 hours.

Separate endives into individual spears; clean and dry. Form mixture into balls and press into the base of each spear. Garnish each spear with watercress.

Variation: Try substituting any other smoked meat such as smoked turkey or ham, or try a blue cheese other than Gorgonzola.

Cocktails on the Terrace

Spanakopeta Triangles

∞

Phyllo Flowers

∞

Smoked Chicken and Gorgonzola in Endive Spears

∞

Petites Gougères

∞

Artichoke Dip

∞

Curry Dip (with Crudités)

∞

Brie with Sun-Dried Tomatoes

Endive Boats with Marinated Smoked Salmon

Exotic, colorful and impressive, this appetizer is a real hit for smoked salmon lovers.

Combine salmon, capers, olive oil, lemon juice, 2 tablespoons of the chives, salt and white pepper to taste, stirring until well blended. Cover and refrigerate for at least 1 hour.

7 oz/200 g smoked salmon, minced
2 tbsp capers
2 tbsp olive oil
1 tbsp fresh lemon juice
4 tbsp chopped fresh chives
salt
white pepper
4 Belgian endives
1 oz/30 g red caviar

Yield: 6 - 8 servings

Remove outer leaves from the Belgian endives. Wash gently, pat dry and chill.

When ready to serve, spoon the marinated filling into the endive leaves. Top with a little red caviar and sprinkle with remaining chives.

Bruschetta

Vine-ripened tomatoes with basil are the taste of summer. This simple but superb Italian appetizer is the perfect starter for a casual outdoor meal.

3 cups peeled, seeded, and diced tomatoes (see index)
5 tbsp chopped fresh basil
1 tbsp minced garlic
¼ cup/60 ml extra virgin olive oil
salt
freshly ground pepper
9 (¾"/2cm) slices Italian bread

Yield: 9 servings

Combine tomatoes, basil, garlic, and oil. Season to taste with salt and pepper. Let the mixture marinate at room temperature for 45 minutes. Toast the bread slices and spoon the mixture generously over them. Serve alone or with an antipasto platter.

> *Even one ripe tomato, if it is good, adds flavour…*
> Anna Del Conte

Herbed Tomato Tart

Baked flat, this is a bit like a pizza; serve in wedges or cut into squares for a cocktail party. Baked in a shallow tart pan, it may also be served on individual plates as an elegant first course with a chilled glass of dry white Burgundy.

Crust:
1¼ cups/165 g flour
¼ tsp salt
½ cup/115 g unsalted butter, chilled
4 tbsp cold water

Filling:
5 medium tomatoes
9 oz/250 g Gruyère, shredded
1 tbsp chopped fresh thyme
1 tbsp chopped fresh oregano
1 tbsp chopped fresh basil
3 tbsp freshly grated Parmesan
freshly ground black pepper

Oven Temp: 375°F/190°C
325°F/165°C
Yield: 8 - 10 servings

Crust: Mix together flour and salt and cut in butter. Add water one tablespoon at a time, mixing with a fork. Gather dough into a ball and flatten into a disk. Wrap in plastic wrap and refrigerate for 30 minutes. Roll on a floured surface to a large round and press into a shallow tart or pizza pan. Freeze for 15 minutes. Line with foil, fill with weights and bake for 15 minutes in a preheated 375°F/190°C oven. Remove weights and foil and bake for another 10 to 15 minutes until golden. Cool.

Filling: Cut tomatoes in ½"/1¼cm slices and drain on paper towels for 15 minutes. Top the crust with Gruyère and then tomatoes, slightly overlapping. Sprinkle with herbs, Parmesan and pepper to taste. Bake for 35 minutes in a preheated 325°F/165°C oven. Cool slightly before cutting.

Crab Squares

½ lb/225 g fresh mushrooms
1 small shallot, minced
1½ tbsp/45 g butter
4 eggs
1 cup/240 ml sour cream
1 cup/240 ml cottage cheese
½ cup/120 ml grated Parmesan
4 tbsp flour
¼ tsp salt
4 drops Tabasco sauce
2 cups/475 ml shredded Emmentaler
1 lb/450 g crabmeat

Oven Temp: 350°F/175°C
Yield: 6 - 8 servings

This crustless quiche is great served as an appetizer, but it could easily be served as a luncheon dish.

Thinly slice mushrooms and sauté them with the shallot in butter; drain on paper towels. Mix eggs, sour cream, cottage cheese, Parmesan, flour, salt and Tabasco in a blender or food processor and pour into a large bowl. Stir in shredded cheese, crab and the mushroom mixture.

Pour into a lightly buttered baking dish and bake in a preheated oven for 45 minutes or until the top is golden brown. Let stand 5 minutes before cutting into squares.

" *My own experience in foreign places had taught me that if someone else ate something with enjoyment, it was probably perfectly palatable once you knew how to peel it, crack it, scoop it, or suck it.* "
Elisabeth Luard

Petites Gougères

A specialty of the Burgundy region of France, this cheese flavored cream puff pastry is traditionally baked in a ring. Try this miniature version of warm cheese appetizers. They go especially well with a red wine from Burgundy.

½ tsp salt
½ cup/115 g unsalted butter
1 cup/240 ml water
1 cup/130 g all-purpose flour, sifted
4 large eggs
2 oz/55 g Gruyère, grated

Oven Temp:
425°F/220°C
400°F/200°C
Yield: 50 - 60 cheese puffs

Combine salt, butter and water in a medium saucepan. Bring to a boil over high heat, stirring constantly with a wooden spoon. Remove the pan from the heat and add the flour all at once. Beat vigorously with a wooden spoon to create a smooth dough. Reheat for 1 minute over medium heat, stirring constantly.

Quickly transfer the dough to the bowl of an electric mixer. Add the eggs and half of the grated cheese and beat at medium speed until the eggs and cheese are thoroughly incorporated into the dough. The dough should still be warm.

Gougère is made with pâte à choux dough, also known as cream puff dough. These little morsels should be crisp on the outside and soft and tender on the inside with a hollow center. If your puffs seem too moist, allow to cool a few minutes in the warm oven with the door propped slightly open; if they seem too dry, use milk in place of the water.

Spoon the dough into a pastry bag fitted with a ½"/1¼cm tube. Squeeze into 1"/2½cm mounds, spacing them about 1"/2½cm apart on 2 nonstick baking sheets. If you do not have a pastry bag, carefully spoon the dough into mounds with a teaspoon.

Sprinkle the tops with the remaining grated cheese. Bake in a preheated 425°F/220°C oven for 10 minutes. Reduce heat to 400°F/200°C and bake until the puffs are an even golden brown, about 10 more minutes. (If the puffs are not baking evenly, allow 1 sheet to bake thoroughly and remove it; then allow the second sheet to bake until golden.) Serve warm.

Variation: For Roquefort Cheese Puffs, use milk in place of water. Stir in 4 oz/115 grams Roquefort cheese, slightly crumbled, instead of Gruyère. Spoon by teaspoonfuls onto baking sheets, brush tops with a beaten egg and sprinkle with 2 tablespoons grated Parmesan cheese. Bake at 375°F/190°C for 10 minutes. Reduce heat to 350°F/175°C and bake 5 to 10 minutes more until puffed and browned.

Smoked Salmon and Chèvre Canapés

*D*iagonally cut 12 thin slices from the baguette. Arrange bread rounds on a baking sheet and brush with olive oil. Bake rounds for 10 minutes or until lightly toasted. Combine mustards, capers, red onion and dill. Spread some chèvre on each bread round and top with mustard mixture and a piece of salmon. Garnish with additional dill.

Variation: For CARAMELIZED ONION AND CHÈVRE CANAPÉS, sauté 1 large chopped onion in 1 tablespoon olive oil. Add 1 tablespoon sugar and sauté until caramelized. Add 1 tablespoon balsamic vinegar and cook for 1 minute longer. Spread chèvre on bread and top with caramelized onions. Garnish with parsley.

1 small baguette
¼ cup/60 ml olive oil
2 tbsp honey mustard
1 tbsp Dijon mustard
1 tbsp drained capers
1 tbsp chopped red onion
2 tsp minced fresh dill
4 oz/115 g soft mild chèvre
3 oz/85 g smoked salmon slices

Garnish:
additional fresh dill

Oven Temp: 350°F/175°C
Yield: 12 canapés

Puttin' on the Ritz

Smoked Salmon and Chèvre Canapés
(Cocktails)
∞
Petite Salade du Sud-Ouest
∞
Asparagus Wrapped in Prosciutto
∞
Coquilles Saint-Jacques à l'Effilochée d'Endives
∞
Gigot d'Agneau Farci en Croûte
∞
White Chocolate Mousse
Raspberry Grand Marnier Sauce

LAST MINUTE APPETIZERS

◆ Stuff hollowed out cherry tomatoes with SUPER GUACAMOLE, soft chèvre or SMOKED TROUT PÂTÉ.

◆ Parboil snow peas just until limp. Cool under running water, drain and wrap around cooked shrimp. Secure with a toothpick and serve with GREEN GODDESS DIP.

◆ Marinate large, raw shrimp in lemon juice, oil and seasonings for several hours. Wrap shrimp with bacon and secure with a wet toothpick. Broil.

◆ Blanch snow peas, cool and drain. Dry well. Open the flat side and fill with SHRIMP SPREAD. Pack filled pods closely together in a flat pan lined with paper towels and chill.

◆ For homemade herbed cream cheese, mix together 16 oz/450 grams cream cheese, ¼ cup/60 ml mayonnaise, 2 teaspoons Dijon mustard, 2 tablespoons each chopped chives and dill, and 1 crushed garlic clove. Serve with crackers.

◆ Stuff mushroom caps with Boursin. Sprinkle with chopped parsley.

◆ Fit wonton skins into lightly greased miniature muffin cups. Bake at 375°F/190°C until crisp and brown. Remove, cool on a rack and fill with shrimp or crab salad. Sprinkle with chopped chives.

◆ Boil new potatoes in their skins. Cool and cut in half. Top with sour cream and a little caviar, crisp bacon or chopped chives.

◆ Put flour tortillas on a baking sheet and top with mixed grated melting cheeses. Sprinkle on topping ingredients (chopped onion, jalapeño slices, diced pepperoni and chopped bell peppers) and bake in a 400°F/200°C oven until the edges of the tortilla are browned and crisp. Cut into 8 wedges and serve hot with salsa or SUPER GUACAMOLE.

◆ In a decorative quiche pan, layer SUPER GUACAMOLE, sour cream and then salsa. Sprinkle with shredded cheddar cheese. Serve with tortilla chips.

◆ Cut a firm chèvre into cubes, add butter and herbs and roll up in phyllo dough (see index). Bake in a hot oven just until brown.

◆ Toast baguette slices, drizzle with olive oil and rub with a garlic clove. Sprinkle with thyme. Put chèvre slices on top and broil. Sprinkle with pine nuts and broil just until nuts are light brown.

Mushroom Croustades

6 tbsp/85 g butter, softened
18 thin slices white bread
4 tbsp minced shallots
½ lb/225 g fresh mushrooms
2 tbsp flour
¾ cup/175 ml heavy cream
½ tsp salt
⅛ tsp cayenne pepper
1½ tbsp finely chopped parsley
1 tbsp lemon juice
grated Parmesan cheese

Oven Temp: 400°F/200°C
350°F/175°C
Yield: 18

Grease bottoms and sides of miniature muffin cups using 2 tablespoons of the butter. Cut a 3"/7½cm round from each slice of bread; fit the rounds carefully into muffin cups. Bake 10 minutes in a preheated 400°F/200°C oven or until edges begin to brown. Remove croustades from tins and cool.

Melt remaining 4 tablespoons butter in a heavy frying pan. Add shallots and stir over moderate heat for 4 minutes. Finely chop the mushrooms and add to the pan; cook until moisture has evaporated, 10 to 15 minutes. Remove pan from heat and stir in flour. Return pan to heat and add cream, stirring until it boils. When thickened, remove from heat and stir in seasonings, parsley and lemon juice.

Just before serving, fill croustades and sprinkle with Parmesan cheese. Bake 5 minutes or until bubbly in a 350°F/175°C oven.

> *A good dinner sharpens wit, while it softens the heart.*
> John Doran

Appetizers

Spanakopeta

Baked in a large pan and cut into squares, this makes a nice first course buffet or luncheon dish. If you prefer, fold the cheese and egg mixture into individual small triangles and use as an appetizer.

1 lb/450 g feta cheese, crumbled
1 lb/450 g dry curd cottage cheese
4 large eggs, slightly beaten
1 bunch green onions, minced
1½ lbs/680 g fresh spinach
¾ lb/340 g butter, melted
1 pkg phyllo dough (20 sheets)

Oven Temp: 350°F/175°C
Yield: 15 squares

Mix the feta with the cottage cheese. Add the 4 eggs and mix well. Chop the spinach, add it and mix thoroughly.

Sauté the green onions in a little of the butter until soft. Stir into the cheese mixture. Unroll room temperature phyllo and keep covered with a slightly damp towel to prevent the fragile sheets from drying out. Remove 1 sheet of phyllo, lightly brush with butter, and place in a buttered 15½"x10½"x1"/36 x 26 x 2cm pan. Continue buttering and layering sheets until there are 10 in the pan. Spread the cheese mixture evenly on top. Repeat the buttering and layering process with the remaining 10 sheets of phyllo and seal edges. Brush butter on top. Refrigerate, uncovered, for 10 to 15 minutes. Score the surface in squares, cutting through only the top few sheets of phyllo, before baking or freezing. Bake for 45 minutes in a preheated 350°F/175°C oven or until golden brown and crisp. Allow to cool slightly before cutting into squares.

To make a day ahead: After baking, cool, cover and refrigerate. Reheat, uncovered, for 20 to 30 minutes in a 250°F/120°C oven until warmed through. To freeze: After scoring, freeze uncooked and uncovered until butter has set. Cover with foil and return to freezer. When ready to bake, follow above instructions except allow 15 minutes extra baking time.

Variation: To make TIROPITA, omit the green onions and spinach.

For individual bite-sized appetizers, butter a sheet of phyllo and top with a second sheet. Cut into six 2"/5cm wide strips. Put a rounded teaspoon of filling at one end of a strip. Fold one corner to opposite side of strip to enclose filling and form a triangle. Continue folding (like a flag) to the end. Repeat filling and folding with each strip. Arrange triangles on a lightly greased baking pan, brush tops lightly with butter and bake in a 400°F/200°C oven for 10 minutes or until golden brown. Remove to a rack to cool.

Phyllo Flowers

A simple and versatile preparation - for a special occasion, make a "bouquet" of flavors.

8 oz/225 g cream cheese, softened
1 large egg
¼ cup/60 ml heavy cream
4 oz/115 g smoked salmon, minced
1½ tbsp chopped fresh dill
salt
freshly ground pepper
4 oz/115 g phyllo dough
unsalted butter, melted

Garnish:
salmon caviar

Oven Temp: 350°F/175°C
Yield: 36

Beat cream cheese until fluffy. Beat in the egg and cream until well blended. Stir in the smoked salmon and dill and season to taste with salt and pepper.

Brush miniature muffin cups with butter. On a clean working surface, lay out 1 sheet of phyllo dough and cut into 3"/8cm squares. (Keep remaining sheets of dough covered with a slightly dampened towel to prevent drying.) Lightly brush phyllo squares with melted butter. Place half the squares on top of the other half to make two layer squares. Arrange two sets of squares at 90° angles and gently ease the dough into the muffin cups. The 4 layers of phyllo should resemble a flower with 8 petals. Repeat cutting squares, one sheet at a time, only after you have used all of the previous sheet.

Spoon the salmon mixture into the phyllo cups, filling it to the top. Bake the filled phyllo in a preheated oven until the filling is lightly puffed and the dough is golden, about 20 minutes. Let cool slightly and gently remove each flower from the pan. Top each flower cup with a small spoonful of salmon caviar and serve hot. (The filled pastry flowers may be baked in advance, removed from the pans and reheated on a baking sheet for 10 to 15 minutes at 350°F/175°C.)

Variation: Replace the salmon and dill with other flavor combinations such as chicken and tarragon or shrimp and basil. On another occasion, vary the cheeses, substituting chèvre or Roquefort for half of the cream cheese. Vary the garnish - do not be afraid to experiment.

> *You can give the same recipe to four different people and each will treat it differently...*
> Frédy Giradet

Appetizers

Brie with Sun-Dried Tomatoes

2 lb/900 g young Brie
5 tbsp minced fresh parsley
2½ tbsp freshly grated Parmesan cheese
10 sun-dried tomatoes, minced
2½ tbsp sun-dried tomato oil
6 garlic cloves, minced
2 tbsp minced fresh basil
3 tbsp chopped toasted pine nuts

Yield: 16 servings

Remove rind from the top of the Brie; place Brie on a serving dish. Combine parsley, Parmesan cheese, sun-dried tomatoes, oil, garlic, basil and pine nuts. Spread on top of Brie. Chill 6 hours. Let stand at room temperature for 30 to 60 minutes before serving with slices of French bread.

Variation: To serve warm, bake at 350°F/175°C for about 15 minutes or just until cheese starts to melt. Serve immediately.

BRIE EN CROÛTE

Baked Brie pastry, a simple and delicious appetizer, may be prepared in various ways. Be sure you have a wheel of Brie (or Camembert), 1 recipe PÂTE BRISÉE, an egg and any one of the following:

◆ 1 package Boursin
◆ 1 jar apricot preserves
◆ mango chutney
◆ Triple Sec (poke holes in top of cheese, pour on Triple Sec and marinate overnight), then top with equal amounts of butter and sugar, melted together, and pecans.

Remove rind from the top of the cheese round, if desired. Leave the bottom and sides to contain cheese. Cut pastry into 2 circles, one 1"/2½cm larger and one 2"/5cm larger than the Brie round. Spread the Brie with one of the toppings, center it on the smaller pastry circle and cover with the second circle, sealing edges. (For a prettier presentation, cut decorative leaves from pastry scraps and arrange on top.) Brush the pastry with a lightly beaten egg and bake for 20 to 25 minutes at 400°F/200°C. Let stand 10 minutes before serving with French bread, crackers, apples or other fruit.

Roquefort Tartlets

1 recipe PÂTE BRISÉE
3 oz/85 g spinach, stems removed
1 egg
⅔ cup/160 ml heavy cream
¾ cup/175 ml grated Emmentaler
¼ tsp freshly grated nutmeg
salt
freshly ground pepper
3 oz/85 g Roquefort cheese, crumbled
2 tbsp pine nuts

Oven Temp: 425°F/220°C
Yield: 18

Prepare the pastry and refrigerate for 3 hours. Remove from the refrigerator 30 minutes before rolling out.

Plunge the spinach into boiling water and cook for 30 seconds. Immediately drain in a colander and rinse with cold water to stop the cooking. Drain again, pressing on the spinach to force out as much water as possible; set aside.

Combine the egg, cream, Emmentaler cheese, nutmeg, salt and pepper to taste, and beat until completely blended. Coarsely chop the spinach and add it to the bowl; stir well.

On a lightly floured board, roll the pastry out as thinly as possible. Cut out 18 (1½"/4cm) rounds. Line 18 individual tartlet pans or miniature muffin pans with the rounds. If using tartlet pans, arrange the lined pans on a large baking sheet. Sprinkle the Roquefort evenly over the pastry. Fill each tartlet with some of the egg mixture and scatter a few pine nuts on top. Place the tartlets in a preheated oven and bake until the filling sets and the crust is golden, about 15 minutes. Serve warm.

MINIATURE QUICHES

Miniature quiche shells, dressed up with a variety of fillings, are always welcome at a cocktail party. To make the custard, mix together 3 eggs, 1½ cups/350 ml heavy cream, salt and pepper. Place a spoonful of filling into the tartlet shells and pour the custard on top. Bake at 375°F/190°C for 15 minutes. Invent your own fillings or use these suggestions:

Classic: crisp bacon, shredded Gruyère
Vegetarian: steamed broccoli, sautéed mushrooms, grated cheddar
Provençal: sautéed zucchini, onion, bell pepper, herbes de Provence
Florentine: cooked chopped spinach, mozzarella
Indian: cooked chicken, curry powder
Seafood: cooked shrimp, dill
Italian: pepperoni, sautéed onion, Parmesan cheese

Smoked Trout Pâté

Blend cream cheese, mayonnaise, horseradish and lemon juice until smooth. Stir in chopped dill. Remove bones from trout, flake and add to mixture. Chill in a lightly oiled, attractive mold.

To serve, unmold and garnish with fresh dill sprigs. Serve with dark bread or crackers.

7 oz/200 g cream cheese, softened
¼ cup/60 ml mayonnaise
1 tbsp horseradish
juice of 1 lemon
1 - 2 tbsp chopped fresh dill
1 (7 oz/200 g) smoked trout

Garnish: dill sprigs

Yield: 1 cup/240 ml

" *Throughout the world, people have dedicated themselves to the noble art of gastronomy. And nowhere does this passion take such imposing and almost possessed forms as in Belgium.* "
Rosine De Dijn

38   Appetizers

Shrimp Spread

1 lb/450 g deveined, cooked shrimp
8 oz/225 g cream cheese
3 tbsp horseradish
¼ cup/60 ml ketchup
2 dashes Worcestershire sauce
1 small onion, minced
juice of ½ lemon

Yield: 2½ cups/600 ml

Mince the shrimp and combine with cream cheese and horseradish. Add ketchup, Worcestershire and onion. Stir in lemon juice slowly so that the mixture does not become too runny. Chill until ready to serve. (May be prepared up to 24 hours in advance.) Serve with toast or crackers, or as a tea sandwich.

Variation: Substitute crab, lobster or any combination of shellfish.

If buying fresh shrimp, 2 pounds/900 grams of shrimp in the shell will yield about 1 pound/450 grams cooked, or 2 cups/475 ml.

Any spread presents an opportunity for tasty tea sandwiches. The key to the perfect sandwich is very thin, high quality, firm white bread. Assemble the sandwiches with a variety of fillings: S HRIMP S PREAD, *paper thin slices of cucumber, Black Forest ham,* E GG S PREAD, *herbed cheese spread and thinly sliced smoked turkey are all possibilities. Vary the tastes with butter, mayonnaise and/or fresh herbs. Once the sandwiches are assembled, remove the crusts with a very sharp knife and cut each sandwich into four squares or triangles. Arrange on a beautiful platter and garnish with watercress or parsley and cherry tomatoes.*

Mousse de Foie de Volaille

Clean the liver. Melt the butter and sauté the liver and shallots. Add salt and pepper. Spoon the mixture into a food processor and blend until smooth. Add port or brandy to taste and blend again. Adjust seasoning. Spoon into a pâté mold, a lightly oiled decorative mold (to be unmolded later) or a crock. Refrigerate several hours. Decorate with aspic and refrigerate up to 3 days. Serve with toast.

Variations: For a spicier version, add 1½ teaspoons of Dijon mustard and ¼ teaspoon anchovy paste. For a lighter version, poach the livers in water with 1 sliced onion, drain and blend, using only ½ cup/115 grams softened butter. Substitute duck liver for chicken liver for a different taste.

1 cup/225 g butter
¾ lb/340 g chicken livers
4 tbsp shallots, finely chopped
1 tsp salt
freshly ground pepper
1 - 2 tbsp port or brandy

Garnish:
aspic

Yield: 1½ cups/350 ml

DECORATING WITH ASPIC/GELEE

Aspic/gelée is a savory gelatin mixture made with meat, poultry or fish stock that is used to glaze chilled foods. If pâté is to be served in a pâté mold or crock, spoon a layer of cooled gelée on top of the chilled pâté and refrigerate until firm. For an elegant presentation, arrange bits of tomato skin, chives, blanched leek or scallion leaves or other thin vegetable skins to make flower designs on the surface of the pâté before spooning on the layer of aspic. If the pâté is to be served unmolded, chill the gelée in a large flat pan, cut into tiny cubes and serve spooned around the pâté.

In Belgium, aspic jelly or gelée, is available in packets (see package instructions). You may also prepare your own by mixing 1 envelope of powdered gelatin into 2 cups/475 ml of clear hot meat, chicken or fish broth (see index). Stir until dissolved and cool until it is the consistency of raw egg white. Spoon over the pâté or chill in a flat pan as above.

The secret to shiny, sparkling aspic is the clarity of the broth. To clarify homemade stock, add 1 slightly beaten egg white and 1 crumpled egg shell to 1 quart/liter of well strained and degreased room temperature broth. Very slowly bring the broth to a slight simmer - the surface should barely ripple. Do not stir or disturb the thick layer of foam that will form on top. Let it barely simmer for 10 to 15 minutes. Gently remove from heat and let stand 15 minutes. Push the scum gently to one side and ladle the clear liquid through a dampened cloth draped in a large strainer.

Artichoke Dip

Rinse and drain the artichoke hearts. Purée all ingredients in a food processor. Bake in an oven-proof dish for 30 minutes. Serve with French bread or crackers.

1 (14 oz/400 g) can artichoke hearts
¾ cup/175 ml mayonnaise
1 cup/240 ml grated Parmesan

Variations: Any or all of the following ingredients may be added to vary the taste: ½ lb/225 grams cooked and crumbled bacon, 4 oz/115 grams shredded mozzarella or mixed cheeses, ½ cup/120 ml diced black olives, paprika, garlic.

Oven Temp: 350°F/175°C
Yield: 6 servings

Chutney Cheese Spread

Mix cheeses, sherry, curry powder and salt together by hand or in a food processor. Spread into a ½"/1 ¼cm thick round on a serving platter. Chill until firm. Before serving, spread the top with the chutney. Finely chop green onions (including tops) and sprinkle on top. Surround with firm crackers.

6 oz/170 g cream cheese, softened
4 oz/115 g cheddar cheese, shredded
1 tbsp dry sherry
¾ tsp curry powder
¼ tsp salt
½ cup/120 ml hot mango chutney
4 green onions

Yield: 10 servings

> *Feeling like a mad chemist, I worked up a blend [of curry] that turned out to be quite delicious.*
> Sheila Lukins

Appetizers   41

Green Goddess Dip

*M*ix ingredients in order given. Serve as a dip for cooked shrimp or crudités.

1 cup/240 ml mayonnaise
3 anchovies, chopped
¼ cup/60 ml chopped fresh parsley
¼ cup/60 ml minced fresh chives
1 tbsp fresh lemon juice
1 tbsp tarragon vinegar
½ tsp salt
freshly ground pepper
½ cup/120 ml sour cream

Yield: 2 cups/475 ml

Crudités are fresh raw vegetables, cut into bite-sized pieces and served as hors d'oeuvres. A crudité platter often includes cauliflower, carrot sticks, snow peas, zucchini sticks, celery sticks, sugar snap peas, broccoli, cherry tomatoes, green onions, cucumber slices, endive spears, bell peppers and/or radishes.

Curry Dip

*C*runchy fresh vegetables are always appreciated at a party, especially when they are accompanied by a delicious dip.

1 quart/liter mayonnaise
1 (9 oz/250 g) jar Major Grey's Chutney
curry powder to taste

Yield: 5 cups/1⅓ liters

Combine mayonnaise, chutney and curry powder, adding curry powder slowly and tasting frequently. Refrigerate until ready to use. Serve with crudités.

Super Guacamole

3 ripe avocados
½ cup/120 ml sour cream
1 tbsp mayonnaise
1 tsp cumin
Tabasco sauce
1 tsp garlic powder
1½ tsp lemon juice
½ green pepper, minced
½ onion, minced
1 tomato, diced

Yield: 2 cups/475 ml

Mash avocados. Mix in sour cream, mayonnaise and spices, carefully adding Tabasco to taste. Stir in lemon juice and the remaining ingredients. If not serving immediately, cover the surface with plastic wrap and refrigerate. Stir before serving with Mexican tortilla chips.

Variation: Sprinkle the guacamole with shredded cheddar cheese before serving.

Avocado darkens after exposure to air, so it is preferable to make this shortly before serving.

Tapenade of Sun-Dried Tomatoes

*P*urée sun-dried tomatoes with a little of the oil. Add the remaining ingredients. Marinate in refrigerator overnight. Serve on wheat crackers.

3 oz/85 g sun-dried tomatoes, in oil
1 tbsp capers
2 tsp minced garlic
1 tsp lemon zest
1 tsp lemon juice
½ tsp herbes de Provence

Yield: 25 crackers

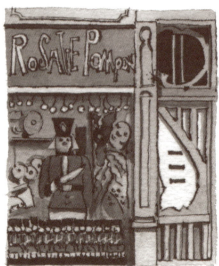

Caviar Pie

*A*ssemble this easy and elegant party dish in a decorative pie plate.

16 oz/450 g cream cheese, softened
1 tbsp Worcestershire sauce
1 tbsp lemon juice
1 cup/240 ml mayonnaise
1 tsp garlic powder
1 tsp seasoned salt
Tabasco sauce
1 (3½ oz/100 g) jar red or black caviar
4 hard boiled eggs, finely chopped
⅓ cup/80 ml minced fresh parsley
1 bunch green onions, finely chopped

Yield: 8 - 10 servings

Combine cream cheese, Worcestershire, lemon juice, mayonnaise and seasonings. Add several dashes Tabasco sauce and stir in. Taste and adjust seasoning. Spoon into a pie plate and spread evenly. Cover with caviar. Layer eggs, parsley and onions on top. Refrigerate. Serve with melba toast or crackers.

> " *Appetite comes with eating...*
> François Rabelais "

Soups

Soups

Bisque de Poisson et Fruits de Mer	49
Black Bean Soup	63
Boursin Soup	59
Brazilian Shrimp and Coconut Soup	56
Chestnut Soup	58
Chicken and Lemon Grass Soup	55
Chilled Cucumber Soup	47
Cream of Broccoli Soup	59
Cream of Fennel Soup	50
Cream of Potato and Leek Soup	57
Goulash Soup	64
Italian Mushroom Soup	53
Lentil Soup	61
Mushroom Brie Soup	52
Roasted Yellow Bell Pepper and Tomato Soup	54
Soupe à l'Oignon Gratinée	60
Spring Carrot Soup	47
Summer Tomato Soup Mozzarella	48
Tortellini Pesto Vegetable Soup	65
Tuscan Bean and Cabbage Soup	62
Winter Vegetable Beef Soup	66

SPECIAL TOPIC
Stocks and Broths 50

Chilled Cucumber Soup

Cooking the cucumbers first makes this soup special.

2 European seedless cucumbers
1 leek, chopped
2 tbsp/30 g butter
1 tbsp flour
4 cups/950 ml chicken broth
1 cup/240 ml heavy cream
juice of ½ lemon
salt
white pepper

Garnish:
chopped fresh dill

Yield: 6 servings

Peel and coarsely chop 1½ cucumbers. Gently sauté cucumber and leek in butter until tender, about 20 minutes. Remove from the heat and stir in the flour. Add chicken broth and simmer covered for 30 minutes. Purée and sieve. Chill several hours or overnight. Peel and coarsely grate remaining half of cucumber. Add cucumber, cream and lemon juice to soup. Add salt and pepper to taste. Chill again at least 30 minutes before serving. Garnish with fresh dill, if desired.

Spring Carrot Soup

A delicious first course before a spring lamb dinner.

1 cup/240 ml sliced carrots
1 medium onion, sliced
1 stalk celery, sliced (with leaves)
1½ cups/350 ml chicken broth
¾ cup/175 ml light cream
½ cup/120 ml cooked rice
salt
pinch of cayenne

Garnish:
chopped parsley

Yield: 6 servings

Put carrots, onion, celery and ½ cup/120 ml of the broth in a saucepan. Bring to a boil and simmer 15 minutes. Transfer to a blender and purée. With motor still running, pour in the rest of the broth, the cream, the rice and the seasonings. Blend until smooth. Chill thoroughly. Before serving, thin with a little more cream if the soup seems too thick. Garnish with parsley.

Soup is an integral part of Belgian family meals. It is served to calm a hunger before the main course and to make use of any remaining vegetables in the kitchen.

Summer Tomato Soup Mozzarella

This cold puréed soup is a refreshing alternative to gazpacho.

¼ cup/60 ml olive oil
2 medium onions, chopped
6 medium tomatoes, peeled (see note)
1 small garlic clove, minced
1 medium beet, peeled and sliced
1 bouquet garni (see note)
½ tsp salt
½ tsp freshly ground black pepper
2 tbsp fresh lemon juice
3 - 4 drops Tabasco sauce
1 tbsp white wine vinegar
4 oz/115 g fresh mozzarella cheese

Garnish:
16 basil leaves

Yield: 4 servings

In a large saucepan, heat the olive oil over moderately high heat. Add the onions and cook, stirring frequently, until softened, about 3 minutes. Quarter five of the tomatoes, reserving one for garnish, and add them to the saucepan with the garlic, beet and bouquet garni. Season with salt and pepper, partially cover the saucepan, and reduce heat to low. Simmer, stirring occasionally, until the tomatoes are stewed, about 45 minutes. Discard the beets and bouquet garni. Transfer the soup to a food processor and purée until smooth. Strain through a fine sieve and let cool to room temperature. Cover and refrigerate until chilled, at least 2 hours or overnight.

A bouquet garni is a bundle of flavorings either tied together or wrapped in cheesecloth. It usually includes bay leaves and fresh herb sprigs, but may also include whole spices, citrus rind and crushed garlic cloves. For this recipe use 2 bay leaves, 2 sprigs fresh thyme or rosemary, and 3 parsley stems.

Just before serving, season soup with lemon juice, Tabasco, vinegar, and salt and pepper to taste. Cut reserved tomato and mozzarella into ½"/1 ¼cm cubes. Arrange tomato and mozzarella cubes in a triangle in the bottom of four chilled soup bowls. Ladle equal amounts of soup over the cubes and garnish with basil leaves. Serve very cold.

To peel and seed a tomato, drop the tomato in boiling water for 30 seconds. Drain, cool under running water and slip off the peel. Cut in half horizontally and squeeze out the seeds. Drain on paper towels.

Bisque de Poisson et Fruits de Mer
Restaurant De Pottekijker (Bruges) - David Cleophas, Chef

Croutons: Melt butter in a skillet. Add oil and lightly crushed garlic cloves to flavor oil. Add bread cubes and sauté over medium heat. Stir until golden brown; transfer to paper towels and drain.

Bisque:
- 7 oz/200 g fillet of salmon
- 7 oz/200 g white fish (bass, monkfish or sole)
- 8 scampi, peeled
- 4 tbsp olive oil
- 2 tsp paprika powder
- 2 tsp cayenne pepper
- 2 tbsp tomato paste
- 2 garlic cloves, chopped
- 3½ oz/100 ml white wine
- 2 oz/60 ml genièvre
- 2 cups/475ml cream
- salt
- freshly ground pepper
- chopped parsley or dill

Accompaniments:
- rouille
- freshly grated Parmesan

Croutons:
- 4 tbsp/55 g butter
- ¼ cup/60 ml olive oil
- 2 garlic cloves
- bread cubes (French bread)

Yield: 4 servings

Cut fish in ¾"/2cm cubes. Heat oil in a sauté pan. When the oil is hot, add the fish and scampi and stir gently.

Add paprika, cayenne pepper, tomato paste and garlic to fish mixture. Stir again. Add white wine and genièvre, without stirring. Carefully flambé (using a long match). When the flame dies, add the cream. Simmer 10 minutes (do not boil), stirring carefully so the fish does not break. Season to taste with salt and pepper and add chopped parsley or dill. Serve in heated bowls. Pass the croutons, rouille and Parmesan.

To make a rouille, pound 4 garlic cloves into a smooth paste with a pestle. Add 2 egg yolks and pound until smooth. Add ¼ cup/60 ml pimiento, continuing to pound. Add ½ cup/120 ml bread crumbs, adding 2 to 3 tablespoons of hot soup broth, drop by drop, to moisten. When the paste is thick and smooth, slowly drizzle in ⅔ to ¾ cup/160 to 180 ml olive oil, pounding at first and then whisking to a consistency like mayonnaise. Add hot pepper sauce or cayenne, salt and pepper to taste. (Rouille should be thick, strong and piquant.) If you like, soak 8 strands of saffron in the soup broth before adding it to the mixture.

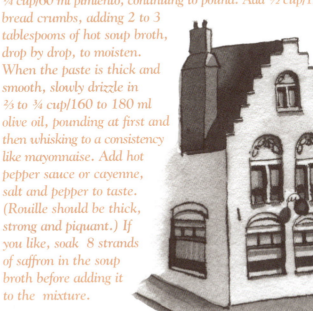

Cream of Fennel Soup

4 tbsp/55 g unsalted butter
1 lb/450 g fresh fennel, chopped
½ cup/120 ml chopped onion
1 cup/240 ml chicken broth
¼ cup/60 ml heavy cream
1 tbsp Pernod or other anise liqueur
⅛ tsp coarsely ground black pepper

Garnish:
sour cream
fennel leaves

Yield: 4 servings

Served warm or chilled this creamy, anise-flavored soup is memorable.

In a 2 quart/liter saucepan, melt the butter. Stir in fennel and onion until well coated. Cover and cook over low heat for 20 to 25 minutes or until very tender, stirring occasionally. Put the fennel mixture and ¼ cup/60 ml of the chicken broth in a food processor. Cover and process until smooth; return to the saucepan. Add the remaining chicken broth, cream, Pernod and pepper. Serve in small bowls, garnished with a dollop of sour cream and a fennel leaf.

STOCKS AND BROTHS

Stock is the liquid obtained by boiling bones with water, usually with other flavorings added. The cooking time depends on the size and type of bones, but ample time is needed to extract all the taste. If you have an appropriate pot, make a large quantity. Reduce the stock and freeze it in small quantities and you will have the base for wonderful sauces at your fingertips. Leftover bones from roasts may also be made into stock as a base for homemade soups and stews. Broth (a clear stock) is usually interchangeable with stock except where clarity is an issue.

◆ **Basic stock techniques:** Always start stocks with cold water and cook them uncovered at a slow simmer. This encourages the foam and fat to the surface. Once skimmed off, the resulting stock will be clearer, leaner, and more digestible. For a brown stock, first brown the bones (with bits of meat attached) in a hot oven in a large roasting pan, turning them and watching carefully so they do not burn. (This can take an hour or more.) For a white stock, do not brown the bones. Do not add salt to a stock since later reduction will produce a concentrated, over-salted product.

◆ **Meat Stock:** Brown the bones (a mixture of veal, beef and chicken) in a large roasting pan. Transfer to a large stock pot. Discard the fat from the roasting pan and pour in some water. Scrape up all the brown bits and pour on top of the bones. Cover bones with cold water. Bring to a simmer, skimming the foam and fat. After an hour, add cut vegetables (carrot, onion, celery, leek, tomato) and

...more on STOCKS AND BROTHS

herbs (parsley, thyme, bay leaf) and a few whole peppercorns. Simmer very slowly for about 10 hours, uncovered. As the water evaporates, add water as needed. Strain through a very fine strainer (chinois). Pour into a clean pot and reduce until it is very flavorful. Cool the stock, refrigerate overnight, and remove any fat that has congealed on the surface. Freeze in small containers or reduce further. For a Demi-Glace (condensed broth) reduce by half. For Glace de Viande (meat glaze) reduce until it is syrupy and large (like caramel) bubbles break on the surface with no steam escaping from them. Watch carefully since it can burn very easily at this point.

◆ Poultry Stock: Follow the same process as above, using only chicken bones (either browned or not) and simmering for only 3 hours.

◆ Fish Stock: Select fish bones (if you use the heads be sure to remove the gills) from non-oily fish. Flat fish such as flounder and sole are the best. Sauté them for a few minutes in butter. Add chopped onion, celery, leek, and parsley sprigs and steam for another few minutes, stirring. Add cold water along with bay leaf, thyme, crushed black peppercorns and about half the quantity of white wine as water. Boil for 35 to 45 minutes. Strain and reduce to desired strength.

◆ Vegetable Broth: Vegetable broth is a wonderful way to use up trimmings and leftover bits of vegetables. Save mushroom stems, scallion tops, celery leaves, corn cobs, tomato peels, and parsley stems as well as the water drained from cooking vegetables. If you add onion skins, your broth will take on a light brown color. Put all your vegetables (suggestions include carrots, beans, leeks, onions, spinach, tomatoes, zucchini, bell peppers, lettuce) in a pot and cover with water. (Eggplant and vegetables in the cabbage family are not recommended.) Add bay leaves, pepper, and herbs if desired and simmer for about an hour. Strain and reduce to desired strength.

◆ Packaged bouillon cubes may be used for recipes where the flavor of the broth is not essential to the success of the dish. Be careful, however, to taste before adding salt as they are quite salty. Good quality glace de viande or beef extract is available in specialty stores.

Mushroom Brie Soup

This velvety rich soup can handle an extra splash of sherry!

Sauté onion and garlic in butter. Add mushrooms and lemon juice; cook 10 minutes. Add flour and cook 2 minutes. Purée mixture, then add chicken broth. Cook over low heat until slightly thickened. Add both creams and brie; heat gently until the brie melts. Stir in sherry, salt and pepper to taste. Serve immediately (or ladle into oven proof bowls and put one slice of brie on top of each; broil until melted).

2 onions, chopped
1 garlic clove, minced
4 tbsp/55 g butter
12 oz/340 g mushrooms, sliced
1¼ tsp lemon juice
2 tbsp flour
1 quart/liter chicken broth
1 cup/240 ml light cream
½ cup/120 ml heavy cream
1 lb/450 g brie, rind removed, chopped
3 tbsp dry sherry
salt
freshly ground pepper

Garnish:
sliced brie (optional)

Yield: 6 - 8 servings

Autumn Dinner

Italian Mushroom Soup
∞
*Magret de Canard à l'Orange
Wild Rice with Walnuts
(Steamed Broccoli)*
∞
Tarte Amandine aux Poires et au Chocolat

"*Beautiful Soup!
Who cares for
fish, game
or any other dish?
Who would not
give all else for two
penney-worth only
of beautiful soup?*"
Lewis Carroll

Italian Mushroom Soup

A satisfying soup to serve before a light main dish.

3 oz/85 g dried porcini (1½ cups)
1½ tbsp/25 g butter
1 tbsp minced onion
1 garlic clove, minced
5 cups/1⅓ liters thinly sliced mushrooms
1 tbsp tomato paste
1 tbsp minced parsley
1 quart/liter rich beef broth
salt
freshly ground pepper
1 egg
1 egg yolk
¼ cup/60 ml grated Parmesan cheese
pinch of nutmeg

Garnish:
½ cup/120 ml croutons

Yield: 6 servings

Put the dried porcini mushrooms in hot water to cover. Let stand for 20 minutes. Lift the mushrooms out of the water, strain the soaking liquid through cheesecloth or a coffee filter and reserve. Cover mushrooms again with hot water and let stand until ready to use.

In a soup pot, heat the butter and sauté the onion and garlic. Drain the mushrooms and squeeze them dry. Add the fresh mushrooms and the soaked mushrooms to the onion mixture and cook until wilted. Add tomato paste and parsley and stir. Add broth and reserved soaking liquid and simmer 1 hour. Add salt and pepper to taste.

Beat whole egg and egg yolk until light and lemon colored. Add the cheese and nutmeg and beat well. Slowly add ½ cup/120 ml of the hot soup to the egg mixture, beating constantly. Remove the soup from the heat and gradually return the egg mixture to the soup, stirring constantly.

Return the pot to low heat and cook, stirring, until the mixture barely begins to simmer. Do not boil.

Divide the soup among 6 soup bowls and sprinkle a few croutons on top.

For homemade croutons, fry firm bread cubes in an oil and butter combination until golden brown and crisp. For garlic croutons, add a lightly crushed garlic clove to the pan. Drain on paper towels.

Roasted Yellow Bell Pepper and Tomato Soup

*Y*ou'll get rave reviews for this elegant soup - well worth the effort!

Bell Pepper Soup:
3 tbsp finely chopped shallot
½ tsp thyme
1 tbsp unsalted butter
6 large yellow bell peppers, roasted, peeled, (see index)
1½ cups/350 ml (or more) chicken broth
¼ cup/60 ml heavy cream
fresh lemon juice to taste
salt
white pepper

Tomato Soup:
3 lb/1½ kg plum tomatoes, quartered
3 unpeeled large garlic cloves
3 tbsp finely chopped shallot
½ tsp oregano
1 tbsp/15 g unsalted butter
1½ cups/350 ml (or more) chicken broth
¼ cup/60 ml heavy cream
fresh lemon juice to taste
salt
white pepper

Serrano Cream:
3 fresh serrano chilies or jalapeños, seeded and minced
1 large garlic clove, minced and mashed to paste with ½ tsp salt
½ cup/120 ml sour cream (see index)

Oven Temp: 350°F/175°C
Yield: 6 servings

Bell Pepper Soup: In a heavy saucepan cook shallot and thyme in the butter over moderately low heat until shallot is soft. Coarsely chop the bell peppers and add along with 1½ cups/350 ml of broth; simmer, covered, for 12 to 15 minutes or until the peppers are very soft. In a blender, purée the soup in batches until it is very smooth, forcing each batch through a fine sieve into a clean pan. Whisk in cream and enough additional broth to reach the desired consistency. Add lemon juice, salt and pepper to taste.

Tomato Soup: Spread the tomatoes, skin side down, in one layer on 2 foil-lined jelly-roll pans. Add the garlic to one of the pans, and bake in a preheated oven for 45 minutes to 1 hour, or until the tomatoes are very soft and the skin is dark brown. Let the tomatoes and garlic cool in the pans. In a heavy saucepan, cook shallot and oregano in butter over moderately low heat, stirring, until the shallot is soft. Add the tomatoes, the garlic (skins discarded), and 1½ cups/350 ml of the broth, and simmer the mixture, covered, for 15 minutes. In a blender, purée the soup in batches until it is very smooth, forcing each batch through a fine sieve set over a clean pan. Whisk in the cream, additional broth if necessary (both soups should have the same consistency), the lemon juice, and salt and pepper to taste.

The soups may be made one day ahead, refrigerated and reheated before serving. The serrano cream may be kept chilled and brought to room temperature before serving.

Serrano Cream: In a blender, blend the chilies, garlic paste, and sour cream until the mixture is well combined. (Be careful not to overblend or the cream may curdle.) Force the mixture through a fine sieve set over a small bowl.

For each serving, ladle ½ cup/120 ml of each soup into 2 measuring cups, pour the soups simultaneously into a shallow soup bowl from opposite sides of the bowl, and drizzle some of the serrano cream on top.

Chicken and Lemon Grass Soup

This elegant, light soup deserves your best chicken broth.

1 stalk fresh lemon grass
1½ quarts/liters rich chicken broth
⅛ tsp freshly ground black pepper
1 fresh jalapeño chili, seeded, minced
1 garlic clove, minced
½ cup/120 ml thinly sliced green onions*
½ cup/120 ml chopped fresh coriander (cilantro)
1 medium tomato, seeded and chopped
3 cups/700 ml shredded cooked chicken
1 avocado, peeled and chopped
cayenne pepper (optional)

Yield: 6 servings

Trim and discard the root end and outer leaves from the lemon grass; cut into 3 pieces. In a large pot, combine lemon grass, broth, pepper, chili and garlic. Bring to a boil, cover and simmer for 30 minutes. Discard the lemon grass. Stir in green onion, fresh coriander, tomato and chicken. Reheat. (If you want the soup a bit spicier, add a pinch of cayenne pepper. If you prefer it less spicy, omit the jalapeño and just use a touch of cayenne.)

Divide the avocado among 6 soup bowls and ladle in the hot soup.

* include the green tops

Lemon grass, a staple in Thai cuisine, has a subtle lemony fragrance and flavor. It comes in stalks, a little like a green onion, and is available in oriental grocery stores. Before using, peel off all the fibrous outer layers until only the center is exposed. If lemon grass is an integral part of a recipe, it must be minced or pounded into a paste. If larger pieces are used to flavor a dish, remove them before serving.

Brazilian Shrimp and Coconut Soup

Based on a Brazilian recipe, this is an appealing soup with an exotic blend of flavors. Served with a bowl of rice it becomes a meal.

2 tbsp/30 g unsalted butter
2 lb/900 g medium shrimp, shelled and deveined, shells reserved
1 large onion, coarsely chopped
5 garlic cloves, finely chopped
2 small Thai or serrano chilies, minced
2 tbsp peeled, grated fresh ginger
1 quart/liter chicken broth or water
2 cups/475 ml plum tomatoes, peeled, seeded, chopped (see index)
14 oz/400 g unsweetened coconut milk
⅔ cup/160 ml roasted unsalted peanuts*
¼ cup/60 ml fresh lime juice
¼ cup/60 ml finely chopped fresh coriander (cilantro)
salt
freshly ground pepper

Garnish:
lime wedges

Yield: 8 servings

Melt the butter in a medium nonreactive saucepan. Add the shrimp shells, onion, garlic, chilies and ginger. Cook over low heat, stirring, until the onion is translucent, about 10 minutes. Add the chicken broth and simmer gently for 15 minutes.

Strain the broth and return it to the pan. Stir in the tomatoes and simmer for 10 minutes.

Purée the coconut milk with the peanuts or peanut butter until smooth. Stir the mixture into the simmering broth. Add the shrimp, lime juice and fresh coriander and simmer gently just until the shrimp curl and turn pink, about 3 minutes. Season the soup with salt and pepper, ladle into warmed bowls and garnish with lime wedges.

* Roasted peanuts may be replaced with ½ cup/120 ml creamy peanut butter.

Cream of Potato and Leek Soup

A touch of bacon makes this soup taste special.

2 tbsp/30 g butter
4 slices of bacon, chopped
4 large leeks, chopped
1 lb/450 g potatoes, peeled, quartered
1 quart/liter of chicken broth
salt
freshly ground pepper
⅔ cup/160 ml milk
freshly chopped parsley

Yield: 6 servings

Melt the butter in a large saucepan, and sauté the bacon until half cooked. Add the leeks and fry gently for 5 minutes; add the potatoes. Pour in the broth, and season with salt and pepper. Bring to a boil, reduce heat and simmer for 30 to 40 minutes. Purée in a blender, add the milk and reheat. Sprinkle with parsley and serve.

Variation: To make a chowder, do not purée. Add a little cream and top with ¾ cup/175 ml grated cheddar cheese.

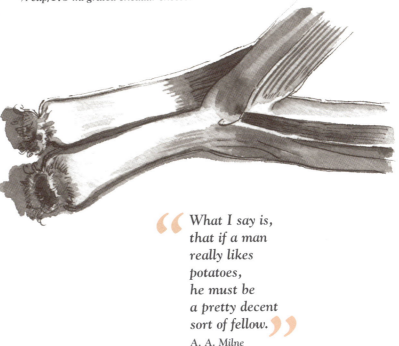

> "What I say is, that if a man really likes potatoes, he must be a pretty decent sort of fellow."
> A. A. Milne

Chestnut Soup

¾ lb/340 g boiling potatoes
1 cup/240 ml coarsely chopped celery
1 cup/240 ml coarsely chopped onion
6 tbsp/85 g unsalted butter
3 cups/700 ml chicken broth
2½ cups/600 ml beef broth
¼ cup/60 ml chopped fresh parsley
1 tbsp chopped fresh thyme
1 tbsp chopped fresh sage
1 tbsp chopped fresh basil
16 oz/450 g chestnuts, drained, chopped
1 cup/240 ml heavy cream
½ cup/120 ml Marsala or Madeira wine
¼ tsp freshly ground white pepper
salt

Garnish:
chopped fresh parsley

Yield: 8 servings

Peel the potatoes and coarsely chop. In a food processor, finely chop the potatoes, celery and onion. In a large heavy pot, cook vegetables in butter over moderate heat, stirring 15 minutes or until softened. Add broths and herbs to vegetable mixture.

In a food processor, purée chestnuts to a thick paste and whisk into the soup. Simmer soup, covered, stirring occasionally until vegetables are soft, about 20 minutes. Stir in the cream, wine, pepper and salt to taste and cook over moderate heat until hot.

Serve soup garnished with additional parsley.

When substituting a dried herb for fresh, use one-third of the amount specified in the recipe.

Boursin Soup

3 medium onions
2 large carrots
6 ribs of celery with leaves
5 leeks, white only
2 quarts/liters chicken broth
3 tbsp/45 g butter
5 tbsp/50 g flour
½ quart/liter milk
1 pkg Boursin cheese
salt
white pepper
chopped parsley

Yield: 10 servings

Finely chop the vegetables and add to the chicken broth. Cook for about an hour or until all the vegetables are thoroughly cooked. (The better your broth, the fuller the flavor of the finished product.) Strain vegetables from the broth, reserving broth. Purée the vegetables and return the purée and broth to the soup pot.

Melt the butter in a saucepan. Add flour and cook a minute before adding the milk to make a cream sauce. Add the cheese and let melt into sauce. Stir a little of the hot soup into the cheese sauce and mix well. Add the sauce to the soup pot and stir to combine. Season to taste with salt and white pepper. Serve topped with a sprinkling of chopped parsley.

Variations: For a lighter version, use skimmed milk and 3 oz/85 grams light Philadelphia herb cheese. For an even richer version, mix together 1 egg yolk and ⅓ cup/120 ml cream and stir into soup. Heat but do not boil.

Cream of Broccoli Soup

1 onion, chopped
3 tbsp/45 g butter
6 cups/1½ liters chicken broth
2⅓ lb/1 kg broccoli, peeled, chopped
1 tsp curry powder
salt
freshly ground pepper
½ cup/120 ml light cream
croutons or chopped green onions

Yield: 6 - 8 servings

In a saucepan, sauté onion in butter over medium heat, stirring, for 4 minutes. Add chicken broth, broccoli, curry powder, salt and pepper to taste. Simmer, covered, for 30 minutes. Purée the mixture, return to low heat and add cream. Allow the soup to heat through gently. Just before serving, put in heated soup bowls and top with croutons or chopped green onions.

Soupe à l'Oignon Gratinée
(French Onion Soup)

*T*he secret to this onion soup is lots and lots of onions!

Heat 3 tablespoons butter and 1 tablespoon oil in heavy skillet. Add onions and stir to coat. Cover pan and cook 20 minutes, stirring occasionally. Uncover pan, raise heat and sprinkle on salt, pepper and sugar. Cook 30 minutes or until onions have turned a deep rich brown. (Watch carefully to be sure the onions do not burn.) Reduce heat and stir in flour, cooking several minutes, until the flour is cooked. Remove from heat and stir in 1 cup/240 ml bouillon; return to the heat and add remaining bouillon, wine, bay leaf and paprika. Cook, covered, for 30 minutes. Taste and correct seasoning if necessary. Remove bay leaf.

Sauté French bread slices with 2 tablespoons butter, 1 tablespoon oil and the 3 chopped garlic cloves until golden brown. Ladle soup into individual oven-proof soup crocks and float bread slices on soup. Top each bowl with lots of Gruyère cheese and then 1 tablespoon cognac. Sprinkle with a little Parmesan cheese. Bake in a preheated oven until hot and bubbling.

3 tbsp/45 g butter
1 tbsp oil
4 lb/1 ¾ kg onions, sliced very thin
salt
freshly ground pepper
½ tsp sugar
1 tbsp flour
1½ quarts/liters beef bouillon
½ cup/120 ml white wine
1 bay leaf
1½ tsp paprika

6 slices French bread
2 tbsp/30 g butter
1 tbsp oil
3 garlic cloves, chopped
grated Gruyère cheese
freshly grated Parmesan cheese
6 tbsp cognac

Oven Temp: 400°F/200°C

Yield: 6 servings

> *Belgium is a country of soup eaters… Men especially feel deprived if their dinner does not start with soup, and I've seen strong men being pitiful about this.*
> Nika Hazelton

Lentil Soup

7 oz/200 g lardons (see index)
2 tbsp olive oil
1 large onion, chopped
3 carrots, coarsely grated
1 tsp marjoram
1 tsp thyme
1 (28 oz/825 g) can tomatoes
7 cups/1¾ liters broth (beef, chicken or vegetable)
1½ cups/350 ml dried lentils (see note)
6 oz/175 ml dry white wine
⅓ cup/80 ml chopped fresh parsley
salt
½ tsp freshly ground black pepper

Yield: 8 - 10 servings

Heat the oil in large saucepan and sauté the lardons until half cooked. Add onions, carrots, marjoram and thyme. Cook, stirring the vegetables, for about 5 minutes. Coarsely chop the tomatoes and add them to the pot along with their juice. Add the broth and lentils. Bring the soup to boil, reduce the heat and simmer, covered, for about 45 minutes to 1 hour or until the lentils are tender.

Add wine, pepper, salt (if needed) and parsley and simmer the soup for a few minutes before serving.

Variations: To make a meaty soup, add some cubed lean ham. For a hearty main dish, serve leftovers hot over rice. For extra spice, add a few dashes of Tabasco sauce.

The most popular lentils are the common brown (lentilles blondes) and the small green (lentilles vertes). Before using, pick out any small stones, wash and drain. Lentils retain their shape better if they are soaked in cold water for one hour before cooking.

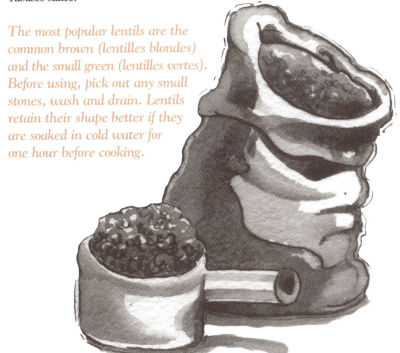

Tuscan Bean and Cabbage Soup

A casual fireside soup to warm your winter day.

1 tbsp/15 g butter
2 tbsp olive oil
1 medium onion, chopped
2 stalks celery, diced
3 garlic cloves, chopped
1 lb/450 g green cabbage, chopped
1½ quarts/liters chicken broth
1 (28 oz/800 g) can tomatoes
2 cups/475 ml canned white beans, drained
2 smoked ham hocks*
¼ cup/60 ml chopped fresh basil
salt
freshly ground pepper

Yield: 6 - 8 servings

Over medium heat, melt the butter with the oil in large pot. Sauté onion, celery and garlic for 5 minutes. Add cabbage and cook 5 more minutes. Watch carefully so it does not scorch. Add remaining ingredients and bring to a boil. Reduce heat and simmer for 45 minutes, stirring occasionally. Dice meat, discarding the bone and return the meat to the soup.

* If you cannot find ham hocks, you may substitute 2 cups/475 ml cubed smoked ham.

Black Bean Soup

1 lb/450 g dried black beans
1 smoked ham hock
6 cups/1½ liters chicken broth
2 tbsp olive oil
1 large onion, diced
1 garlic clove, chopped
¾ tsp chili powder
2 tbsp vinegar
1½ tsp fresh coriander (cilantro)
salt
freshly ground pepper

Yield: 10 servings

Soak beans overnight. Drain beans and place in a stock pot with ham. Simmer until tender. Strain ham and beans, reserving broth. Purée half of the beans. Set aside both puréed bean mixture and remaining whole, cooked beans. In a large stock pot, heat oil and sauté onion and garlic. Add chili powder and reserved broth and simmer for 20 minutes. Add puréed beans, whole beans, vinegar, fresh coriander and chopped ham (from the ham hock). Bring to a boil and simmer for 5 minutes. Season to taste with salt and pepper.

This Black Bean Soup is delicious on its own, but here are some simple and attractive accompaniments. Pick your favorites or use them all for a festive occasion: dry sherry (served in a small pitcher), rice, chopped onions, thin lemon slices, sliced hard boiled eggs, chopped fresh parsley, avocado slices, tomato slices, sour cream and Tabasco sauce.

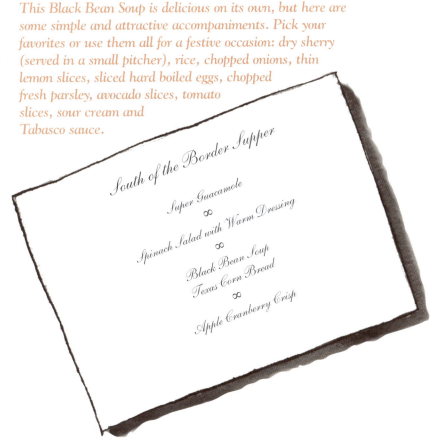

South of the Border Supper

Super Guacamole
∞
Spinach Salad with Warm Dressing
∞
Black Bean Soup
Texas Corn Bread
∞
Apple Cranberry Crisp

Soup

Goulash Soup

A hearty rendition of a regional European soup.

5 thick slices bacon, chopped
3 lb/1½ kg stewing beef, cubed
2 tbsp vegetable oil
4 medium onions
3 garlic cloves, minced
3 tbsp paprika (Hungarian sweet)
1½ tsp caraway seeds
⅓ cup/45 g all-purpose flour
¼ cup/60 ml red wine vinegar
¼ cup/60 ml tomato paste
5 cups/1⅓ liters beef broth
5 cups/1⅓ liters water
½ tsp salt
2 red bell peppers, chopped
4 large baking potatoes
freshly ground pepper

Yield: 12 servings

In a heavy 8 quart/liter pot, cook bacon over moderate heat, stirring, until crisp. Transfer with a slotted spoon to a large bowl. In the fat remaining in the pot, brown beef in small batches over high heat. As it browns, transfer meat to a bowl with a slotted spoon.

Reduce heat to moderate and add oil. Add onions and garlic and cook, stirring, until golden. Stir in paprika, caraway seeds and flour. Cook for 2 minutes, stirring. Whisk in vinegar and tomato paste. (Mixture will be very thick.) Stir in broth, water, salt, bell peppers, bacon and beef. Bring to a boil. Cover and simmer soup, stirring occasionally for 45 minutes.

Peel potatoes and cut into ½"/1¼cm pieces. Add to the soup and simmer, covered, stirring occasionally until tender, about 30 minutes. Adjust the salt if necessary and season the soup with pepper to taste.

> *... there's little I've eaten in Belgium that wouldn't be ideal on a cold day.*
> Lynn Rossetto Kasper

Tortellini Pesto Vegetable Soup

Vegetable soup that tastes even better with your own homemade PESTO.

1 small onion, chopped
2 garlic cloves, minced
1 tbsp/15 g butter
6 cups/1½ liters chicken broth
1 bunch broccoli, in florets
2 carrots, sliced or chopped
2 leeks, white only, chopped
½ zucchini, chopped
9 oz/250 g cheese spinach tortellini
¼ cup/60 ml pesto
¼ cup/60 ml freshly grated Parmesan

Yield: 8 - 10 servings

In a large saucepan, cook onion and garlic in butter just until tender. Stir in chicken broth, broccoli and carrots and simmer for 5 minutes. Add leeks and zucchini and bring to a boil. Stir in tortellini and return to a boil. Reduce heat, cover and simmer until tortellini is tender but firm. Stir in pesto. Ladle into serving bowls and top with cheese.

> **The best way to enjoy meals is with family or friends.**
> Jacques Pepin

Winter Vegetable Beef Soup

3 quarts/liters beef broth
2 cups/475 ml large white beans (see note)
¼ cup/60 ml chopped fresh basil
2 tsp finely chopped garlic
3 cups/700 ml meatless spaghetti sauce
1 lb/½ kg lean beef
2 carrots, diced
4 ribs celery, diced
1 medium onion, diced
1 zucchini, diced
1 large potato, peeled and diced
¼ cup/60 ml pepe pasta
3 fresh Italian plum tomatoes, diced
salt
freshly ground pepper
½ lb/225 g fresh spinach, washed, chopped
freshly grated Parmesan cheese

Yield: 15 servings

Bring broth to a boil; add drained beans. Simmer beans until almost tender (according to package directions). Add basil, garlic and spaghetti sauce. Simmer 15 minutes. Cut beef into small cubes and add to the pot with the carrots, celery and onion and simmer 15 minutes. Add zucchini and potato, simmer another 5 minutes, stirring frequently. Add the pasta and tomatoes and cook another 5 to 10 minutes. Stir in spinach and cook until wilted. Season soup with salt and pepper to taste. Serve with Parmesan cheese.

Most dried beans need to be soaked before cooking, usually in cold water to cover, for 8 hours or overnight. Before soaking carefully pick over the beans to remove any small stones; then wash and dry. To quickly soak dried beans, cover with water, bring to a boil and boil hard for 2 minutes. Cover and let stand 1 hour before draining.

Salads

Salads

Arugula Salad with Avocado, Shiitakes and Prosciutto	71
Asparagus Salad Vinaigrette	82
California Pasta Salad	91
Cashew, Shrimp and Pea Salad	88
Cole Slaw	98
Crottin de Chavignol Salade	74
Curried Chicken, Pasta and Apple Salad	92
Endive, Pear, Roquefort and Walnut Salad	77
Endive Salad with Roquefort	77
Four Bean Chicken Salad	73
French Potato Salad	85
Fresh Cucumber Mold	97
Golden Chicken and Spiced Wheat Salad	93
Greek Couscous Salad	94
Mesclun aux Lardons	76
Mesclun aux Timbales de Chèvre	75
Mixed Greens with Fennel, Pears and Parmesan	78
Orange Avocado Salad	79
Oriental Chicken Salad	72
Pasta Salad with Roasted Peppers, Basil and Cheese	90
Petite Salade du Sud-Ouest	69
Potato Salad with Caraway	86
Salade Liègeoise	84
Salade Niçoise	96
Sesame Noodle Salad	89
Snow Pea Salad	83
Spinach Salad with Chutney Dressing	80
Spinach Salad with Warm Dressing	81
Tomatoes Provençal	87
Warm Scampi Salad	70

Dressings

Apple Honey Mustard Vinaigrette	77
Basic Vinaigrette	99
Blue Cheese Salad Dressing	101
Caesar Salad Dressing	100
Creamy Dill Dressing	88
Herbed Vinaigrette	99
Lemon Leek Salad Dressing	78
Mayonnaise	102
Oriental Dressing	72
Poppy Seed Dressing	79
Sweet and Sour Dressing	100

SPECIAL TOPICS

Goat Cheese/Chèvre	74
Herbed Vinegar/Flavored Oil	101
Salad Greens	94
Tomatoes	87

Petite Salade du Sud-Ouest

Wash and shake the greens, one at a time, keeping them separate. Place the duck legs under a preheated broiler and grill for 10 to 12 minutes, turning occasionally. Remove from oven and take the meat off the bones, reserving 1 teaspoon duck fat.

various salad greens (including frisée)
4 whole legs of duck confit
2 tart apples, peeled and diced
freshly ground pepper
12 walnut halves
12 cherry tomatoes, halved

Dressing:
2 minced shallots
1½ tbsp cider vinegar
1 tsp Dijon mustard
salt
freshly ground pepper
½ tbsp walnut oil
3 tbsp vegetable oil

Yield: 4 servings

Sauté the shallots (for the dressing) in reserved duck fat just until tender. Remove from the pan and cool. In the same pan, cook the apples until tender. Add pepper to taste and set aside.

A salad may also be served as a first course - be sure the portions are smaller and it is compatible with the rest of the meal.

To make the dressing, combine the vinegar, mustard, salt, pepper and both oils. Stir in reserved shallots.

Lightly brown the walnuts on a baking sheet. Arrange the greens decoratively on a plate with the frisée in the center. Put the apples on the frisée and arrange the duck pieces on top. Pour dressing on the greens. Arrange the walnuts and cherry tomato halves on each salad.

Variation: Substitute slices of smoked poultry (chicken, duck or turkey) for the duck confit.

Warm Scampi Salad
Castello Banfi - Ruane Breeda, Chef

To make the vinaigrette dressing, whisk all dressing ingredients together. Wash and dry the salad greens and tear into pieces. Place in a salad bowl.

selection of salad greens*
1 lb/450 g scampi
3 tbsp olive oil
1 lb/450 g sliced tomatoes

Vinaigrette Dressing:
3 tbsp balsamic vinegar
9 tbsp olive oil
salt
freshly ground pepper

Garnish:
2 tbsp chopped fresh basil
1 small red bell pepper, chopped

Yield: 4 servings

De-vein the scampi, wash and dry (see index). In a large frying pan, fry the scampi in hot olive oil until golden brown, 1 to 2 minutes. Remove immediately from the pan.

Toss the salad greens with just enough dressing to make the leaves glisten; reserve the remaining dressing. Arrange the greens on 4 plates, making sure that there is some height in the center. Make a circle with the sliced tomatoes around the salad. Divide the scampi among the plates. Garnish with basil and red pepper. Drizzle scampi with just a touch of reserved vinaigrette. Serve immediately.

* Selection may include raddichio, oak leaf lettuce, white frisée and arugula.

Arugula Salad with Avocado, Shiitakes and Prosciutto

Set the stage for your main dish with this very special first course salad.

1 large red bell pepper
16 fresh shiitake mushrooms
6 oz/170 g arugula
1 avocado
¼ cup/60 ml (or more) olive oil
3 oz/85 g prosciutto, thinly sliced
2 tbsp balsamic vinegar
2 to 3 dashes of Tabasco sauce
freshly ground black pepper

Yield: 4 servings

Roast the pepper, cut into thin strips and set aside (see note). Pull off the shiitake stems, including the hard center, and slice the caps into thin strips. Set them aside.

Remove any coarse stems from the arugula and arrange the leaves on four salad plates. Arrange the pepper strips around the edge. Peel and slice the avocado and divide among the plates.

Fry the prosciutto in oil in a large heavy skillet over medium heat until crisp. As the pieces cook, transfer them to a plate lined with a paper towel. When cool, crumble them coarsely. Drain excess fat into a measuring cup and return 2 tablespoons of the oil to the skillet. Heat over moderately high heat. Add the mushrooms and sauté quickly until they are seared and juicy. Using a slotted spoon, remove them from the pan and divide among the plates.

Pour any drippings from the pan into the measuring cup. Add enough olive oil to make a ¼ cup/60 ml and return to the pan. Whisk in the vinegar, Tabasco and pepper to taste. Drizzle the warm dressing evenly over the salads. Sprinkle the crumbled prosciutto on top and serve immediately.

To roast a bell pepper, place the pepper on a broiler pan and roast under a hot broiler, turning occasionally, until it is evenly blistered and charred on all sides. Place in a brown paper or plastic bag and set aside until cool enough to handle. Slide the skin off and scrape out the stem, seeds and ribs. Pat the flesh dry.

> *Les amours sont comme les champignons, on ne sait si elles appartiennent à la bonne ou à la mauvaise espèce que lorsqu'il est trop tard.*
> Tristan Bernard

Oriental Chicken Salad

*P*oach the chicken breasts in water (or white wine) just until cooked. Remove, cool and cut into small pieces.

4 skinned chicken breast halves
½ lb/225 g snow peas
1 can water chestnuts, sliced
6 green onions, sliced
lettuce

Blanch the snow peas in boiling water for 20 seconds, refresh in ice water and drain.

In a bowl, combine chicken, water chestnuts, green onions and snow peas. Pour on ORIENTAL DRESSING and mix. Serve on a bed of lettuce.

Yield: 4 servings

Dressing:
2 tbsp fresh lemon juice
2 tbsp soy sauce
2 tbsp peanut oil
2 tbsp oriental sesame oil
1 tsp peeled, minced fresh ginger
1 - 2 tbsp fine granulated sugar

Yield: ½ cup/120 ml

Oriental Dressing

Whisk together lemon juice, soy sauce, oils, ginger and sugar to taste.

Variation: Try this dressing with sliced cucumbers or crisp fresh bean sprouts.

Four Bean Chicken Salad
American Women's Club of Brussels - Michel Thomasset, Chef

Combine all the marinade ingredients. Pour over the chicken breasts, cover and refrigerate overnight.

To make the dressing, whisk together all dressing ingredients.

Combine the cooked green beans and dried beans, the onions, shallots and parsley. Pour on the dressing and mix well. Set aside.

Broil the chicken until just cooked through. Cut in diagonal slices.

Serve the bean salad on a bed of lettuce leaves and decorate with tomato wedges, olives, nuts and cheese. Top with slices of broiled chicken.

4 boned, skinned chicken breast halves
1 cup/240 ml cooked green beans
4 cups/960 ml cooked mixed dried beans (see note)
½ cup/120 ml chopped green onions
½ cup/120 ml minced shallots
chopped parsley
soft leaf lettuce leaves

Marinade:
2 tbsp fresh lime juice
2 tsp honey
1 large garlic clove, minced
1 tsp Worcestershire sauce
dash of Tabasco sauce
2 tbsp fresh coriander (cilantro), chopped

Dressing:
½ cup/120 ml vinegar
¾ cup/180 ml mixed corn and olive oils
½ tsp salt
freshly ground black pepper
½ tsp oregano
½ tsp basil
3 garlic cloves, crushed
1 tbsp dry red wine
grated rind and juice of ½ lemon

Garnish:
tomato wedges
pitted black olives
slivered almonds or chopped pistachios
grated cheddar cheese

Yield: 6 - 8 servings

When selecting dried beans, choose three similarly sized beans of different colors for the nicest presentation, such as kidney, garbanzo, white, pinto or black beans. Dried beans will yield at least double their volume cooked. Each type of bean must be cooked separately.

Salads

Crottin de Chavignol Salade

4 pieces Crottin de Chavignol
honey
herbes de Provence
6 oz/170 g salade de blé
8 green onions, sliced
¼ cup/60 ml pine nuts, slightly toasted

Balsamic Vinegar Dressing:
2 tbsp balsamic vinegar
6 tbsp extra virgin olive oil
salt
freshly ground pepper
1 tsp honey (optional)

Oven Temp: 400°F/200°C
Yield: 4 servings

Whisk together dressing ingredients. Slice each Crottin de Chavignol horizontally and put on a baking tray, cut side up. Brush with honey and sprinkle with herbes de Provence. Bake approximately 10 minutes in a preheated oven until soft, but not runny.

Toss salade de blé with green onions, pine nuts and dressing. Arrange salad on plates and put two pieces of cheese on each salad. Serve immediately.

GOAT CHEESE/CHÈVRE

Goat Cheese/Chèvre is available in several textures and strengths of taste. All forms can be heated in the oven, however the crottin maintains its shape the best when heated. Mild and creamy Montrachet and buttery Boucheron are two of the most readily available and popular of the chèvres.

- Crottin de Chavignol is a firmly textured chèvre which is sold in a disk shape. It comes from a specific region and is marked with an AOC (Appellation d'Origine Contrôlée) stamp to prove its authenticity.
- Chèvre affiné is a softer textured chèvre with a strong taste.
- Chèvre pavé is soft and has a moderate taste.
- Chèvre frais, such as Chavroux, is a very soft cheese with a mild taste.

Mesclun aux Timbales de Chèvre

1 lb/450 g mild, creamy chèvre
4 eggs
¾ lb/340 g mesclun*
fresh thyme leaves
black olives

Vinaigrette:
2 tbsp tarragon or white wine vinegar
2 tsp Dijon mustard
salt
freshly ground pepper
6 tbsp olive oil
2 tbsp minced fresh tarragon, chervil, basil, dill or chives

Oven Temp: 350°F/175°C
Yield: 6 servings

In a food processor, combine chèvre and eggs and process until smooth. Divide the cheese mixture among 6 buttered ½ cup/120 ml ramekins and smooth the tops. Set the ramekins in a bain marie (see index). Bake in a preheated oven for 20 to 25 minutes, or until tops are puffed and golden. Remove the ramekins from the water bath and let cool until warm. (The timbales may be made ahead of time. Before serving, remove timbales from ramekins, put on a cookie sheet and gently warm in the oven.)

To make the vinaigrette, whisk together vinegar and mustard. Add salt and pepper to taste. Slowly drizzle in olive oil, whisking constantly. Stir in 2 tablespoons of minced fresh herbs.

In a large bowl, toss the mesclun with the vinaigrette. Invert a timbale onto each of 6 serving plates and surround the timbale with salad. Top each timbale with thyme leaves and olives.

* mixed baby salad greens

Olive oil is used where the flavor of the oil enhances the dish. The best quality oils, green and fruity extra virgin and virgin, are "cold-pressed" from hand-picked olives and have a rich taste. Lesser quality olive oil is extracted, using heat and chemical solvents, from subsequent pressings of the residue and is not as flavorful. If you like a delicate olive oil taste, mix a fine quality olive oil with safflower or corn oil.

Mesclun aux Lardons
Le Café Camille - Olivier Bellaches, Chef

To make the dressing, brown the lardons in a very hot frying pan. When the lardons are well done, drain the grease and add the brown sauce to the lardons. Remove from the heat and add the vinegar. Put back on the heat and reduce for 2 minutes; add the butter and reduce for 1 minute more, whisking until creamy and thickened.

Gently toss the salad greens with the warm dressing. Arrange on salad plates and serve immediately, topped with chives, pine nuts, apple and tomatoes.

To make the brown sauce, whisk together 5 teaspoons of meat fond de sauce (brown sauce powder) and 17 oz/500 ml water.

1 lb/450 g salade de blé frisée (red and green)
1 bunch chives, chopped
3½ oz/100 g pine nuts, toasted
1 Golden Delicious apple, diced
2 tomatoes, cut in wedges

Dressing:
14 oz/400 g lardons (see index)
17 oz/500 ml brown sauce (see note)
7 oz/200 ml sherry vinegar
½ cup + 3 tbsp/150 g butter

Yield: 8 servings

Endive, Pear, Roquefort and Walnut Salad

The deliciously sweet dressing is a perfect complement to the sharp greens in the salad.

2 Belgian endives
1 medium head radicchio
1 head soft leaf lettuce or mixed greens
2 pears, sliced
½ cup/120 ml walnuts, chopped
4 oz/115 g Roquefort, crumbled

Wash and pat dry the endives, radicchio and lettuce; separate the leaves. In a large bowl, mix the endive leaves with the radicchio and lettuce and pour on just enough APPLE HONEY MUSTARD VINAIGRETTE to lightly coat the leaves. Toss well and place on individual salad plates. Arrange pears around the salad and top with walnuts and Roquefort cheese.

Yield: 8 servings

Apple Honey Mustard Vinaigrette
Combine vinaigrette ingredients in a jar and shake for 5 to 10 seconds.

Vinaigrette:
⅓ cup/80 ml extra virgin olive oil
⅓ cup/80 ml honey
⅔ cup/160 ml apple juice
3 tbsp grainy mustard
2 tbsp white wine vinegar

Yield: 1½ cups/350 ml

Endive Salad with Roquefort

2 lb/900 g endive (about 6)
1 cup/140 g walnuts, chopped
6 oz/170 g Roquefort, crumbled
1 apple, chopped (optional)

Separate endive leaves, wash thoroughly and pat dry. Place leaves, whole or chopped, in a large salad bowl. Add walnuts, cheese (and apple). To make the dressing, mix lemon juice and salt; whisk in oil. Pour the dressing on the salad and toss well. Serve immediately.

Variation: Include raisins and sun-dried tomatoes (drained and chopped) for an additional burst of flavor.

Dressing:
2 tbsp fresh lemon juice
¼ tsp salt
¼ cup/60 ml walnut oil

Yield: 6 servings

> "I think I could talk forever about the 'white lady,' but it would not be right. Some people hate her, even Belgians, you know!"
> — Michel Thomasset

Salads 77

Mixed Greens with Fennel, Pears and Parmesan

For those who love the anise taste of fennel, add a little more!

3 bunches watercress, stems removed
3 cups/700 ml coarsely torn salad greens
1 small head radicchio, separated
1 cup/240 ml sliced fennel
3 tbsp pine nuts, toasted
2 pears, peeled, cored, thinly sliced
1 cup/240 ml shaved Parmesan cheese

Yield: 6 - 8 servings

Toss the watercress, salad greens, radicchio, and fennel together in a large salad bowl. Scatter the pine nuts, pears, and Parmesan over the greens. Toss the salad with enough LEMON LEEK SALAD DRESSING to coat and refrigerate remaining dressing. Serve immediately.

Lemon Leek Salad Dressing

Dressing:
1 large egg yolk
2 tbsp Dijon mustard
½ cup/120 ml fresh lemon juice
3 tbsp tarragon vinegar
1 leek, minced
3 tbsp tarragon
1½ cups/350 ml vegetable oil
2 cups/475 ml extra virgin olive oil
salt
freshly ground pepper

Yield: 1 quart/liter

Whisk the egg yolk and mustard together in a mixing bowl. Whisk in the lemon juice and vinegar. Add the leek and tarragon and whisk to combine. Continue to whisk, pouring in the oils in a thin, steady stream. Season to taste with salt and lots of pepper. Store, covered, in the refrigerator.

Try using this dressing on a mixed green salad, topped with grilled shrimp.

Orange Avocado Salad

This refreshing fruit salad is appropriate for lunch or as a dinner accompaniment.

1 large orange
1 lb/450 g salad greens, torn in pieces
1 large avocado, peeled and sliced
1 cup/240 ml salted cashews

Cut the orange in half and section with a grapefruit knife. Combine the orange with the greens, avocado and cashews. Drizzle enough Poppy Seed Dressing *over the salad to coat well. Serve on chilled plates. (Refrigerate remaining dressing.)*

Yield: 8 servings

Poppy Seed Dressing

Combine sugar, mustard, vinegar and onion. Mix well and whisk in oil. Add poppy seeds. Keep refrigerated.

Dressing:
1½ cups/300 g fine granulated sugar
2 tsp dry mustard
⅔ cup/160 ml vinegar
1 tbsp grated onion
2 cups/475 ml olive oil
3 tbsp poppy seeds

Yield: 1 quart/liter

Salads

Spinach Salad with Chutney Dressing

*D*elicious as a salad or topped with sliced chicken for a light meal. Reserve a little dressing to flavor the chicken!

Spread the pecans on a baking sheet and toast in a preheated oven for 12 minutes, watching carefully that the pecans do not burn.

1 cup/240 ml pecan halves (4 oz)
1½ lb/680 g young spinach
2 red apples
½ cup/120 ml raisins
½ cup/120 ml chopped green onions

Wash, stem and dry the spinach. Core, halve and thinly slice the unpeeled apples crosswise. Put the spinach, apples, pecans, raisins, and green onions in a large salad bowl.

Chutney Dressing:
½ cup/120 ml vegetable oil
4 tbsp mango chutney
1 tsp curry powder
1 tsp dry mustard
½ tsp salt
2 tbsp lemon juice

To make the dressing, stir together the oil, chutney, curry powder, dry mustard, salt and lemon juice. Add the dressing to the salad and toss gently to coat all ingredients. Serve immediately.

Variation: Substitute salade de blé for the spinach.

Oven Temp: 300°F/150°C
Yield: 4 - 6 servings

Spinach Salad with Warm Dressing

¼ cup/60 ml pine nuts
2 tbsp/30 g butter
¼ tsp celery salt or Beau Monde
1 lb/450 g mushrooms, sliced
½ lb/225 g lardons (see index)
1 lb/450 g spinach
6 green onions, chopped
½ cup/120 ml finely grated Parmesan
½ cup/120 ml finely grated feta

Warm Dressing:
⅔ cup/160 ml vegetable oil
¼ cup/60 ml red wine vinegar
2 tbsp white wine
2 tsp soy sauce
1 tsp sugar
1 tsp dry mustard
½ tsp pepper
1 garlic clove, minced
reserved lardon drippings

Yield: 6 - 8 servings

Over low heat, sauté the pine nuts in 1 tablespoon of the butter. When pine nuts are lightly browned, remove with a slotted spoon and place on a paper towel to drain. Sprinkle celery salt on the pine nuts while they are still warm. Melt the remaining tablespoon of butter and sauté the mushrooms until tender. Set aside. Cook the lardons until crisp. Remove the lardons from the pan, reserving drippings for the dressing.

To make the dressing, combine in a jar the oil, vinegar, white wine, soy sauce, sugar, dry mustard, pepper and garlic and shake well. Pour into the pan with reserved lardon drippings and heat (do not boil).

Wash, stem and dry the spinach and combine it with the green onions in a large salad bowl. Add the pine nuts, mushrooms, lardons and cheeses. Toss in the warm dressing and serve immediately.

> To eat is to commune - first of all with the person responsible for what's on your plate. Beyond that, in its fullest, most satisfying sense, to eat is to absorb the essence of a place: a landscape, an economy, a way of life all condensed into a special sensory experience.
>
> G. Y. Dryansky

Asparagus Salad Vinaigrette

Especially good in the spring when the asparagus is young and tender.

2 lb/900 g fresh asparagus
1 head soft leaf lettuce

Vinaigrette Dressing:
2 tbsp white wine vinegar
1½ tsp Dijon mustard
¼ tsp salt
freshly ground pepper
1 tbsp minced green onions
1 tbsp minced fresh parsley
6 tbsp vegetable oil
¼ tsp oriental sesame oil

Yield: 6 servings

Wash asparagus and cut off the woody bottom of each stalk. If the asparagus is thick, peel the outer stalk at the bottom with a vegetable peeler. Simmer the spears until just tender when pierced at the bottom. Drain spears well. Cover and chill.

To make the vinaigrette, whisk together the vinegar, mustard, salt, pepper (to taste), green onions and parsley. Slowly whisk in the vegetable oil until blended. Add sesame oil to taste. (Just a faint nutty flavor should be present.) Cover and refrigerate.

Just before serving, arrange the asparagus on a bed of lettuce. Spoon the vinaigrette over the salad and serve cold.

> *Nature, with its changing seasons, varies our diet beautifully...*
> Delia Smith

Snow Pea Salad

½ lb/225 g fresh snow peas
1 large red bell pepper
½ lb/225 g fresh mushrooms
2 tbsp sesame seeds, toasted

Dressing:
⅓ cup/80 ml oil
2 tbsp white wine vinegar
1 tbsp fresh lemon juice
1 garlic clove, minced
1 tbsp fine granulated sugar
½ tsp salt

Yield: 4 servings

Remove strings from snow peas and blanch them for 1 minute in boiling water. Immediately rinse with cold water to stop cooking. Drain well. Slice the snow peas in half diagonally. Cut pepper into thin 2"/5cm strips and thinly slice mushrooms. Combine the peppers and mushrooms with the snow peas.

To make the dressing, combine oil, vinegar, lemon juice, garlic, sugar and salt; mix well. Pour dressing over the salad and gently toss to coat.

Refrigerate up to 24 hours. Just before serving, add sesame seeds and toss the salad again.

> **I could quite happily live on salads.**
> Anton Mosimann

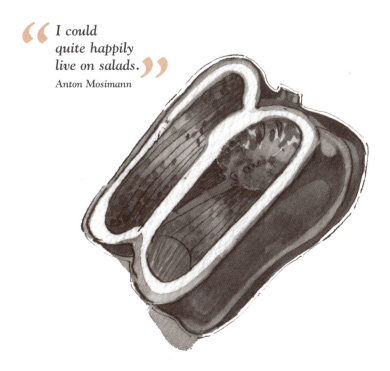

Salade Liègeoise
American Women's Club of Brussels - Michel Thomasset, Chef

This hearty salad from Liège is perfect for a buffet luncheon or as an accompaniment to a simple main dish.

6 medium potatoes
7 oz/200 g lardons (see index)
2 tbsp/30 g butter
2 tbsp oil
4 shallots, thinly sliced*
1 lb/450 g large green beans
freshly ground black pepper
4 - 6 tbsp cider or balsamic vinegar
chopped parsley

Yield: 4 servings

Boil the potatoes in their skins until barely tender. Let cool until lukewarm and peel. Cut in half and then into thick slices. In a large skillet, fry the lardons until crisp; remove. Add butter and oil to the same pan and sauté the potatoes and shallots until light brown.

Trim the ends from the beans and cook the beans in boiling salted water. When just tender, rinse quickly in cold water just enough to stop the cooking and to set the color, but not enough to cool them completely. Put the beans in a serving dish and add a generous amount of pepper. Add the warm potatoes and onions and top with the lardons.

Deglaze the skillet with vinegar and pour over the salad. Sprinkle with chopped parsley and serve warm.

* or sliced sweet onion

> "Two things are too serious to joke about - marriage and potatoes."
> Irish Proverb

French Potato Salad

2 lb/900 g waxy potatoes
4 tbsp white wine
2 tbsp chicken broth
3 tbsp chopped parsley

Dressing:
2 tbsp wine vinegar
1 tsp Dijon mustard
¼ tsp salt
freshly ground pepper
6 tbsp olive oil
2 tbsp minced shallots, chives or onion

Yield: 4 - 6 servings

Boil the potatoes in salted water until just tender; drain. When cool enough to handle, peel and cut the potatoes into very thin slices. Put in a bowl. Pour the wine and broth over the warm potatoes and toss very gently. Set aside for a few minutes until the potatoes absorb the liquids.

To make the dressing, whisk together the vinegar, mustard, salt and pepper in a small bowl until the salt dissolves. Then whisk in the oil by droplets. Stir in the shallots, chives or onion.

Pour the dressing over the potatoes and toss gently to blend. Serve warm or chilled, sprinkled with parsley.

Potato Salad With Caraway

*T*his tasty salad is even more flavorful the day after it is made.

3 lb/1⅓ kg waxy potatoes
¼ cup/60 ml tarragon vinegar
3 tbsp fine granulated sugar
¼ tsp paprika
salt
freshly ground black pepper
⅓ cup/80 ml chopped green bell pepper
¼ cup/60 ml chopped green onions
1 tsp caraway seeds, crushed
¼ tsp celery seeds
½ cup/120 ml sour cream
½ cup/120 ml mayonnaise

Garnish:
soft lettuce leaves
3 tbsp snipped fresh chives

Yield: 6 servings

Cook potatoes in a large pot of boiling water until just tender; drain and cool slightly. Cut the potatoes into ¼"/½cm slices. Combine vinegar, 2 tablespoons of the sugar, paprika, salt and a generous amount of pepper in a large bowl. Mix in the warm potatoes and let marinate 45 minutes. Gently mix in the bell pepper, green onions, caraway seeds and celery seeds. Combine the sour cream and mayonnaise and mix into the salad. Adjust seasonings and add the remaining 1 tablespoon sugar, if desired. Cover and refrigerate until well chilled.

Let salad stand at room temperature 30 minutes before serving. Line a large shallow bowl or platter with lettuce. Top with the potato salad and sprinkle with chives.

Green onions are also called spring onions or scallions.

Tomatoes Provençal

This delicious salad may be made in advance and is especially nice in summer when tomatoes are ripe and full of flavor.

12 large tomatoes
salt
freshly ground black pepper
2 large garlic cloves, minced
2 tbsp extra virgin olive oil
12 large fresh basil leaves

Dressing:
2 tbsp extra virgin olive oil
2 tbsp balsamic vinegar

Garnish:
24 fresh basil leaves
24 cured black olives
watercress sprigs

Oven Temp: 400°F/200°C
Yield: 24 tomato halves

Skin the tomatoes by pouring boiling water over them. Let stand for 1 minute; drain, cool, and remove skins. Cut each tomato in half and place the halves in a shallow, oiled roasting pan, cut side up. Season with salt and pepper. Sprinkle on the garlic, distributing it evenly among the tomatoes. Drizzle a few drops of olive oil on each tomato and top each with half a basil leaf, turning the leaf over to coat with oil.

Place the roasting pan on a rack in the top half of a preheated oven and roast the tomatoes for 50 to 60 minutes, or until the edges are slightly blackened. Remove the pan from the oven and allow the tomatoes to cool. (May be done several hours ahead.)

Transfer tomato halves to individual serving plates or a serving platter. To make the dressing, whisk the oil and balsamic vinegar together and drizzle it over the tomatoes. Top each tomato with a fresh basil leaf and an olive; decorate with sprigs of watercress.

TOMATOES

Tomatoes are their tastiest from May to September; however, good ones are available throughout the year from other parts of the world. In addition to the standard tomato used in salads and vegetable dishes, look for the following alternatives:

- *Cherry Tomatoes/Tomates Cerises are slightly larger than an olive. They are crisp and flavorful and may be eaten plain, grilled or stuffed. In addition to red, yellow are sometimes available.*
- *Plum Tomatoes/Tomates Roma are oval-shaped and fleshy and are often used in preparing Italian dishes.*
- *Vine Tomatoes/Tomates en Grappes are sold on the vine and have a "fresh from the garden" flavor and aroma.*

Cashew, Shrimp and Pea Salad

A delicious summer salad for dinner in the garden.

1 cup/240 ml roasted cashews
4 cups/950 ml frozen tiny peas, thawed and drained
1 cup/240 ml thinly sliced green onions
2 ribs celery, ½"/1 ¼cm diagonal slices
¾ lb/340 g tiny cooked, shelled shrimp
salt
freshly ground pepper

6 - 8 large soft lettuce leaves

Yield: 4 servings

Set aside ¼ cup/60 ml of cashews. In a large bowl, stir together remaining cashews, peas, green onions, celery and shrimp. Add CREAMY DILL DRESSING to shrimp mixture. Season to taste with salt and pepper. Line bowl or platter with lettuce leaves. Spoon salad into center and sprinkle reserved cashews on top.

Light Summer Luncheon

Tomatoes Provençal
∞
Cashew, Shrimp and Pea Salad
Crusty Yeast Rolls
∞
Cold Lemon Soufflé
Sugar Cookies

Dressing:
¼ cup/60 ml mayonnaise
¼ cup/60 ml sour cream or fromage frais
1 tbsp lemon juice
1 tbsp minced fresh dill

Yield: ½ cup/120 ml

Creamy Dill Dressing

Blend dressing ingredients together in a small bowl. Keep refrigerated.

" *The chapter of green peas is still continuing,
the impatience to eat them,
the pleasures of having eaten them,
and the anticipated joy of eating them again.* "
Madame de Maintenon

Sesame Noodle Salad

10 oz/280 g Chinese egg noodles or thin spaghetti
3 tbsp soy sauce
4 tbsp oriental sesame oil
2 tbsp balsamic vinegar
6 sliced green onions
⅓ cup/80 ml chopped peanuts
1 cucumber, peeled and julienned

Sauce:
2 tbsp soy sauce
½ tsp ground hot red pepper
2 tbsp packed brown sugar
¾ cup/175 ml peanut butter
2 tsp peeled, grated fresh ginger root
1 cup/240 ml chicken broth

Garnish:
scallion brushes

Yield: 6 servings

To make the sauce, combine 2 tablespoons soy sauce, hot red pepper, brown sugar, peanut butter, ginger and chicken broth in a saucepan. Simmer, stirring until thick and smooth, about 2 minutes. Let cool slightly.

Cook noodles, run under cold water and drain. Combine the 3 tablespoons soy sauce, sesame oil and balsamic vinegar and toss into the noodles. Add peanut sauce and combine well. Serve at room temperature, topped with green onions, peanuts and cucumbers. Garnish with scallion brushes (see note).

Variation: For a more authentic taste, substitute 1 teaspoon of oriental chili paste with garlic for the hot red pepper.

To make a scallion (green onion) brush, trim off the root of the green onion. Cut off a 3"/5cm length from the white end of the green onion and lay it flat. Make 6 or 8 lengthwise cuts ½"/1¼cm into each end, rotating it as you cut, to make frills at each end. Be careful to keep the piece intact. Place in ice water and refrigerate for about half an hour until the frilled ends open up and curl.

Pasta Salad with Roasted Peppers, Basil and Cheese

*T*his tasty, colorful salad must be prepared in advance - perfect for a summer buffet.

To make the vinaigrette mix together the mustard, vinegar and garlic. Whisk in the oil and let stand for 30 minutes.

Cook fusilli al dente. Drain pasta and cool immediately under cold water. Drain well.

Roast peppers (see index) and cut into thin strips. Steam snow peas until bright green and barely crisp/tender; run under cold water and drain. Cut in half diagonally.

Mix peppers, snow peas, pasta, basil and cheese. Whisk vinaigrette thoroughly and toss into salad. Season with salt and pepper to taste. Cover salad and let stand for 4 to 5 hours. Serve at room temperature, sprinkled with pine nuts if desired.

Variation: For a more pungent version, try Pecorino Romano cheese instead of Parmesan.

1 lb/450 g fusilli pasta
6 oz/140 g snow peas
4 bell peppers (green, red, yellow)
½ cup/120 ml fresh basil, chopped
3 oz/85 g Parmesan cheese shavings
salt
freshly ground pepper
¼ cup/60 ml toasted pine nuts (optional)

Garlic Vinaigrette:
2 tsp Dijon mustard
2 tbsp red wine vinegar
2 garlic cloves, minced
⅔ cup/160 ml olive oil

Yield: 6 - 8 servings

Summer Barbecue

Bruschetta
∞
Pasta Salad with Roasted Peppers, Basil and Cheese
Balsamic Chicken
Cucumber Mold
∞
Cheesecake Supreme
Summer Fruit Compote

California Pasta Salad

1 lb/450 g penne pasta
1½ lb/680 g large shrimp, cooked
1½ cups/350 ml tiny frozen peas
¼ cup/60 ml chopped green onions
1 cup/240 ml chopped artichoke hearts
½ cup/120 ml sliced pitted black olives
2 cups/475 ml quartered cherry tomatoes
2 avocados, peeled and diced
1 cup/240 ml freshly grated Parmesan

Dressing:
3 tbsp green onions, finely chopped
4 garlic cloves
1½ tsp dry mustard
1½ tsp salt
3 tbsp sugar
¾ tsp pepper
½ cup/120 ml salad oil
⅓ cup/80 ml olive oil
⅓ cup/80 ml cider or wine vinegar
3 tbsp water
½ tsp basil
¼ tsp oregano

Yield: 8 servings

To make the dressing, process the green onions and garlic in a food processor until smooth. Add mustard, salt, sugar and pepper and process again. With the machine running, slowly add the oils. Add vinegar, one tablespoon at a time, processing after each addition. Add water, basil and oregano and process briefly. Refrigerate at least 2 hours.

Cook penne al dente. Drain pasta and cool immediately under cold water. Drain well.

Thaw and drain the peas. In a large salad bowl, gently combine all salad ingredients and toss with the dressing. Sprinkle with Parmesan cheese just before serving.

> *No one is indifferent to garlic. People either love it or hate it, and most good cooks seem to belong to the first group.*
> Faye Levy

Salads

Curried Chicken, Pasta and Apple Salad

Cook fusilli al dente. Drain, rinse with cold water and drain again. Put chicken breast, onion, peppercorns, celery stalk and salt in a saucepan. Add cold water just to cover. Bring to a simmer and cook gently until the chicken is just firm to the touch. Cool in broth. Drain the chicken and shred the meat.

12 oz/340 g fusilli pasta
1 boned, skinned whole chicken breast
1 small onion
4 peppercorns
1 small celery stalk
1 tsp salt
3 medium red apples, with peel, diced
½ cup/120 ml raisins
1 cup/240 ml chopped celery
½ cup/120 ml sliced pitted ripe olives
½ cup/120 ml sliced green onions
¼ cup/60 ml slivered almonds, toasted
lettuce leaves
chopped parsley or chives

Dressing:
1 cup/240 ml mayonnaise
¼ cup/60 ml light cream
2 tsp curry powder
1½ tsp salt
⅛ tsp cayenne
1 tbsp lemon juice

Yield: 6 - 8 servings

Blend dressing ingredients in a small bowl. Combine chicken, apples, raisins, celery, olives, green onions, almonds and pasta. Pour about half the dressing over the salad and toss lightly. Cover and refrigerate at least 1 hour.

Mix in the remaining dressing just before serving. Serve mounded on a bed of lettuce and sprinkled with parsley or chives.

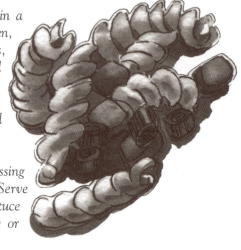

> *…there is nothing like a good lunch to give us an appetite for dinner.*
> Peter Mayle

Golden Chicken and Spiced Wheat Salad

1 tbsp mango chutney
1 tbsp mild curry paste
2 tsp ground turmeric
½ cup/120 ml olive oil
1½ lb/680 g boned, skinned chicken breasts
2 tbsp white wine vinegar
1 cup/240 ml bulgur wheat
7 oz/200 ml boiling water
salt
freshly ground pepper
2 tbsp chopped fresh chives
6 oz/170 g cherry tomatoes, halved*
1 bunch green onions, chopped
1 tbsp minced fresh mint leaves

Garnish:
mint sprigs

Yield: 6 servings

Mix together the chutney, curry paste and turmeric. Stir in half of the oil. Cut the chicken into small pieces and toss into the mixture. Cover and marinate for 30 minutes or overnight in the refrigerator. Spread the chicken and marinade in a foil-lined broiler pan. Broil 10 to 12 minutes or until the chicken is cooked. Transfer the chicken and pan juices to a bowl and stir in the remaining oil and the vinegar. Let cool.

Place the bulgur wheat in a bowl and cover with the boiling water. Cover and let soak for 5 to 10 minutes or until all the water has been absorbed (unprocessed bulgur wheat from health food shops will take about 25 minutes). Season with salt and pepper and stir in the chives.

Drain the oil mixture from the chicken and stir the oil into the wheat. Spoon the wheat onto a platter.

Combine the tomatoes, green onions, mint and chicken; spoon over the bulgur wheat. Garnish with sprigs of mint if desired.

* yellow and red if available

Greek Couscous Salad

*P*lace the couscous in a medium bowl and cover with boiling water. Stir to combine, cover and set aside for 10 minutes. Fluff with a fork.

⅔ cup/160 ml couscous
1 cup/240 ml boiling water
¾ cup/175 ml chick peas (drained)
½ cup/120 ml chopped bell pepper
⅓ cup/80 ml sliced pitted black olives
⅓ cup/80 ml chopped red onion
3 tbsp chopped fresh mint
3 tbsp olive oil
2 tbsp fresh lemon juice
¾ cup/175 ml crumbled feta cheese
salt
freshly ground pepper

Yield: 4 - 6 servings

Add chick peas, bell peppers, olives, onion and mint. Toss with olive oil and lemon juice and gently stir in the cheese. Season with salt and pepper to taste. Refrigerate until ready to serve.

SALAD GREENS

◆ *Arugula/Roquette* has small, tender, dark green leaves and imparts an aggressive peppery taste. It perks up mild lettuces and is especially delicious with ripe tomatoes and an olive oil and balsamic vinaigrette.

◆ *Belgian Endive/Chicon* is Belgium's best known member of the lettuce family. This long, oval-shaped vegetable has crisp, creamy white leaves tipped in yellow with a mildly bitter taste. The whiter the leaf, the less bitter the flavor. It combines well with Boston lettuce, watercress, arugula or radicchio. Try creamy dressings or a walnut flavored vinaigrette.

◆ *Boston/Salade Pommée* has a loose head with soft leaves and is available in pale green and red varieties. It has a buttery flavor that mixes well with Bibb, endive, spinach or watercress. Use a gentle white wine vinaigrette or buttermilk dressing.

◆ *Cabbage/Chou* is available in green or red. It has a tight head and tough, crisp, strongly flavored leaves. Traditionally used for cole slaw, it may also be mixed with carrots, onions or bell peppers and dressed with a poppyseed or vinaigrette dressing. Cabbage may also be fermented to become sauerkraut or cooked as an accompaniment to pork or corned beef.

◆ *Cressonette* has tiny leaves and a spicy taste. It is used primarily as a garnish, but may also be minced and combined with other herbs and mayonnaise to make a sauce.

◆ *Fennel/Fenouil* is a green and white bulb-shaped vegetable which is eaten raw or cooked. Its anise flavor mixes well with mild lettuces.

◆ *Frisée* has pale green, slender, curly leaves with a yellowish-white heart. This mildly bitter lettuce mixes well with arugula and oak leaf. Try a fruity or nutty vinaigrette.

◆ *Iceberg* lettuce is pale, with a tight head and crisp leaves. Its mild flavor blends well with other greens. Use substantial dressings such as Russian, Roquefort or French.

...more on SALAD GREENS

- Iceberg lettuce is pale, with a tight head and crisp leaves. Its mild flavor blends well with other greens. Use substantial dressings such as Russian, Roquefort or French.
- Lamb's Lettuce/Salade de Blé has deep green leaves which grow in a rosette. The delicate, sweet/nutty taste and is best eaten alone or with Belgian endive. It has a special affinity for raspberry, walnut or citrus vinaigrette. Try it cooked as an alternative to spinach.
- Leaf Lettuce/Batavia is a soft textured green lettuce with a frilly edge. Also available as Red-Tip Leaf/Batavia Rouge, both have a delicate, sweet flavor. Leaf lettuce is often mixed with arugula, radicchio, watercress, fennel or sorrel. It is delicious with either a red, white or cider vinaigrette.
- Mesclum/Mesclun is a mixture of tiny greens that may include arugula, chervil, dandelion, chickweed or oak leaf lettuce. Its delicate flavor mixes well with a light wine vinegar and nut oil vinaigrette.
- Oak Leaf/Feuille de Chêne has long leaves tipped in burgundy. Its delicate flavor mixes well with a mild vinaigrette.
- Radicchio/Trevise has ruby colored leaves and grows in a tight bulb. Its chewy leaves have a slightly bitter, peppery flavor. It combines well with Boston, leaf lettuce, spinach, Belgian endive or arugula. In Belgium, radicchio is mixed with Belgian endive and salade de blé for a winter salad. The assertive taste calls for a strong vinaigrette or dressing.
- Romaine is a long-stalked lettuce with medium green or red leaves. It is crisp, with a sweet/nutty flavor that mixes well with spinach, arugula or watercress. It is particularly delicious with garlic or anchovy dressings and is the ideal lettuce for a CAESAR SALAD.
- Spinach/Epinards has long stemmed, dark green oval leaves. It has a mildly hearty flavor and can be eaten raw or cooked. It mixes well with aggressive fruity or smoky dressings.
- Sorrel is a delicate salad green with smooth, arrow shaped, bright green leaves and a sharp, tangy lemon taste. Eat it raw mixed with other salad greens or cooked in soups, cream sauces or stuffings.
- Watercress/Cresson has small, dark green, glossy leaves. Part of the mustard family, its spicy flavor compliments romaine, Boston, leaf lettuce or Belgian endive. It makes a lovely garnish, enhances a salad dressed with a nutty vinaigrette, or adds a spicy taste to soup.

Salade Niçoise

Whisk together vinaigrette ingredients in a small mixing bowl. Set aside until ready to use.

Steam potatoes until tender, about 15 to 20 minutes. Peel and slice. Toss slices with green onions, vermouth, salt and pepper. Set aside.

Blanch green beans in 3 quarts/liters boiling salted water for 3 to 5 minutes. Drain the beans and chill them in ice water. Drain again and dry well.

Separate the lettuce leaves and toss the whole leaves of lettuce with 2 tablespoons of the vinaigrette. Arrange the leaves on the bottom of a large, round platter. Put the potato slices in a ring on top of the lettuce and arrange the beans and tomatoes in a decorative pattern. Flake the tuna into a mound in the center of the dish; sprinkle with capers and olives. Put the anchovies on top of the halved eggs and arrange them around the tuna. Whisk the dressing, spoon it over the salad and serve at once.

8 new potatoes
1 tbsp minced green onions
3 tbsp dry vermouth
salt
freshly ground pepper
½ lb/225 g green beans
2 heads soft leaf lettuce
4 ripe tomatoes, quartered
2 (7 oz/200 g) cans tuna, drained
3 tbsp tiny capers
½ cup/120 ml Niçoise olives
1 (2 oz/55 g) can rolled anchovies
3 hard boiled eggs, peeled, halved

Vinaigrette:
⅔ cup/160 ml olive oil
1 tbsp lemon juice
3 tbsp wine vinegar
2 tbsp Dijon mustard
1 garlic clove, minced
1 tbsp chopped fresh basil
1 tbsp chopped fresh parsley (or dill)
salt
fresly ground pepper

Yield: 4 - 6 servings

Fresh Cucumber Mold

A cooling accompaniment to a spicy main dish.

2 envelopes unflavored gelatin
½ cup/120 ml cold water
4 medium cucumbers
¾ cup/175 ml sour cream
¾ cup/175 ml mayonnaise
2½ tbsp prepared horseradish
2 tbsp grated onion
1 tsp salt
¼ tsp white pepper
1 cup/240 ml heavy cream

Garnish:
watercress
cucumber
radishes

Yield: 8 servings

Soften gelatin in cold water in a glass measuring cup. Place the cup in very hot water until the gelatin dissolves. Peel cucumbers, cut in half lengthwise and remove seeds. Chop cucumbers and purée. Measure 3 cups/700 ml purée and combine with sour cream, mayonnaise, horseradish, onion, salt and pepper. Stir in the dissolved gelatin. Chill until thickened, about 45 minutes.

Whip cream and fold into the cucumber mixture. Turn into a lightly oiled 1½ quart/liter salad mold. Chill at least 4 hours or until set. Unmold and garnish with watercress, thinly sliced cucumbers and radishes.

Cole Slaw

An all-American salad for your next barbecue!

3 cups/700 ml finely shredded cabbage
1 cup/240 ml shredded carrots
2 tbsp chopped onion
pinch of cayenne pepper

Dressing:
⅔ cup/160 ml mayonnaise
2 tbsp vinegar
4 tsp sugar
½ tsp salt
½ tsp celery seed

Yield: 6 servings

Mix all dressing ingredients together and stir until sugar dissolves. Mix together cabbage, carrots, onion and cayenne in a large bowl. Toss with dressing and refrigerate overnight.

Variation: Add minced green pepper, raisins and/or pineapple if desired.

Basic Vinaigrette

Combine vinegar, mustard, lemon juice, sugar, salt and pepper. Whisk in oil and chill.

2 tbsp red wine vinegar
1 tsp Dijon mustard
1 tsp lemon juice
1 tsp fine granulated sugar
1 tsp salt
freshly ground pepper
6 tbsp olive oil

Yield: ½ cup/120 ml

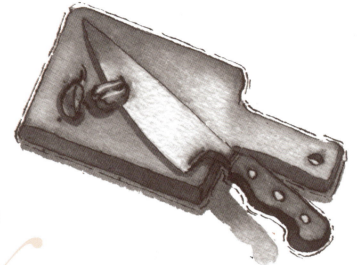

Herbed Vinaigrette

Whisk together all ingredients. Pour into a jar and refrigerate. Shake before using.

⅓ cup/80 ml vegetable oil
⅓ cup/80 ml olive oil
⅓ cup/80 ml white wine vinegar
1 tbsp chopped fresh parsley
1 tbsp chopped fresh dill
1 tbsp chopped fresh basil
1 tsp Dijon mustard
½ tsp crushed garlic
2 tbsp freshly grated Parmesan

Yield: 1¼ cup/300 ml

In addition to the familiar heads of garlic everyone knows, Belgians are treated to two other types - mild fresh garlic in the spring and rich smoked garlic, sold in braids, in the fall. The fresh garlic is wonderful sliced on antipasto. Smoked garlic adds depth to cooked dishes and, as an added benefit, the smoking process helps the garlic stay juicy for months.

Salads

Caesar Salad Dressing

2 anchovy fillets
¼ tsp salt
2 - 3 garlic cloves, minced
¼ cup/60 ml olive oil
juice of ½ lemon
1 tsp Dijon mustard
2 dashes Worcestershire sauce
1 egg yolk
3 tbsp freshly grated Parmesan

Yield: ½ cup/120 ml

Mash together the anchovy fillets, salt and garlic until they form a paste. Add olive oil, lemon juice, mustard, Worcestershire, egg yolk and Parmesan. Whisk until well blended and smooth. Pour into a jar and refrigerate. Shake before using.

For a traditional Caesar Salad, make the dressing in a wooden salad bowl and toss with a head of romaine lettuce leaves torn into small pieces. Top with homemade croutons (see index), additional grated Parmesan cheese and lots of freshly ground black pepper.

Sweet and Sour Dressing

¾ cup/150 g fine granulated sugar
1 cup/240 ml oil
⅓ cup/80 ml ketchup
¼ cup/60 ml white wine vinegar
1 tsp Worcestershire sauce
1 medium onion, chopped
7 oz/200 g lardons, cooked (see note)
pinch of salt
2 garlic cloves, crushed

Yield: 2 cups/475 ml

Absolutely the best on a fresh spinach salad!

Mix sugar and oil together. Add remaining ingredients plus a little of the drippings from the fried lardons. Whisk until well combined and refrigerate.

In Belgium, it is easy to find packaged lardons. If you wish to make your own, simply cut thickly sliced smoked bacon into thin strips.

Blue Cheese Salad Dressing

Put all ingredients except the blue cheese in a blender and mix until smooth. Crumble cheese and stir into dressing.

1 cup/240 ml mayonnaise
½ cup/120 ml sour cream
1 tbsp fine granulated sugar
2 tbsp cider vinegar
¼ tsp salt
white pepper
4 oz/115 g blue cheese (1 cup)

Yield: 2½ cups/600 ml

HERBED VINEGAR/FLAVORED OIL

Vinegar: Pack fresh herb sprigs, whole garlic cloves, chili and/or whole spices or peppercorns into sterilized jars. Pour in warmed cider vinegar or white wine vinegar. Cover with vinegar-proof lids. Let stand two weeks. Strain into clean, glass bottles with cork stoppers. Insert a few fresh herb sprigs, if desired. Store in a cool dark place and use within a year.

Oil: Choose a combination of fresh herbs, chilis, peeled garlic cloves, peppercorns, and/or zest strips. Place in a sterilized glass jar. Cover with a good quality light olive oil or corn oil. Let stand in a cool, dark place for at least two weeks, shaking the jar daily. Discard the garlic (if used) and leave for another two weeks. Strain the oil into a sterilized, dry, decorative bottle. Add a fresh herb sprig, if desired. Use within six months.

Do not skimp on the vinegar or oil. The better the quality, the better the finished product!

Mayonnaise

There is no secret to a great mayonnaise - just be sure that all the ingredients are at room temperature.

Mix the oils together in a measuring cup and set aside. In a medium bowl, whisk the egg yolks until light and thick. Whisk in the mustard, lemon juice, and a little salt and pepper. Continue beating until the mixture is smooth and thick. In a fine drizzle, gradually add some of the oil, whisking, until the mayonnaise begins to thicken. Add the rest of the oil in a slow and steady stream, whisking continually. Whisk in the vinegar and the boiling water. Taste the mayonnaise and adjust the seasonings. Cover and refrigerate. Use within 5 days.

½ cup/120 ml light olive or vegetable oil
½ cup/120 ml corn or peanut oil
3 large egg yolks
1 tsp Dijon mustard
1 tbsp freshly squeezed lemon juice
salt
freshly ground white pepper
1 tbsp white wine vinegar
1 tbsp boiling water

Yield: 1½ cups/350 ml

Homemade mayonnaise is a wonderful base for a gourmet sauce. Add minced fresh herbs such as chervil, parsley, cressonette, chives, and/or green onions, and serve with poached salmon or fresh asparagus. Mayonnaise seasoned with curry powder and a dash of lemon juice is a perfect accompaniment to artichokes.

Seafood

Seafood

Anguilles au Vert	110
Broiled Swordfish with Mustard Sauce	122
Cassolette de Palourdes au Champagne	138
Cod with Chèvre and Roasted Peppers	127
Cold Cucumber Sauce	117
Coquilles Saint-Jacques à l'Effilochée d'Endives	135
Creamy Seafood Sauce	115
Crêpes aux Fruits de Mer	125
Ginger Salmon	120
Goujonnettes de Filets de Sole aux Jeunes Pousses d'Epinards	107
Grilled Salmon Steaks	121
Halibut with Mango Sauce	124
Homard Braisé et Mousseline de Tomates	128
Moules Marinière	137
Mussels with Leeks, Saffron and Cream	136
Raie au Beurre Noisette	111
Salmon Braids with Saffron Sauce	113
Salmon Croquettes	117
Salmon Wellington	114
Salmon with Pink Peppercorn Raspberry Sauce	118
Salmon with Sorrel Sauce	119
Scallops in Saffron Sauce	134
Scallops with Leeks and Truffles	133
Scampi and Papaya with Hot Sweet and Sour Sauce	131
Shrimp Etouffée	129
Shrimp on the Bar-B	132
Sole Meunière	106
Spicy Cod with Snow Peas	126
Swordfish Brochette	123
Truite de l'Abbé Gourmand	112
Waterzooi de Lotte	105
Whole Poached Salmon	116

SPECIAL TOPICS

Fish	108
Mussels	136
Shellfish	130

Waterzooi de Lotte

This monkfish version of Waterzooi is a delicious alternative to the famous Belgian classic Waterzooi de Volaille à la Gantoise.

2 tbsp/30 g butter
2 tbsp olive oil
6 leeks, chopped
6 carrots, chopped
1 quart/liter fish stock
3 onions, chopped
2 1/3 lb/1 kg monkfish, in chunks
1/2 cup/120 ml dry white wine
2 cups/475 ml heavy cream
salt
freshly ground pepper

Garnish:
chopped fresh parsley

Yield: 6 - 8 servings

In a large stock pot, heat half the butter with half the olive oil. Add the leeks and carrots and sauté until soft. Add the fish stock and simmer for 45 minutes.

In a frying pan, melt remaining butter and oil. Sauté the onion. Add the monkfish and sauté until pale gold. Add the monkfish mixture, wine and cream to the stock pot. Simmer gently for 15 minutes. Season to taste with salt and pepper.

Serve in a large tureen or individual bowls, sprinkled with parsley.

Waterzooi is a Flanders specialty from Ghent. Resembling a soup or a stew, it may be made with either chicken or fish in a rich creamy broth. Waterzooi is often served in a deep soup plate and accompanied by brown bread, boiled potatoes and a good Belgian beer.

" *A fine kettle of fish...* "

Seafood 105

Sole Meunière

*E*njoy with FRITES *and a Belgian beer.*

8 whole sole* (see note)
milk
¾ cup/100 g flour
1 tbsp garlic powder
1 tsp salt
½ tsp pepper
1 cup/225 g butter
2 tbsp oil
juice of 1 lemon
½ cup/120 ml chopped fresh parsley

Garnish:
8 lemon halves

Yield: 8 servings

To mellow the flavor, soak the sole in milk to cover and refrigerate for 20 minutes. Mix together flour, garlic powder, salt and pepper. Drain the sole and dredge in the seasoned flour. Set aside.

Heat ½ cup/115 grams butter with the oil in a large, heavy frying pan. Brown the sole for 6 to 7 minutes on each side over moderately low heat. Drain and place on a heated serving platter in a warm oven. Wipe out the pan with a paper towel and add the remaining butter to the pan. Brown the butter to a nutmeg color. Add the lemon juice and parsley. Stir and pour over the fish.

Serve with lemon halves wrapped in squares of cheesecloth, tops tied with narrow ribbon.

* ½ lb/225 grams each

Ask for the sole to be cleaned with the head, black skin, fins, tail and side bones removed. Leave on the tender white bottom skin, but be certain all the scales are removed. If your guests are big eaters, buy larger sole. A pound of fresh sole will yield about 6 ounces/170 grams of edible fish.

" ...a whole big flat sole...handsomely browned and still sputteringly hot under its coating of chopped parsley... "
Julia Child

Goujonnettes de Filets de Sole aux Jeunes Pousses d'Epinards
Les Brasseries Georges - Jean-Claude Demurger, Chef

4 whole sole, filleted*
4 large handfuls young spinach leaves
2 tomatoes
1 tbsp sherry vinegar
2 tbsp peanut oil
2 tbsp walnut oil
olive oil
juice of 2 lemons
salt
freshly ground pepper

Garnish:
1 bunch of chives, chopped

Yield: 4 servings

Ask the fishmonger to clean and fillet the fish; cut each fillet diagonally into 4 or 5 pieces (goujonnettes). Season with salt and pepper.

Wash the spinach thoroughly, drain and remove thick stalks.

Submerge the tomatoes in boiling water for 20 seconds. Cool under running water and peel. Cut in half, remove seeds and dice.

Prepare the vinaigrette by combining the sherry vinegar, salt and pepper. Whisk in the peanut oil and walnut oil.

Season the spinach with the vinaigrette and place in a mound in the center of each serving plate.

Pour the olive oil into a very hot nonstick pan and fry the seasoned goujonnettes briefly on both sides until cooked. Drain on absorbent paper and arrange around the spinach. In the same pan, heat lemon juice and tomato cubes over low heat and season with salt and pepper. Spoon over the sole fillets. Garnish with chives.

* 3½ lb/1½ kg total weight before filleting

FISH

Belgium is a wonderful country for beautifully fresh fish. If you have the time for a seafood adventure, a good place to start is on the coast. Oostende is a lovely city and the perfect place to strike a bargain with a fishmonger. Starting in the spring, street vendors line the boardwalk and sell the freshest of fish at enticing prices. Put a cooler in your trunk and stay for dinner at a local seafood restaurant. If you prefer something closer, Place St. Catherine is the seafood center of Brussels. The fish vendors open before daybreak and close in the early afternoon, making way for the brisk lunch trade in the seafood restaurants of this beautiful area.

When purchasing fresh fish from a fishmonger, apply the following test: eyes bright and clear, gills red or pink, scales shiny, flesh firm, absolutely no fishy odor. You will be assured of a fresh, tasty fish. For perfectly cooked fish, whether whole (lay whole fish flat), fillets or steaks, measure the fish at the thickest point and cook it 10 minutes for every 1"/2½cm of thickness. This applies to pan-frying, broiling, poaching, steaming or baking (at 450°F/230°C).

The following are some of the most popular fish available in Belgium:
- Bass/Loup de Mer (Bar) is a dense, flaky white-fleshed fish with a mild flavor. This versatile fish can be baked, stuffed, broiled, sautéed, poached or fried.
- Bream/Daurade has a firm texture and a delicate taste. It is best served with aromatic herbs or sauces which lend flavor to the fish. Pan-fry or broil.
- Cod/Cabillaud is a lean, firm, white fish with a mild taste. Usually sold as fillets or steaks, this fish falls into large, tender flakes when cooked. Cod is poached, broiled, or used in chowder. Scrod is cod that weighs under 3 pounds/1⅓ kilos.
- Eel/Anguille is an oily, strong-tasting Belgian specialty. It is often sold smoked.
- Flounder/Limande has sweet, fragile, white meat with a delicate flavor. This fish is usually filleted and pan-fried or sautéed with buttery sauces.
- Haddock/Aiglefin is a slightly softer, but more flavorful member of the cod family. Best filleted and poached.

...more on FISH

- ◆ Halibut/Flétan (Elbot) has lean, firm, white flesh with a delicate, slightly sweet flavor. This larger relative of the flounder family is usually sold in steaks and baked or broiled.
- ◆ John Dory/St. Pierre is a firm, fine-textured white fish with a mild taste. It is most commonly sold in fillets and lightly sautéed. Serve with a delicate sauce.
- ◆ Monkfish/Lotte is a firm, white fish with a delicate, sweet flavor and the texture of lobster. It is a good substitute in scallop and lobster recipes. Purchase in small fillets or steaks and use for chowders and brochettes or bake and serve with rich sauces.
- ◆ Salmon/Saumon is a firm, pink, dense fish with a pronounced flavor. It is usually sold whole, filleted or in steaks, and is delicious poached, barbecued, broiled, baked or used in mousses. Salmon is also cured or smoked and sold in very thin slices.
- ◆ Skate (Ray)/Raie has a tender texture, similar to scallops, with a mild taste. It is usually poached and served with capers and browned butter.
- ◆ Sole/Sole has lean, white, firm flesh with a delicate flavor. The only true sole is Dover Sole, indigenous to European waters. Lemon Sole, Gray Sole and Rex Sole, all of which have a softer flesh, are actually varieties of flounder. Pan-fry whole or gently sauté the fillets.
- ◆ Swordfish/Espadon has firm flesh and a rich flavor. Usually sold in thick slices, it is wonderful broiled with butter and lemon or included in a seafood brochette.
- ◆ Trout/Truite is a delicate white fish with a very mild flavor. It is usually sold whole and pan-fried, poached or baked.
- ◆ Whiting (Hake)/Merlan is a white fish with a very mild, delicate, buttery taste. It is often used in chowders as it keeps its texture and flavor through longer cooking.

Other Belgian fish specialties:
- ◆ Maatjes herring, a seasonal whole fish that looks like a large sardine, makes its appearance at every fish counter in mid-summer. They are eaten whole, bones and all, as a snack. Serve with brown bread, chopped onions and a beer.
- ◆ Small marinated fresh anchovies are available at traiteurs, fishmongers and grocery store delicatessen counters. Serve as a snack with French bread.

There is a wide variety of smoked fish available in Belgium. Try them out in dips, quiches, spreads, mousses, or simply steamed and served with boiled potatoes.

Anguilles au Vert
(Eel with Spinach and Sorrel)

You cannot go wrong ordering eel in Belgian restaurants. Here is one version of a popular preparation to try at home, served with FRITES, of course!

2⅓ lb/1 kg small eels
½ cup/115 g butter
¼ lb/115 g spinach, chopped
¼ lb/115 g sorrel, chopped
1⅓ cup/320 ml dry white wine
bouquet garni (see index)
2 tbsp chopped fresh parsley
2 tbsp chopped fresh sage
2 tbsp chopped fresh tarragon
salt
freshly ground pepper
2 large egg yolks
2 tbsp lemon juice

Yield: 4 - 6 servings

Skin and prepare small eels; cut each one into 4 (2"/5cm) pieces. In a sauté pan, melt the butter and cook the eel until they have stiffened. Add the spinach and sorrel leaves. Reduce the heat and continue cooking until the leaves are soft. Add the dry white wine, a bouquet garni, parsley, sage and tarragon. Season with salt and pepper and simmer for 10 minutes.

Mix the egg yolks with the lemon juice and add a few spoonfuls of the hot liquid. Off the heat, add the eggs to the sauté pan. Return the pan to the heat and gently reheat the mixture, without allowing it to boil, until it thickens. Serve hot, in shallow bowls.

Eels are an essential item on a Belgian seafood menu. The river towns of Temse in Flanders and Esquelsmes in Wallonia are famous for their eels. Before cooking, eels must be skinned and the head and intestines removed. Fortunately, a good fishmonger will prepare them. Be sure to purchase eels just before cooking as they deteriorate rapidly.

Raie au Beurre Noisette

1 pkg court-bouillon
3⅓ lb/1½ kg ray (skate) wings
7 tbsp/100 g butter
3 tbsp capers
1 tbsp cider vinegar

Garnish:
chopped parsley

Yield: 4 servings

Prepare the court-bouillon according to package directions; cool.

Wash the ray under cold water. Cut into 4 serving pieces. Add to the cold court-bouillon and simmer over low heat, without boiling, about 10 to 15 minutes, depending on the thickness of the ray. Drain, scrape off any skin that remains and keep warm on a heated plate.

In a small saucepan, melt 4 tablespoons/55 grams of the butter. Cook until it turns a nutty brown. Remove pan from heat and add remaining 3 tablespoons/45 grams butter, capers and vinegar.

Immediately pour onto the warm fish, decorate with parsley and serve immediately.

Court-bouillon may be purchased in any Belgian supermarket. Court-bouillon packets may be found on the shelf near the stock cubes. A homemade court-bouillon (see page 128) is even better!

> **Food as a Solace and Joy,
> a sensual delight,
> never to be taken for granted,
> but to be sung and extolled…**
> Arthur Frommer

Truite de l'Abbé Gourmand
Les Quatre Saisons, Royal Windsor Hotel - André Smit, Chef

*P*eel and clean the shrimp (see index). Season the trout fillets with salt and pepper and lightly dredge them in flour. Sauté the trout and shrimp in a hot frying pan with 3 tablespoons/45 grams butter. Place the trout and shrimp on individual plates and keep warm.

Discard the cooked butter from the pan. Melt 2 tablespoons/30 grams of butter in the same pan, and sauté the shallots, mushrooms and thyme. Add the beer, bring to a boil and reduce until one-third of the liquid remains. Over low heat, add remaining ½ cup/115 grams butter, little by little, whisking until thickened. Add parsley, lemon juice and salt and pepper to taste.

Pour the sauce next to the fish and serve hot.

* bière blanche

12 medium shrimp
4 (5 oz/140 g) trout fillets
salt
freshly ground pepper
flour
3 tbsp/45 g butter

Sauce:
½ cup + 2 tbsp/115 g + 30 g butter
2 tbsp minced shallot
4 oz/115 g mushrooms, sliced
thyme
½ cup/120 ml white beer*
2 tbsp chopped parsley
lemon juice
salt
freshly ground pepper

Yield: 4 servings

Salmon Braids with Saffron Sauce

Sit back and collect the compliments - this lovely presentation requires little effort.

1 ¾ lb/800 g salmon fillet (see note)
14 oz/400 g turbot
8 tbsp frozen peas
salt
freshly ground pepper
½ cup/120 ml dry white wine
½ cup/120 ml fish stock

Saffron Sauce:
3 shallots, minced
⅔ cup/160 ml dry white wine
⅔ cup/160 ml fish stock
1 ¼ cup/300 ml heavy cream
salt
freshly ground pepper
¼ tsp saffron powder
7 tbsp/100 g butter, softened
2 tbsp chopped fresh parsley
2 tbsp chopped fresh chives
2 tbsp chopped fresh tarragon
2 tbsp chopped fresh dill

Oven Temp: 400°F/200°C
Yield: 8 servings

Salmon Braids: Cut 16 long strips of salmon (½"/1cm thick) and 8 long strips of turbot. All strips must be of equal length and thickness. Make 8 braids, each using 2 strips of salmon and 1 strip of turbot. Form a crown with each braid by joining the two ends together. Place the crowns in an oven-proof dish and put 1 tablespoon of peas into the center of each crown. Season with salt and pepper. Mix together wine and fish stock and pour over the fish. Cover the dish with buttered aluminum foil and bake in a preheated oven, 12 to 15 minutes.

Sauce: In a saucepan, reduce the shallots and wine for a few minutes. Add the fish stock and reduce again. Add the cream. Boil and reduce to desired consistency. Season with salt and pepper. Add the saffron and remove from heat. Just before serving, whisk in butter, bits at a time, and stir in the chopped herbs. Reheat gently.

Transfer braids to warmed plates and spoon warm sauce around fish.

Buy the fillet from the thicker (head) end of the salmon. It should be 1"/2½cm thick and 9"/23cm long. Cut 4 (½"/1¼cm wide) lengthwise strips from the thinner (belly) side of the salmon and 6 from the thicker side. Cut the 6 strips in half lengthwise for a total of 16 strips, ½"/1¼cm in diameter. Cut 8 (9"/23cm) strips of turbot to match.

Salmon Wellington

Pastry: Blend butter and cream cheese. Add flour and mix until well incorporated. Shape into 2 flat balls and refrigerate for several hours or overnight.

3½ lb/1½ kg salmon fillet (see note)
1 egg yolk
1 tbsp milk
CREAMY SEAFOOD SAUCE

Pastry:
1 cup/225 g butter, softened
8 oz/225 g cream cheese, softened
2 cups/260 g all-purpose flour

Mushroom-Artichoke Filling:
1 (8 oz/225 g) can artichoke bottoms
3 tbsp/45 g butter
1 onion, chopped
1 lb/450 g mushrooms, chopped
¼ cup/60 ml Madeira wine
salt
freshly ground pepper

Oven Temp: 425°F/220°C
Yield: 8 servings

Mushroom-Artichoke Filling: Rinse, drain and chop artichoke bottoms. Melt butter in a frying pan and sauté artichokes and onions until lightly browned. Add mushrooms and Madeira and cook, stirring, until most of the liquid has evaporated. Season to taste with salt and pepper. Cool.

Roll half the pastry on a floured board into a 12"x14"/31 x 36cm rectangle. Cut into 4 equal rectangles, trimming edges. Repeat with remaining dough.

Place the salmon pieces (see note) on a greased baking sheet tucking the thinner (belly side) under to make the pieces the same thickness. Divide the filling equally among the fillets and spread evenly on top. Cover each fillet with a rectangle of pastry, tucking edges under fillet. (Do not cover entire bottom of fillet with pastry or it will become soggy.) Mix egg yolk with milk and brush the top and sides of the pastry, being careful not to let the glaze drip. Scraps of dough may be rerolled and cut into small decorations. Place decorations on Wellingtons and glaze the entire pastry again. (May be refrigerated up to 8 hours.)

Before serving, bring Wellingtons to room temperature for 1 hour. Bake in a preheated oven for 20 to 25 minutes or until the pastry is golden. Spoon a pool of CREAMY SEAFOOD SAUCE onto each plate, place the fish on the sauce and pass the remaining sauce.

Variations: Use a purchased puff pastry if you prefer. For the seafood lover, replace the Mushroom-Artichoke filling with ¼ lb/115 grams bay scallops per serving and season with salt and pepper.

Buy a large (at least 3½ pound/1½ kilo) fillet of salmon with the skin and small bones removed. It should be at least 1"/2½ cm thick at the thickest point. Starting at the head end, cut 8 equal portions of salmon, about 6 oz/170 g each. If the salmon is 1"/2½cm thick, the pieces should be 2½"/7½cm wide. Reserve the thin tail section for another use. If you cannot find a large fillet, buy the head end of 2 smaller fillets.

Creamy Seafood Sauce

Enhance any beautifully fresh poached or grilled seafood with this special sauce.

6 tbsp/90 ml dry white wine
6 tbsp/90 ml white wine vinegar
2 tbsp minced shallots
1½ cups/350 ml heavy cream
¼ tsp salt
white pepper
2 tbsp chopped fresh chives or parsley

Yield: 1 cup/240 ml

Place the wine, vinegar and shallots in a medium saucepan and bring to a boil. Lower the heat and simmer until slightly thickened and reduced to 4 tablespoons. Slowly whisk in the cream. Simmer, stirring occasionally, until the sauce reduces to the desired consistency. Season with salt and pepper and stir in chives or parsley. (Sauce may be kept at room temperature for up to 4 hours or refrigerated overnight. Reheat and thin with more cream before serving.)

Variations: To the basic sauce, add 1 tablespoon minced fresh ginger or vary the fresh herbs. A dash of sherry or a pinch of saffron would particularly complement shellfish.

Whole Poached Salmon

This salmon goes very well with Cold Cucumber Sauce and is always a party favorite!

1 quart/liter fish stock
2 shallots, chopped
½ cup/120 ml white wine
1 (2½ lb/3 kg) whole salmon
salt
freshly ground pepper
¼ cup/60 ml fresh dill
¼ cup/60 ml fresh thyme
¼ cup/60 ml fresh parsley

assorted garnishes

Oven Temp: 350°F/175°C
Yield: 15 servings

Bring the fish stock, shallots and wine to a boil. Set aside. Wash the fish under cold running water and snip out the gills with a pair of kitchen scissors. Pat the inside cavity dry and sprinkle liberally with salt, pepper, dill, thyme and parsley. Lay the fish flat on its side and measure the thickness at the thickest part.

To fashion a fish poacher with rack, tear off three 12"/30cm long strips of 18"/46cm wide heavy-duty foil. Fold them like an accordion until they are roughly 2"/5cm wide and 18"/46cm long. Brush them with oil. Lay them across a deep roasting pan large enough to fit the whole salmon, positioning them where the fish head, middle and top of the tail will be. Place the fish on its stomach, bending it into a "U" shape to fit into the pan. Wrap a piece of foil around the tail to protect it. Place a ball of foil under the jaw to keep the mouth closed.

Cover the fish completely in a tent of oiled aluminum foil. Seal the edges, leaving the corner by the head open. (Be careful not to press down on the fish.) Pour in the hot stock mixture. It should come half way up the sides of the pan. Seal in a way that marks the corner by the head. In a preheated oven, cook the fish 10 minutes per inch of thickness at the thickest part. To see if the salmon is fully cooked, carefully peek at the head. If the eyes are white and bulging, the fish is done.

Carefully remove from the oven and let cool completely, still covered with foil. When cool, peel off the skin and scrape away any gray flesh. Grasp the folded pieces of foil on either side of the fish and lift the salmon onto a decorative platter. Carefully slide out the foil strips, wipe away any juices and decorate the fish with sprigs of fresh herbs, fresh flowers, cold green beans, cherry tomatoes, lemon wedges, sprouts or cucumber.

Cold Cucumber Sauce

This refreshing cucumber sauce is even better with homemade MAYONNAISE. *It is the perfect complement for* WHOLE POACHED SALMON, *or try it with* SALMON CROQUETTES *as an alternative to tartar sauce.*

2 large cucumbers
1 cup/240 ml mayonnaise
1 cup/240 ml sour cream
2 tbsp Dijon mustard
1 tbsp lemon juice
½ tsp salt
¼ tsp pepper
½ cup/120 ml chopped fresh dill
¼ cup/60 ml chopped fresh chives

Peel, seed and grate the cucumbers. Squeeze dry in a clean towel. Mix with the remaining ingredients and chill for up to 24 hours.

Yield: 3 cups/700 ml

Salmon Croquettes

When leftover salmon is this delicious, you will be tempted to poach extra!

1 tsp celery salt
3 green onions, minced
½ small green pepper, minced
¾ cup/175 ml bread crumbs*
1 tbsp mayonnaise
1 jalapeño, seeded and minced
salt
freshly ground pepper
2 large eggs, beaten
2 cups/475 ml flaked poached salmon
oil for frying

Mix all ingredients except the eggs and salmon and adjust seasoning. Stir in eggs and gently fold in salmon. Shape mixture into croquettes with your hands. Heat the oil in a heavy frying pan over medium heat. Fry the croquettes until golden brown, turning once.

Serve on a bed of lettuce with COLD CUCUMBER SAUCE *and some finely grated carrots.*

* may be dry or fresh

Yield: 4 servings

Salmon with Pink Peppercorn Raspberry Sauce

A wonderfully tasty sauce with fresh salmon. On another occasion, serve the sauce with sautéed duck breasts.

6 (1"/2½cm thick) salmon steaks
PINK PEPPERCORN RASPBERRY SAUCE

Heat the sauce in a large sauté pan. Gently poach the salmon in the sauce, covered, for 10 minutes. (If a "custardy" salmon is preferred, reduce the cooking time to 6 minutes.)

Garnish:
fresh raspberries

Yield: 6 servings

Lift the salmon onto a warmed serving dish. Turn up the heat and allow the sauce to bubble briskly for 1 minute. Spoon the sauce around the salmon and garnish with raspberries.

> "One fish
> two fish
> red fish
> blue fish."
> Dr. Seuss

Variation: Add 1 tablespoon of chopped fresh dill to the sauce just before serving.

Pink Peppercorn Raspberry Sauce

Sauce:
1 lb/450 g fresh raspberries*
2¼ cups/530 ml dry white wine
4 tsp red currant jelly
2 tsp pink peppercorns, crushed
juice of ½ lemon
salt

Yield: 2½ cups/600 ml

Put the raspberries and white wine into a saucepan. Simmer for 10 minutes. Strain the liquid into a clean saucepan. Add the red currant jelly, crushed pink peppercorns, lemon juice and salt to taste. Stir over a low heat until jelly has dissolved.

* If fresh raspberries are not available, buy unsweetened frozen raspberries and thaw slightly before using.

Salmon with Sorrel Sauce

Perfect for a romantic dinner for two - just add candles.

12 oz/340 g center-cut salmon fillet

Sorrel Sauce:
6 oz/170 g mushrooms, chopped
6 shallots, finely chopped
¼ cup/60 ml dry white vermouth
1 cup/240 ml dry white wine
¾ cup/175 ml fish stock
1 tsp fresh lemon juice
¾ cup/175 ml heavy cream
salt
freshly ground white pepper
2 cups/475 ml fresh sorrel

Yield: 2 servings

Sauce: In a saucepan, combine mushrooms, shallots, vermouth, white wine, fish stock and lemon juice. Boil until reduced to a syrupy consistency. Stir in cream and bring to a boil for a few seconds. Remove from heat and strain into another saucepan.

Salmon scallops are very thin diagonal slices cut crosswise from a boneless, skinless fillet. Run your fingers over the top of the salmon before slicing. If any tiny bones remain, remove them with tweezers.

Clean sorrel and strip the tender leaves from the stem. Tear into small pieces and drop into the sauce. Rapidly boil until reduced and slightly thickened, stirring with a wooden spoon. Taste, season with salt and pepper, and keep warm.

Cut salmon into 12 thin (¼"/½cm) scallops. Season on one side. Preheat a nonstick frying pan until very hot. Cook scallops without butter or oil, about 40 seconds on each side. Do not brown.

Divide sorrel sauce between two warmed plates. Arrange 6 salmon scallops in the center of each plate and serve.

Sorrel, oseille in French, may be found during the winter and early spring. If it is not with the salad greens, look in the fish section near the salmon. Do not use metal utensils when cooking sorrel.

> "When I fell in love, which I did with great frequency in my hooligan youth, I would cook beautiful suppers for the object of my desire."
> Elisabeth Luard

Ginger Salmon

This preparation is superb with salmon, but don't hesitate to substitute any other firm fish.

1 lb/450 g salmon fillet
3 tbsp mirin
2 tbsp chopped fresh ginger
2 tbsp soy sauce
2 tbsp minced green onions
4 garlic cloves, minced
1 tsp honey
¼ tsp Tabasco sauce
1 piece (1"/2½cm) fresh ginger
3 cups/700 ml hot cooked rice
coriander sprigs

Yield: 4 servings

Rinse the salmon, pat dry and remove bones. Cut into 4 to 6 pieces. In a large glass pie dish, whisk together the mirin, the 2 tablespoons of chopped ginger, soy sauce, green onions, garlic, honey and Tabasco sauce. Add the salmon and turn to coat both sides. Refrigerate for 1 hour.

Mirin is a Japanese cooking wine found in specialty stores. If unavailable, substitute dry sherry.

To create a steamer, put a rack in a large frying pan with ¾"/2cm water in the bottom. Bring to a boil. Place the pie plate containing the fish and marinade on the rack, cover, and steam fish for 10 minutes, keeping the water at a low simmer.

Peel the pieces of ginger and cut it into fine julienne. Place the rice on a serving platter and arrange the fish on the rice, reserving the marinade. Sprinkle the fish with the ginger and coriander sprigs. Keep warm.

Strain the marinade into a saucepan and bring to a full boil. Pour into a serving bowl and serve as a dipping sauce for the fish.

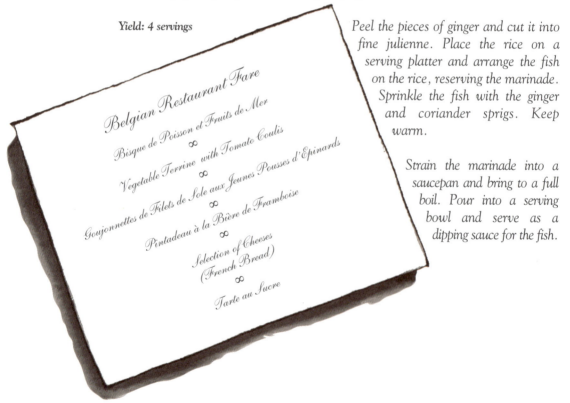

Belgian Restaurant Fare

Bisque de Poisson et Fruits de Mer
∞
Vegetable Terrine with Tomato Coulis
∞
Goujonnettes de Filets de Sole aux Jeunes Pousses d'Épinards
∞
Pintadeau à la Bière de Framboise
∞
Selection of Cheeses
(French Bread)
∞
Tarte au Sucre

Grilled Salmon Steaks

The mayonnaise seals in the juices and keeps the salmon moist - serve with a crisp white wine.

4 (1"/2½cm thick) salmon steaks
1 tbsp chopped fresh dill
juice of 1 lemon
salt
freshly ground pepper
4 tbsp mayonnaise

Yield: 4 servings

Remove any scales from the steaks. Put the steaks on a cookie sheet lined with greased foil. Mix dill, lemon juice, salt and pepper into the mayonnaise. Spread 1 tablespoon seasoned mayonnaise on top of each steak. Broil the salmon for 10 minutes or until the mayonnaise has colored. Be careful not to overcook the steaks. Remove from the oven when the slightest bit of pink remains in the center. Let stand a minute or two to finish cooking before serving.

To remove the odor of fish, rub your hands with fresh lemon juice and salt.

Variations: *Be creative by varying the flavors. A splash of tequila and a squeeze of lime stirred into the mayonnaise is lovely for summer; or mix mayonnaise with grated fresh ginger and soy sauce and serve with SESAME BROCCOLI ORIENTAL.*

" *Yet there are certain things that are undeniably fundamental in any culinary repertoire, and roast chicken, sautéed steak and grilled fish are three. Ageless and timeless, they are, like little black dresses, great on their own, but even better when accessorized for the moment.* "

Kristine Kidd
Karen Kaplan

Broiled Swordfish with Mustard Sauce

4 (8 oz/225 g) swordfish steaks
2 tbsp olive oil
2 tbsp fresh minced basil

Mustard Sauce:
¼ cup/60 ml dry white wine
2 tbsp minced green onions
⅔ cup/160 ml heavy cream
¾ cup/170 g butter, chilled
¼ cup/60 ml fresh lemon juice
2 tbsp Dijon mustard
salt
freshly ground white pepper

Garnish:
basil sprigs

Yield: 4 servings

To make the sauce, bring wine and green onions to a boil in a small saucepan. Cook until the liquid is reduced to 3 tablespoons. Add the cream and reduce the mixture by half. Remove from the heat and whisk in 2 tablespoons/30 grams butter until blended. Return to low heat and whisk in remaining butter, one tablespoon at a time, being sure each addition has blended smoothly before adding more. Remove the pan from the heat if sauce begins to separate. (If the sauce breaks, remove from heat and add 2 more tablespoons butter.) Add lemon juice, mustard and salt and pepper to taste, whisking until smooth. Remove the sauce from the heat and keep over warm water, whisking occasionally.

Brush the swordfish steaks with olive oil and sprinkle with basil. Let stand for 5 minutes. Broil fish 3 to 5 minutes per side until firm to the touch. Divide the sauce among 4 warm dinner plates. Top with the fish and garnish with basil sprigs.

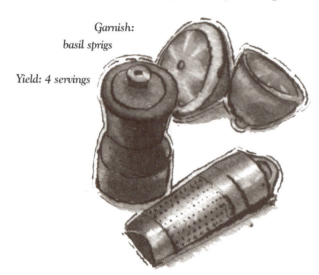

Swordfish Brochette

*F*inely chop the garlic with the herbs, add pepper and bread crumbs and set aside. Place the mushroom caps in a small saucepan with the lemon juice and enough water to cover. Bring to a boil, then drain immediately. Set aside.

1 small garlic clove
1 tsp fresh rosemary
1 tsp fresh thyme
1 tsp fresh sage
freshly ground black pepper
¾ cup/175 ml dry bread crumbs
8 large mushroom caps
juice of ½ lemon
2 bell peppers
1 ¾ lb/800 g thick swordfish steaks
6 strips bacon
8 large roasted garlic cloves
1 sweet onion
salt
3 tbsp/45 ml extra virgin olive oil

Yield: 4 servings

Core and seed the peppers and cut them into 16 (2"/5cm) squares. Trim the skin from the swordfish and cut the fish into 12 uniform pieces. Wrap each in half a strip of bacon. Peel the roasted garlic cloves. Peel and quarter the onion, and separate it into layers.

Thread the ingredients equally on each of 4 skewers, starting and ending with a mushroom cap. Lightly season the brochettes with salt and pepper, brush with olive oil, and roll in the bread crumb mixture to coat lightly. Grill or broil the brochettes 6 to 8 minutes, turning them as they brown.

To roast garlic, preheat the oven to 350°F/175°C. Place the unpeeled head of garlic in a small baking dish and cover it completely with 2 cups/500 grams kosher salt. Roast the garlic for about 45 minutes. Remove the garlic from the salt and refrigerate until ready to use.

> *You should enjoy the art of dining, having fun with your friends, the community of spirit, of being together at the table.*
> Martha Stewart

Seafood

Halibut with Mango Sauce

When mangos are ripe, this refreshing combination is just right for a barbecue.

6 (¾"/2cm thick) halibut steaks
¼ cup/60 ml lime or lemon juice
1 tbsp minced garlic
1 tbsp olive oil

Mango Sauce:
1½ cups/350 ml peeled, chopped mango
¼ cup/60 ml chopped red bell pepper
3 tbsp chopped green onions
1 tsp brown sugar
½ tsp minced garlic

Garnish:
fresh parsley sprigs

Yield: 6 servings

Place the halibut steaks in a shallow glass dish. Combine lime juice, 1 tablespoon garlic and olive oil. Pour the marinade over the steaks. Cover and refrigerate for 1 hour, turning occasionally.

To make the sauce, combine mango, red pepper, green onions, brown sugar and ½ teaspoon garlic in a small saucepan. Cook over medium heat for 6 minutes or until thoroughly heated, stirring frequently.

"Barbecue", derived from the French language, refers to grilling fish from the "barbe" (beard) to the "queue" (tail).

Remove fish from marinade. Oil a grill rack and place on the grill over medium-hot coals. Cook the halibut 4 minutes on each side or until the fish flakes easily when tested with a fork.

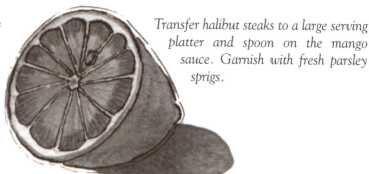

Transfer halibut steaks to a large serving platter and spoon on the mango sauce. Garnish with fresh parsley sprigs.

Crêpes aux Fruits de Mer
(Seafood Crêpes)

Served with a salad, this makes a perfect luncheon dish!

4 large or 8 small CRÊPES

8 oz/225 g haddock or cod, boned
¼ cup/60 ml dry white wine
4 oz/115 g peeled prawns
4 sea scallops, quartered
4 tbsp/55 g butter
4 oz/115 g mushrooms, thinly sliced
1 tsp lemon juice
salt
white pepper
1 medium onion, minced
2 tbsp flour
½ cup/120 ml milk
4 tbsp heavy cream
4 tbsp grated Gruyère cheese

Garnish:
8 whole cooked prawns
chopped parsley

Yield: 4 servings

Place the fish and wine in a saucepan and poach over gentle heat for 10 minutes. Add the prawns and scallops to the pan and cook 2 to 3 minutes longer. Drain, reserving the liquid. Flake the fish.

Melt half the butter in a sauté pan. Add the mushrooms, lemon juice, salt and pepper. Cook, covered, for a few minutes until mushrooms are soft. Set aside.

Melt the remaining butter in a large pan. Add the onion and cook gently until soft. Add the flour and cook for 1 to 2 minutes, stirring. Add the reserved fish juices and milk. Bring to a boil and cook for 2 to 3 minutes, stirring. Add the cream, fish, scallops, mushrooms and prawns and reheat. Taste and adjust the seasoning, thinning the sauce with additional milk if it seems too thick.

Roll up some of the mixture in each crêpe and place in a buttered oven-proof dish. Sprinkle the cheese over the top. Broil until the cheese melts and bubbles, about 7 minutes.

Serve hot, garnished with whole prawns and chopped parsley.

Spicy Cod with Snow Peas

This delicious Caribbean taste is perfect with tender flaky cod, but feel free to experiment with perch, monkfish or halibut.

1 tbsp chili oil
1 tbsp peanut oil
2 lb/900 g cod fillet
1 large onion, finely chopped
2 garlic cloves, crushed
2 tsp curry powder
½ tsp ground cardamom
½ tsp ground cumin
10 oz/280 g coconut cream/milk
2½ oz/75 ml water
1 tbsp lemon juice

Snow Peas:
1 small red bell pepper
2 tbsp/30 g butter
8 oz/225 g snow peas

Yield: 4 servings

Heat chili oil and peanut oil in a sauté pan and gently cook the fish just until sealed, 3 to 5 minutes. Remove and drain on absorbent paper.

Add onion, garlic, curry, cardamom and cumin to the sauté pan. Cook, stirring constantly, until the onion is soft. Add coconut cream, water, and lemon juice. Bring to a boil and simmer for 4 minutes. Cut the fish into bite-sized pieces, add to the sauce and heat through. Keep warm.

Thinly slice the red pepper. Melt butter in a wok or frying pan and add the snow peas and red pepper slices. Stir-fry until the peas are just tender.

Reheat the fish to just below boiling and serve with the snow peas.

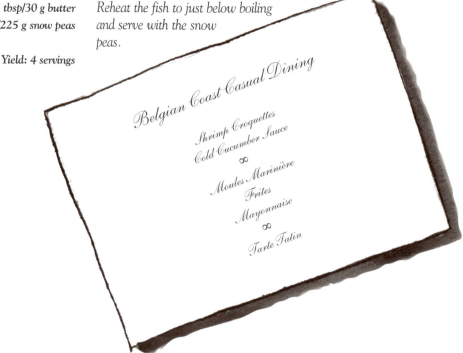

Belgian Coast Casual Dining

Shrimp Croquettes
Cold Cucumber Sauce
∞
Moules Marinière
Frites
Mayonnaise
∞
Tarte Tatin

Cod with Chèvre and Roasted Peppers

Heat oil in a large frying pan. Add the onions and cook until transparent. Set aside.

Roast, peel and seed the bell peppers (see index) and cut them into strips. Drain and chop tomatoes. Add the tomatoes, pepper strips and basil to the onions and heat.

Lightly oil a large baking dish. Layer three-quarters of the pepper mixture on the bottom of the dish. Top with the fish and sprinkle with garlic salt and lemon pepper. Spread the goat cheese on the fish and top with the remaining pepper mixture.

Bake in a preheated oven for 15 minutes or until the fish flakes easily.

3 medium onions, sliced
2 - 3 tbsp olive oil
1 yellow bell pepper
1 red bell pepper
1 green bell pepper
1 (14 oz/400 g) can plum tomatoes
4 tbsp chopped fresh basil
garlic salt
lemon pepper
11 oz/310 g soft chèvre
8 (4 oz/115 g) slices cod

Oven Temp: 350°F/175°C
Yield: 4 servings

To make garlic salt, bury three peeled and slightly crushed garlic cloves in ½ cup/120 ml salt. Keep three days in a covered glass jar and remove the garlic.

> *Fish and guests in three days are stale.*
> John Lyley

Homard Braisé et Mousseline de Tomates
La Truite d'Argent - Michel Smeesters, Chef

Prepare a spicy court-bouillon in a large pot. Bring to a boil and drop in the whole lobsters. When the water comes back to a boil, cook for 8 minutes. Remove from heat, leaving lobsters in the pot.

To make the mousseline, quarter the tomatoes, remove seeds and crush the tomatoes. In a heavy pan, sauté the onion in butter until lightly colored. Add the tomatoes and let cook over low heat. Add bay leaf, thyme branch, sugar, tomato paste, white wine, saffron and Ricard. Cook over low heat until the mixture reaches a light consistency. Remove the thyme branch and bay leaf and purée the mixture. Sieve the purée, pour back into the pot and bring to a boil. Season with salt and pepper to taste. Let the sauce cool. Whip cream until firm and delicately incorporate into the tepid sauce.

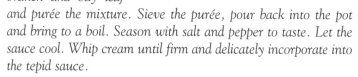

Cut the lobsters in half lengthwise and crack the claws. Place the lobster halves on 4 oven-proof plates. Spoon sauce over the lobster halves and broil until lightly browned. Serve with black squid pasta, garnished with fennel leaves.

To make a court-bouillon, add chopped aromatic vegetables (onion, celery stalks and leaves, parsley and carrots) to water or a mixture of water and white wine. Add other flavorings (bay leaf, thyme, lemon slices, peppercorns) and simmer until vegetables have softened and the liquid is flavorful.

Ingredients

court-bouillon (see note)
2 (1¾ lb/800 g) lobsters
8 oz/225 g black squid pasta, cooked

Mousseline:
8 ripe tomatoes
1 medium onion, minced
1 tbsp butter
1 bay leaf
1 branch fresh thyme
1 tsp sugar
2 tbsp tomato paste
1 cup/240 ml dry white wine
1 thimble saffron
3 tbsp Ricard (aniseed aperitif)
salt
freshly ground pepper
1 cup/240 ml heavy cream

Garnish:
fennel leaves

Yield: 4 servings

Shrimp Etouffée

1 cup/225 g butter
½ cup/65 g flour
2 garlic cloves, chopped
1 cup/240 ml chopped green onions
1 cup/240 ml chopped yellow onions
½ cup/120 ml chopped green bell pepper
½ cup/120 ml chopped celery
1 bay leaf
¼ tsp thyme
8 oz/225 g tomato sauce
2 tsp salt
½ tsp freshly ground pepper
1 tbsp Worcestershire sauce
Tabasco sauce
2 cups/475 ml white wine or vermouth
1 tbsp lemon juice
1 tbsp lemon rind
¼ cup/60 ml minced fresh parsley
2 tbsp brandy
2 lb/900 g shrimp, peeled and cooked

Yield: 6 servings

To be completely authentic, use a wooden spoon to stir the roux for this spicy Cajun specialty.

In a large saucepan, combine ½ cup/115 g butter and all the flour. Cook until it becomes a walnut color, stirring constantly with a wooden spoon. Stir in the vegetables, bay leaf and thyme. Add the remaining butter and sauté, covered, over medium heat for 20 minutes, stirring occasionally. Add the tomato sauce, salt, pepper, Worcestershire, Tabasco to taste, wine and lemon juice. Bring to a boil. Reduce heat and simmer uncovered for 1 hour, stirring occasionally.

Remove from heat and add the lemon rind, parsley, brandy and shrimp, cooking just until the shrimp is pink. Serve over white rice.

" The first shrimp was a test of courage and honor for me, because of my conditional aversion to its general shape, but once I tackled it, my whole life changed… "
M.F.K. Fisher

Seafood

SHELLFISH

Shellfish fall into one of three categories:
- Crustaceans including crabs, crayfish, lobsters, prawns and shrimp
- Mollusks including clams, mussels, oysters and scallops
- Cephalopods including squid and octopus

These are some of the shellfish available in Belgium:
- Clams/Palourdes have a slimy texture when eaten raw. They are also served steamed or baked depending on the variety of clam.
- Crayfish/Ecrevisses are freshwater crustaceans which resemble 4"/10cm lobsters. The white tail meat is sweet and the fat from the head adds richness to seafood stocks.
- Langoustines are crayfish-sized members of the lobster family. This saltwater delicacy is indigenous to European waters.
- Lobsters/Homards have sweet white meat in the tail and claws (depending on the variety).
- Mussels/Moules are a Belgian specialty served in large pots with flavorful broths and sauces and eaten with FRITES.
- Sea Scallops/Coquilles Saint-Jacques are a mild, tender, sweet white muscle. The orange crescent-shaped coral (roe), commonly still attached in European fish markets, is also a delicacy. Bay Scallops/Pétoncles, about one-quarter the size of sea scallops, are even more tender.
- Shrimp/Crevettes are saltwater crustaceans with a firm texture and the sweet flavor of the sea. Prawns, or Scampi in Italian, are found in fresh water. Prawns and Scampi, however, have come to designate any large shrimp in the United States. Two types of tiny shrimp, Crevettes Grises and Crevettes Roses, are considered a Belgian delicacy. They are most often served plain, in salad or with cocktail sauce.

Scampi and Papaya with Hot Sweet and Sour Sauce
Jaco's - Yann Blanchet, Chef

¾ cup/150 g caster sugar
3½ oz/100 ml wine vinegar
1 tbsp tomato purée
17 oz/500 ml water
3 sprigs of fresh mint
2 papayas
24 scampi
2 tbsp oil
2 zucchini
2 tbsp/30 g butter
3½ oz/100 g rice
1 tsp chili paste (optional)

Garnish:
fresh mint leaves

Yield: 4 servings

To make the sauce, combine sugar, vinegar, tomato purée and water. Boil for 10 minutes and set aside.

Chop the mint leaves. Peel the papaya, remove the seed, scoop out little balls of fruit and set aside. Heat oil and fry the scampi on both sides; reserve. Cut the zucchini into long, thin "spaghetti" and fry them lightly in butter. Cook the rice and keep warm.

Heat the sauce. Add the mint, (chili paste), scampi and papaya balls. Immediately divide the mixture among 4 serving plates, placing it to one side. Twist the fried zucchini into "nests" and arrange them on the plates. Add a small mound of rice to each plate and decorate with mint leaves.

Shrimp on the Bar-B

This is hot, spicy and delicious!

Marinate peeled and deveined shrimp (see index) in marinade ingredients for 1 to 2 hours. Thread on skewers. Barbecue until just pink and curled. To make the sauce, combine mayonnaise and chili pepper. Serve shrimp with the sauce.

When peeling shrimp, save the shells and broil them until they turn very brown. You may then use them to flavor sauces, soups and stocks. (Lobster and crab shells may be used in the same fashion.) Add them to liquid in the recipe or create a flavorful stock by boiling them with water or white wine. Strain out the shells and reduce the liquid to desired intensity.

2½ lb/1¼ kg large shrimp

Marinade:
⅓ cup/80 ml vegetable oil
1½ tbsp honey
1½ tbsp minced chili peppers
1 tbsp lemon juice
4 green onions, finely chopped
2 tbsp parsley
¼ tsp cayenne pepper
¼ tsp cinnamon

Sauce:
1 cup/240 ml mayonnaise
1 tbsp chopped chili pepper

Yield: 6 servings

Seafood Mixed Grill

Green Goddess Dip with Crudités Platter
∞
Shrimp on the Bar-B
Swordfish Brochette
Rice Pilaf
Orange Avocado Salad
∞
Chocolate Tart Gourmandise
(Whipped Cream and Fresh Raspberries)

Scallops with Leeks and Truffles
Restaurant 't Pandreitje (Bruges) - Guy Van Neste, Chef

A perfect fish course served as part of a formal multi-course dinner. Minced truffles may be substituted for the truffle oil if you are feeling extravagant.

2 leeks, julienned 4 tbsp butter truffle oil	Sauté leeks in butter until soft; add a little truffle oil to taste and keep warm.
olive oil balsamic vinegar salt	Drizzle a little olive oil and a little balsamic vinegar around the outside edge of individual serving plates.
freshly ground pepper 12 sea scallops, halved	Rub the scallops with olive oil, season with salt and pepper and grill quickly on both sides. Mound the leeks in the center of each plate. Surround with the scallops and serve.

Yield: 4 servings

> *Si j'avais un fils à marier, je lui dirais: 'Méfie-toi de la jeune fille qui n'aime ni le vin, ni la truffe, ni la musique.'*
> Colette

Seafood 133

Scallops in Saffron Sauce

A special occasion dish! Serve as a romantic dinner for two or a first course for four.

16 sea scallops, coral attached
½ cup/120 ml fish stock
½ cup/120 ml dry white wine
1 shallot, chopped
1 bouquet garni (see index)
6 black peppercorns
pinch of saffron threads
4 tbsp hot water
1¼ cups/300 ml heavy cream
3 tbsp chopped fresh parsley
salt
freshly ground pepper

Yield: 2 - 4 servings

Put the scallops into a large sauté pan with the fish stock, wine, shallot, bouquet garni (1 bay leaf, 1 sprig fresh thyme, 3 stalks parsley) and peppercorns. Cover the pan and bring the liquid to just below a boil. Remove the pan from the heat and allow the scallops to poach in the hot liquid for 10 to 15 minutes. The scallops are cooked when they are just firm to the touch. Remove them from the liquid and keep warm.

Strain the scallop cooking liquid into a small saucepan and boil rapidly until it is reduced by half. Soak the saffron in the 4 tablespoons of hot water for 5 minutes, until the color has infused. Add the saffron water, heavy cream and parsley to the reduced cooking liquid and season to taste with salt and pepper. Bring the sauce back to just below boiling point.

Arrange the scallops on individual serving plates and top with the warm sauce.

Variations: Use this sauce and preparation for other types of poached fish.

> *… good eating remains an everyday pleasure, central to life. At table - not on the pillow - relationships are hammered out.*
> Catharine Reynolds

Coquilles Saint-Jacques à l'Effilochée d'Endives
(Sautéed Sea Scallops with Creamed Endives)

½ lb/225 g Belgian endives
3 tbsp/45 g unsalted butter
salt
freshly ground pepper
1 tsp granulated sugar
½ cup/120 ml heavy cream
1 lb/450 g sea scallops
1 tbsp all-purpose flour
1 tbsp minced fresh chervil or parsley

Yield: 4 servings

Cut the endives into fine shreds, lengthwise.

Heat 1 tablespoon/15 grams butter in a small saucepan and add endive shreds, salt, pepper and sugar. Cover and cook over low heat for 15 minutes. Add the cream and correct the seasoning. Simmer, uncovered, another 10 minutes. Keep warm.

Sprinkle the scallops with salt, pepper and flour. Over high heat, melt remaining butter in a nonstick pan. Brown the scallops in two batches, 2 to 3 minutes per batch, until cooked through.

Warm 4 individual serving plates. Ladle the sauce onto each plate and arrange scallops on top. Sprinkle with chervil or parsley.

Mussels with Leeks, Saffron and Cream

A delicious alternative to the usual preparations, this recipe is proportioned to be a starter.

4 dozen mussels
2 tbsp/30 g butter
2 large leeks
2 fish bouillon cubes
1 cup/240 ml dry white wine
8 fresh parsley sprigs
10 saffron threads, crumbled
½ cup/120 ml heavy cream
2 tbsp minced fresh parsley
salt
freshly ground pepper

Yield: 4 servings

Scrub and de-beard the mussels (see note).

Melt butter in a large, heavy deep pan over medium-low heat. Thinly slice the leeks, including some of the pale green part. Add the leeks to the pan and sauté until tender, about 8 minutes.

Combine fish bouillon cubes, wine and parsley sprigs in a large pot and bring to a boil. Add mussels; cover and cook over high heat just until the mussels open, about 6 minutes. Do not overcook. Using tongs, transfer the mussels to a large bowl, discarding any that did not open. Strain clear mussel juices into the leeks. (Do not pour off any sandy residue at the bottom of the pot.)

Add saffron and cream to the leeks. Boil until reduced to sauce consistency, about 2 minutes. Stir in minced parsley and season with salt and pepper. Add mussels and any accumulated juices to the pan. Stir over medium heat until heated through, about 2 minutes. Divide mussels among 4 bowls. Pour on the sauce and serve immediately.

MUSSELS/MOULES

Mussels in Brussels are a must! The traditional season for mussels is September to April, the months with "R" in the name, but Belgians only do without during the hottest summer months. Fresh mussels must be kept cold and cooked as soon as possible. Clean them no more than an hour before cooking. Thoroughly scrub the shells under cold running water, pulling off the fibrous beard clinging to the shell. Mussels with cracked or partly opened shells which do not close when lightly tapped must be discarded. They are not safe to eat. Plan on ¾ kilo or a generous 1½ pounds per person as a main course. Serve with FRITES, homemade MAYONNAISE, a Belgian beer and several large, empty bowls for the shells.

Moules Marinière
(Classic Mussels)

3 tbsp/45 g butter
2 cups/475 ml chopped vegetables
(shallots, celery, onion)
1½ cups/350 ml dry white wine
1 tbsp chopped fresh parsley
1 tsp chopped fresh thyme
1 bay leaf
freshly ground black pepper
6½ lb/3 kg mussels, well cleaned

Yield: 4 servings

Melt the butter in a large pot with a tightly fitting lid. Add the chopped vegetables and sauté over medium heat for 5 minutes. Add the wine and simmer 15 minutes. Stir in the herbs and pepper and add the mussels. Cover tightly and bring to a boil over high heat. Cook for 5 to 6 minutes or until the mussels open. (Discard any that do not open.)

Serve in bowls with the broth and vegetables spooned on top.

Variations: For MOULES MARINIÈRE À LA GUEUZE, replace the white wine with a Belgian beer such as a gueuze. For MOULES À L'AIL ET AUX FINES HERBES, add 6 minced garlic cloves, 4 tablespoons of lemon juice and 4 tablespoons each of chopped fresh parsley, basil and fresh coriander (cilantro). For MOULES PROVENÇALE, add garlic, oregano, chopped tomatoes and hot red pepper flakes to the vegetable and wine mixture, and reduce before adding the mussels. For MOULES À LA CRÈME, spoon cooked mussels into bowls and add heavy cream or BÉCHAMEL SAUCE to cooking juices; reduce until thickened.

Leftover mussels: Pick mussels from shells and refrigerate in their own juices, tightly covered, for up to 3 days. Stuff small mushroom caps with mussels, drizzle with garlic butter, sprinkle with Parmesan cheese and broil. Add mussels to a seafood risotto or a favorite seafood pasta sauce. Use leftover broth as the beginning of a seafood soup; stir in cooked mussels just before serving. Mix mussels with minced shallot, celery and garlic and add mayonnaise or vinaigrette for a delicious salad.

For a richer sauce, remove cooked mussels to serving bowls and rapidly boil the sauce until concentrated and thickened. Spoon over the mussels and serve.

> "Recipes are like folktales, small parcels of culture."
> Martha Stewart

Cassolette de Palourdes au Champagne
Café Restaurant de l'Ogenblik - M. Gonzalo Gomez, Chef

2⅕ lb/1 kg clams (palourdes)
2 tbsp olive oil
2 shallots, chopped
1 leek, minced
2 celery sticks, minced
2 carrots, minced
¾ cup/175 ml champagne
7 oz/200 g fresh spinach
fresh coriander (cilantro), chopped
1 tomato, diced
¼ cup/60 ml MOUSSELINE SAUCE
¼ cup/60 ml heavy cream

Yield: 4 servings

Thoroughly scrub the clams. Cook, covered, in hot olive oil with the shallots and champagne until the clams begin to open. Add leeks, celery and carrots and cook another 5 minutes. Remove the clams and reduce the sauce by half. Add the fresh coriander and tomato. To finish the sauce, thicken it with the mousseline sauce and cream. Keep warm.

Blanch the spinach in boiling water and drain. Cover the bottom of a shallow casserole with spinach. Reserving 4 whole clams for decoration, remove the clams from the shells and layer the clams over the spinach.

Cover the clams with the sauce and broil until lightly browned. Serve with reserved clams on top.

Poultry, Game and Meat

Poultry, Game and Meat

Poultry	Algerian Brochette	147
	Balsamic Grilled Chicken	148
	Chicken and Leek Lasagne	152
	Chicken Breasts in Phyllo	155
	Chicken Breasts on Wild Mushroom Ragoût	154
	Chicken in White Wine	153
	Chicken Niçoise	142
	Chicken Piccata	146
	Chicken Saté	144
	Chicken with Cashews	145
	Malaysian Chicken Pizza	149
	Raspberry Chicken	147
	Roast Breast of Turkey with Corn Bread, Spinach and Pecans	156
	Roast Garlic Herb Chicken	143
	Waterzooi de Volaille à la Gantoise	141
	Wild Rice and Turkey Casserole	158
Game	Lapin à la Moutarde	162
	Magret de Canard à l'Orange	161
	Pintadeau à la Bière de Framboise	160
	Pintadeau à la Moutarde	159
	Rich Venison and Beef Stew	163
Meat	Beef Burgundy	179
	Blanquette de Veau	170
	Braised Veal Shanks with White Beans and Tomatoes	169
	Carbonnade de Boeuf à la Gueuze	177
	Carbonnades Flamandes	178
	Chili Con Carne	183
	Escalope de Veau Normande	172
	Filet Mignon avec Sauce Béarnaise au Vin Rouge	184
	Filet Mignon with Green Peppercorn Sauce	185
	Gigot d'Agneau Farci en Croûte	176
	Herb and Garlic Roast Pork	166
	Herbed Pork Loin with Bourbon Gravy	168
	Herbed Rack of Lamb	174
	Lamb Brochette	174
	Lamb with Almonds	175
	Lasagne	182
	Lemon Braised Veal Chops	173
	Pork and Stilton Stroganoff	167
	Pork Tenderloin with Mustard Sauce	165
	Saltimbocca	171
	San Jacinto Pork Fajitas	164
	Veal Marsala	173

Sauces, etc.

Béchamel Sauce	152
Garlic Herb Butter	143
Pizza Crust	149
Shashlik Sauce	186
Spicy BBQ Sauce	186

SPECIAL TOPICS

Balsamic Vinegar	148
French Cider	172
Game	158
Meat	180
Mushrooms	150
Pepper	185

Waterzooi de Volaille à la Gantoise
La Maison du Cygne - Richard Hahn, Chef

1 (2 lb/900 kg) chicken
2½ cups/600 ml chicken broth
2 carrots, finely julienned
2 celery ribs, finely julienned
1 leek, finely julienned (white only)
½ cup/120 ml heavy cream
2 large egg yolks
2 tbsp chopped fresh chervil
salt
freshly ground black pepper

Yield: 2 servings

In a large saucepan of boiling salted water, blanch the chicken for 3 minutes and drain. In a heavy saucepan just large enough to hold the chicken, combine the chicken with the broth (the broth should come about one-third of the way up the chicken), bring the broth to a boil and simmer the chicken, covered, for 15 to 20 minutes or until tender.

Meanwhile, heat water to a boil in a large saucepan and, one vegetable at a time, add carrots, celery and then leek, returning the water to a boil between each. After adding the leek, return the water to a boil, remove from heat and let stand.

When the chicken is tender, transfer it to a cutting board. Remove and discard the skin and bones. Tear the chicken into pieces, place into a warmed tureen and keep warm, covered with foil.

Boil the broth until it is reduced to about 1⅓ cups/320 ml. In a bowl, whisk together the cream and the yolks, add hot broth in a thin stream, whisking, and then return the sauce to the pan. Cook the sauce over moderately low heat, whisking continuously, until it is slightly thickened. (Do not let it boil.) Remove the pan from the heat and stir in the chervil, salt and freshly ground black pepper to taste.

Pour the vegetables into a large strainer and drain well. Add them to the tureen and pour the sauce over the chicken and vegetables. To serve, ladle into large shallow soup bowls.

Chicken Niçoise

*T*his uncomplicated dish is light and refreshing. It is even better made ahead and reheated so all the flavors are absorbed by the chicken.

4 lb/1⅘ kg chicken, in serving pieces
juice of 1 lemon
2 tsp thyme
salt
freshly ground black pepper
3 tbsp olive oil
½ cup/120 ml lardons (see index)
4 onions, minced
2 garlic cloves, peeled
5 tomatoes, quartered*
2 bay leaves
½ cup/120 ml dry white wine
½ cup/120 ml black or oil-cured olives
½ cup/120 ml chopped fresh basil

Yield: 6 servings

Dry the chicken thoroughly and sprinkle with lemon juice, thyme, salt and pepper. Heat the olive oil in a large heavy pan. Add the lardons and chicken. Sauté for 15 minutes, turning the pieces on all sides. Remove the lardons and chicken from the pan with a slotted spoon and add the onions. Cook over low heat for 10 minutes, adding more oil if necessary. Add the garlic cloves, tomatoes, bay leaves, and wine and cook for 10 minutes. Return the lardons and chicken to the pan and cook slowly, uncovered, for 35 to 40 minutes, basting frequently. Taste and correct the seasoning.

Shortly before serving, remove the bay leaves and garlic cloves and add the olives. Heat gently, sprinkle with basil and serve immediately.

* or ¾ cup/175 ml canned tomatoes

Bistro Fare
(Belgian Beer)
∞
Mesclun aux Lardons
∞
Chicken Niçoise
Rosemary Roasted Potatoes
(Steamed Baby Carrots)
∞
Apple Tart
Caramel Sauce

Roast Garlic Herb Chicken

Roast chicken is a classic throughout Belgium and France.

To make the herb butter, combine butter, rosemary, thyme, garlic and lemon peel in a small bowl and stir to blend. Season to taste with salt and pepper.

1 (7 lb/3 kg) roasting chicken
¼ cup/60 ml dry white wine
1 cup/240 ml chicken broth
2 tbsp flour
salt
freshly ground pepper

Rinse chicken and pat dry. Gently loosen the skin of the chicken breast from the meat. Setting aside 2 tablespoons of herb butter, rub half of the remaining herb butter on the chicken breast meat under the skin. Spread remaining half of the herb butter over the outside of the chicken. Season chicken with salt and pepper and truss.

Garlic Herb Butter:
½ cup/115 g butter, softened
2 tbsp chopped fresh rosemary
2 tbsp chopped fresh thyme
3 large garlic cloves, minced
1½ tsp grated lemon peel
salt
freshly ground pepper

Place chicken in a roasting pan. Roast in a preheated 450°F/230°C oven for 20 minutes. Reduce oven temperature to 375°F/190°C. Roast about 1 hour and 15 minutes longer, until a meat thermometer inserted into the thickest part of the inner thigh registers 175F/90°C and juices from the thigh run clear when pierced with a skewer. Lift chicken and tilt slightly, emptying any juices from the cavity into the roasting pan. Transfer chicken to a serving platter. Tent with aluminum foil to keep warm.

Garnish:
lemon wedges
rosemary sprigs

Oven Temp: 450°F/230°C
375°F/190°C
Yield: 4 servings

Belgians often serve their steak topped with a round slice of garlic herb butter. To serve the Belgian way, make this GARLIC HERB BUTTER, form into a cylinder with plastic wrap or foil, freeze and slice as needed.

Pour pan juices into a large glass measuring cup. Spoon fat from the top. Deglaze roasting pan with wine, scraping up any browned bits. Pour wine mixture into the cup with the pan juices. Add enough broth to measure 2½ cups/600 ml liquid. Melt reserved 2 tablespoons herb butter in a heavy saucepan over moderately high heat. Add flour, whisking until smooth and light brown, about 3 minutes. Gradually whisk in pan juices. Boil until thickened, whisking occasionally, about 7 minutes. Season gravy with salt and pepper. Arrange lemon wedges and rosemary around the chicken and serve with gravy.

Chicken Saté

A wonderful combination of flavors - easily barbecued or broiled.

3 tbsp soy sauce
2 tbsp vegetable oil
1 tbsp lemon juice
½ tsp curry powder
1 garlic clove, minced
1 lb/450 g boned, skinned chicken breasts
paprika

Dipping Sauce:
2 tbsp thinly sliced green onions
½ tsp peeled, minced ginger root
⅛ tsp hot red pepper flakes
¼ cup/60 ml peanut butter
½ cup/120 ml water
½ tbsp soy sauce

Yield: 4 servings

Combine soy sauce, oil, lemon juice, curry and garlic in a bowl. Cut chicken into 1"/2½cm pieces and add to marinade, turning pieces to coat evenly. Cover and refrigerate at least 2 hours.

To make the sauce, combine onions, ginger root and red pepper in a saucepan. Stir in peanut butter, water and soy sauce and warm over low heat until combined, stirring constantly.

Thread chicken pieces onto 4 bamboo skewers. Sprinkle paprika over chicken. Broil or grill about 5 minutes on each side. Serve with the sauce.

" *Whether for comfort or celebration, what matters most is the sharing of memories - and there is no memory more powerful than that shared around the kitchen table.* "
Elizabeth Luard

Chicken with Cashews

So easy to prepare, it's almost like going out for dinner!

Cut chicken into bite-sized pieces and combine with cornstarch, sherry and ginger root. Set aside for 20 minutes. In a small bowl, combine hoisin sauce, soy sauce, sugar and water and set aside.

Heat oil in a large sauté pan or wok over high heat. Add garlic and chicken mixture and cook 2 minutes. Remove garlic and reduce heat to medium. Stir in soy sauce mixture and cook another 5 minutes. Add cashews and drizzle with sesame oil. Serve immediately with rice.

1 lb/450 g boned and skinned chicken
2 tsp cornstarch
2 tsp sherry
½ tsp peeled, grated ginger root
2 tbsp hoisin sauce
2 tbsp dark soy sauce
1 tsp sugar
1 tbsp water
4 tbsp oil
1 garlic clove, slightly crushed
1 cup/240 ml blanched cashews, toasted
1 tsp oriental sesame oil

Yield: 4 servings

Poultry, Game and Meat

Chicken Piccata

Great for a family meal - serve with ITALIAN GREEN BEANS and rice.

8 boned, skinned chicken breast halves
½ cup/65 g flour
1 tsp salt
½ tsp paprika
¼ tsp freshly ground pepper
4 tbsp/55 g butter
2 tbsp olive oil
4 tbsp dry white wine
3 tbsp fresh lemon juice
3 - 4 tbsp capers, drained
Garnish:
lemon slices
Yield: 6 - 8 servings

Flatten chicken breasts between sheets of wax paper or plastic wrap. Combine flour, salt, paprika and pepper. Dredge chicken pieces in the flour mixture, shaking off excess.

In a large frying pan, heat butter and olive oil until it sizzles. Sauté chicken breasts on both sides until lightly browned, about 3 to 4 minutes per side. Remove chicken to an oven-proof serving platter and keep in a warm oven.

Add wine to the hot pan, scraping up any browned pieces. Stir in lemon juice and simmer 1 minute. Return chicken to the frying pan. Add capers and simmer 2 minutes. Return chicken to the serving platter and cover with sauce. Garnish with lemon slices.

Variation: Use veal scallops instead of chicken for VEAL PICCATA.

> *La bonne cuisine est celle où les choses ont le goût de ce qu'elles sont.*
> Auguste Escoffier

Poultry, Game and Meat

Algerian Brochette

The yogurt marinade tenderizes and flavors the chicken. Serve with couscous or LEMON RICE.

4 boned, skinned chicken breast halves
¼ cup/60 ml olive oil
2 cups/475 ml plain yogurt
1 tsp lemon juice
1 tbsp chopped fresh oregano
1 tbsp minced garlic
1 tsp ground cumin
1 tbsp cracked peppercorns
2 small green bell peppers
2 small red bell peppers

Yield: 4 servings

Cut the chicken breasts into 2"/5cm pieces (about 4 to 6 pieces per breast). Mix olive oil, yogurt, lemon juice, oregano, garlic, cumin and peppercorns to make a marinade. Marinate the chicken breasts in the refrigerator for 6 hours.

Cut each bell pepper into 1"/2½cm squares and blanch the squares in boiling water. Arrange chicken and peppers alternately on metal skewers. Grill or broil 4"/10cm from heat for 8 to 10 minutes, turning often.

Raspberry Chicken

It's hard to imagine anything this easy being so delicious!

4 boned, skinned chicken breast halves
salt
flour
2 tbsp/30 g butter
¼ cup/60 ml minced shallots
3 tbsp raspberry jam or jelly
3 tbsp red wine vinegar
¼ cup/60 ml heavy cream

Garnish:
fresh raspberries

Yield: 4 servings

Salt and lightly flour the chicken. Melt butter in a large sauté pan and cook chicken over medium heat for about 5 minutes per side. Sprinkle shallots around the chicken and continue cooking for 5 minutes more. Remove chicken and keep warm.

Add jam and vinegar to the pan and cook, scraping up brown bits in the pan. Bring to a full boil and cook for 1 minute or until slightly reduced. Stir in cream and heat to boiling.

Pour the sauce over the warm chicken. Garnish with fresh raspberries.

Balsamic Grilled Chicken

Great for your next big barbecue, or reduce the quantity for a family meal. The marinade makes the chicken extra tender and juicy and gives it a slightly sweet teriyaki flavor.

5 lb/2¼ kg boned, skinned chicken breasts

Marinade:
1 cup/240 ml vegetable oil
½ cup/120 ml balsamic vinegar
3 tbsp granulated sugar
3 tbsp ketchup
1 tbsp Worcestershire sauce
2 green onions, tops included, minced
1 tsp salt
½ tsp cracked pepper
1 tsp dry mustard
1 garlic clove, minced
Tabasco sauce

Yield: 16 - 20 servings

Combine all marinade ingredients. Arrange the chicken in one layer in stainless or glass baking dishes. Pour marinade over the chicken, turning to coat. Cover and refrigerate chicken at least 6 hours, preferably overnight, turning occasionally.

Bring chicken to room temperature. Remove chicken from marinade and grill on a barbecue for 7 to 8 minutes per side, basting occasionally.

Variation: Chicken cut into serving pieces may also be used; however, first oven-bake the chicken in the marinade for 30 to 40 minutes at 325°F/165°C. Remove chicken from marinade and grill 4 to 5 minutes per side, basting occasionally.

BALSAMIC VINEGAR

This intense, sweetly tart vinegar from Northern Italy is made from the unfermented juice of the white Trebbiano grape. The juice is boiled down to a syrup which concentrates the sugar. It is then slowly fermented in wood. To be labeled Aceto Balsamico Tradizionale, the vinegar must have been aged at least twelve years, but the very finest balsamic vinegar can be aged for decades. This extremely expensive vinegar blends sweetness and acidity, lending richness and complexity to recipes. Avoid inexpensive balsamic vinegars which often contain ordinary wine vinegar and caramel. Use moderately priced balsamic for marinades, strong salad dressings, and heavy sauces, reserving the finest, slowly-aged vinegar to use as a flavoring when the intense taste can be appreciated using only a few drops.

Malaysian Chicken Pizza

Combine first 8 ingredients in a bowl and whisk until well combined. Set aside.

Oil a large, nonstick frying pan and place over medium heat until hot. Cut chicken into bite-sized pieces and add to the pan; sauté 2 minutes. Remove and set aside.

Pour vinegar mixture into the frying pan and bring to a boil over moderately high heat. Cook 6 minutes or until slightly thickened. Return chicken to pan and cook 1 minute or until chicken is cooked. (Mixture will be the consistency of thick syrup.)

Sprinkle cheeses over prepared crust, leaving a ½"/1 ¼cm border; top with chicken mixture. Bake on the bottom rack of a preheated oven for 12 minutes. Remove pizza to a cutting board, sprinkle with green onions and let stand 5 minutes before serving.

Pizza Crust

In a large bowl, dissolve sugar and yeast in warm water; let stand 5 minutes. Stir in 2¾ cups/360 g flour, salt and oil to form a soft dough.

Turn the dough out onto a lightly floured surface. Knead until smooth and elastic (about 5 minutes); add enough of remaining flour, one tablespoon at a time, to prevent dough from sticking to hands.

Place dough in a lightly oiled bowl, turning dough to oil top. Cover and let rise in a warm place for 1 hour or until doubled in bulk.

Coat pizza pans or baking sheets with oil and lightly sprinkle with cornmeal. Punch dough down and divide in half. On a lightly floured surface, roll each half of dough into a 12"/30cm circle. Place dough on prepared pans. Crimp edges of dough with fingers to form a rim. Cover and let rise in a warm place, 30 minutes. Top and bake according to recipe directions.

12"/30 cm Pizza Crust

¼ cup/55 g firmly packed brown sugar
¾ cup/175 ml rice wine vinegar
¼ cup/60 ml soy sauce
3 tbsp water
2 tbsp chunky peanut butter
1 tbsp peeled, minced ginger root
½ tsp hot red pepper flakes
4 garlic cloves, minced
8 oz/225 g skinned, boned chicken breast
½ cup/120 ml shredded Swiss cheese
¼ cup/60 ml shredded mozzarella cheese
¼ cup/60 ml chopped green onions

Oven Temp: 500°F/260°C
Yield: 4 servings

Crust:
1 tbsp sugar
1 pkg dry yeast
1 cup/240 ml warm water (110°F/43°C)
3 cups/400 g all-purpose flour
¼ tsp salt
1 tsp olive oil
1 tbsp cornmeal

Yield: 2 pizza crusts

This recipe makes two crusts - freeze the extra dough for a delicious homemade Italian pizza.

MUSHROOMS

Europeans take their mushrooms seriously and fill baskets with treasures from the woods; the novice, however, should exercise caution since many edible mushrooms have poisonous look-alikes. Some pharmacists in Belgium are trained to distinguish poisonous mushrooms, but it is perhaps wiser to purchase your fungi from the local shops or markets and remember that there are bold mushroom hunters and old mushroom hunters, but few bold, old mushroom hunters!

Mushrooms are low in calories and high in vitamins. Select plump, firm mushrooms with closed caps and no blemishes or slimy spots. Since mushrooms absorb water like sponges, it is best to brush or wipe them clean; if you must wash them, do it quickly and dry them thoroughly. Most of the flavor and texture is in the skin, so leave the peel on. If you do not need the stems in your recipe, save them for adding flavor to stock. The following varieties should be available in the local markets when they are in season or at specialty stores most of the year.

Cêpes/Porcini/Boletus/Steinpiltz - good grilled, sautéed, and in sauces; they have a chewy, meaty texture and earthy flavor.

Chanterelle/Girolle - best sautéed with a touch of garlic or shallot; use in lightly flavored sauces or omelets to appreciate the delicate flavor.

Shiitake - a Japanese mushroom with a thick, meaty, dark brown cap and a hearty flavor; good in stir-fry, soup and stew. The tough stem must be completely removed.

Oyster/Pleurote - best quickly sautéed to highlight the delicate flavor and texture.

Morel/Morille - this honeycombed beauty gives a deep, woodsy flavor to game and other flavorful meats. Sauté in butter before adding to sauces; they must be cooked to remove a poisonous alkaloid present in the raw mushroom. Clean very carefully as they tend to be quite sandy.

...more on MUSHROOMS

Death Trumpet/Trompette-des-Morts - these small, black, "withered-looking" mushrooms have a pronounced wine-like flavor and enhance meats, game and other strongly flavored preparations.

Sheep's Foot/Pieds-de-Mouton - a firm, fleshy mushroom ideal to sauté or use in cooked dishes.

Button/Champignons de Paris - a cultivated, versatile mushroom with a firm texture which can be eaten raw or cooked. As they age, they lose moisture and the caps open, so be sure to select the freshest ones with tightly closed caps.

Truffle/Truffe - Although very expensive, the truffle is appreciated for its intense flavor. Shavings are ideally suited to mild flavors such as scrambled eggs, risotto, potatoes and pasta. Even in season (October to March), they are rarely available fresh, but good quality truffles are readily available in cans. The most prized are the black truffles from Perigord and the white Italian truffle. Beware of the inferior quality truffle imported from China. If you do find fresh truffles, choose ones that are firm, highly perfumed and reasonably clean. Before using, they should be washed well and scrubbed clean. Pare carefully or rub off the skin and use these bits to flavor sauces. Truffles should be shaved into fine slices and added at the end of the cooking time or used as a garnish. Truffles spoil rapidly; they can be kept refrigerated, submerged in rice for six to ten days. If you use only part of a truffle, place the remainder in a jar and cover with good quality oil. Keep the jar covered and refrigerated for up to one month. The perfumed oil that results is a bonus! You may also freeze truffles immersed in Madeira or sherry.

Dried Mushrooms - Many varieties of wild mushrooms come dried. Soak them in just enough warm water to cover for about one-half hour or until swelled and softened. Lift them carefully from the soaking liquid, without disturbing the bottom, squeeze gently and pat dry. Let the soaking liquid settle and pour off the clear liquid at the top or strain through several layers of cheesecloth or a coffee filter to remove any sand. Use this flavorful liquid in your recipe.

Chicken and Leek Lasagne

3 lb/1⅓ kg chicken, in serving pieces
½ quart/liter water
¾ cup/175 ml dry white wine
1 onion, sliced
1 celery stalk, in chunks
1 bay leaf
5 peppercorns
1 lb/450 g leeks, chopped
2 garlic cloves, minced
5 tbsp/70 g butter
7 oz/200 g lasagne noodles
6 oz/170 g Gruyère, shredded
6 oz/170 g mozzarella, diced
1 (10 oz/290 g) jar sun-dried tomatoes
4 tbsp grated Parmesan cheese
5 tbsp pine nuts, lightly toasted

Béchamel Sauce:
5 tbsp/70 g butter
5 tbsp flour
1¼ cups/300 ml chicken broth
½ cup/120 ml white wine
1¼ cups/300 ml heavy cream

Oven Temp: 350°F/175°C
Yield: 8 servings

In a large pot, combine chicken with water, wine, onion, celery, bay leaf and peppercorns. Bring to a boil and simmer gently just until the chicken is cooked, about 20 minutes. Let cool in broth until cool enough to handle. Cut the chicken into small pieces, putting bones and skin back into the pot. Continue to simmer the broth for 30 minutes. Strain and measure 1¼ cups/300 ml broth; set aside.

Sauté the leeks and garlic in butter until soft. Add the chicken pieces, season with salt and pepper, and set aside.

To make the Béchamel Sauce, melt butter in a saucepan. Add flour and stir to make a roux. Cook 1 minute, but do not let it brown. Gradually add the broth, wine and cream and whisk until sauce is smooth and thick. Set aside.

Cook the pasta al dente according to package directions; drain and rinse with cold water. Drain the sun-dried tomatoes and pat dry; chop coarsely. Ladle a little sauce on the bottom of a 9"x13"/24 x 34cm baking pan. Layer noodles, chicken mixture, Gruyère, mozzarella, sun-dried tomatoes and sauce. Repeat twice. Sprinkle with Parmesan and pine nuts and bake until sauce bubbles and top is lightly colored, about 30 minutes if the ingredients are warm, or 45 to 55 minutes if the lasagne has been refrigerated.

Variation: Add chopped artichoke hearts and sauté with the leeks and garlic.

> "Cooking with butter, cream and wine is still the best. Cut these out and, to my taste, something is missing. And of course, one needs a glass of wine for health."
> André Soltner

Chicken in White Wine

Cooking for a crowd is easy with this wonderful party dish - serve with RICE PILAF.

24 boned, skinned chicken breast halves
1 cup/225 g butter
2 cups/475 ml minced onion
8 oz/225 g small mushrooms
2 garlic cloves, minced
½ cup/65 g flour
½ tsp salt
½ tsp pepper
½ tsp dried thyme
3½ cups/830 ml chicken broth
4 chicken bouillon cubes
2 cups/475 ml dry white wine

Garnish:
chopped fresh parsley

Oven Temp: 350°F/175°C
Yield: 24 servings

In a large frying pan, melt some of the butter and brown chicken breasts, a few at a time, adding more butter as needed. Set the browned breasts aside. In the same pan, sauté onions, mushrooms and garlic, stirring for about 5 minutes. Remove from the heat.

Mix flour, salt, pepper and thyme; stir into the onion mixture. Gradually stir in chicken broth and crumble in bouillon cubes. Return to the heat and bring to a boil; reduce heat and add wine.

Put 8 breast halves into each of three 2 quart/liter casseroles and cover each with a third of the sauce. Bake in a preheated oven for 1 hour or until bubbly. Garnish with parsley before serving.

To freeze and bake later: Line the casserole dishes with foil. Put in chicken and sauce as above. Fold foil over chicken and freeze until solid. Remove foil package from casserole, wrap, seal and return to freezer. To bake, remove wrap from as many packages as desired. Put each 8-person serving in a casserole; bake in a 400°F/200°C oven, covered, for 1 hour. Uncover and bake another 30 minutes, or until bubbly.

Chicken Breasts on Wild Mushroom Ragoût

Rich and flavorful, the wild mushrooms turn humble chicken breasts into gourmet fare. Delicious with WILD RICE WITH WALNUTS and CARROT FLANS.

2 cups/475 ml chicken broth
2 oz/55 g dried cêpes and/or morels
1 lb/450 g fresh mushrooms
6 tbsp/85 g unsalted butter
8 chicken breast halves, boned
½ cup/120 ml minced shallots
salt
freshly ground black pepper
1 cup/240 ml Port wine
1 cup/240 ml heavy cream

Yield: 6 - 8 servings

Bring chicken broth to a boil. Pour over the dried mushrooms and let stand for 2 hours.

Meanwhile, trim stems from the fresh mushrooms and cut into thin slices. Melt the butter in a frying pan, add the chicken and brown lightly on both sides. Cover and simmer over low heat for about 15 minutes, turning the chicken breasts over after half the cooking time. Remove the chicken from the pan, pour a little of the butter over them and keep warm while preparing the sauce.

> *The table can establish or augment a mood, for it is in fact a stage set...*
> Martha Stewart

Pour off all but about 2 tablespoons of the drippings from the pan and add the shallots. Sauté gently for about 5 minutes without browning. Carefully lift the dried mushrooms from the broth and roughly chop them, reserving the liquid. Add the dried and fresh mushrooms to the pan and simmer for 10 minutes, stirring occasionally. Taste and season with salt and pepper.

Strain the reserved soaking liquid through dampened cheesecloth, or a coffee filter, and add it to the mushrooms along with the Port. Simmer for 5 minutes, or until slightly thickened. Add cream and simmer until sauce is thick enough to coat a spoon.

If you prefer, remove the skin from the chicken breasts before placing them on top of the mushroom mixture. Cover the frying pan and simmer for 5 minutes before serving.

Chicken Breasts in Phyllo

8 boned, skinned chicken breast halves
salt
freshly ground pepper
8 oz/225 g phyllo dough
½ cup/115 g butter, melted
4 tbsp/55 g cold butter

Stuffing:
2 cups/475 ml chopped spinach leaves
1 cup/240 ml shredded Swiss cheese
½ cup/120 ml ricotta cheese
½ medium onion, chopped
2 hard boiled eggs, chopped
1 garlic clove, minced
1 tbsp green peppercorns, crushed
½ tsp salt

Madeira Sauce:
2 tbsp/30 g butter
2 tbsp flour
2 tbsp Madeira wine
1 cup/240 ml chicken broth
2 tsp tomato paste
⅓ cup/80 ml sour cream
⅓ cup/80 ml chopped chives
½ tsp salt
white pepper

Oven Temp: 400°F/200°C
Yield: 8 servings

Pound the chicken breasts until they are very thin. Sprinkle with salt and pepper.

Combine stuffing ingredients until the crushed peppercorns are well distributed. Spread stuffing over each chicken breast. Beginning at one end, roll once, then fold in sides and roll like a jelly roll. Place 1 sheet of phyllo on a damp towel. (Keep remaining phyllo covered.) Brush phyllo with some melted butter. Fold in half width-wise. Turn phyllo so narrow end faces you. Place one rolled chicken breast about 2"/5cm from the end of the phyllo. Top chicken with ½ tablespoon of cold butter. Roll phyllo over chicken once and then fold in sides. Continue rolling to end. Place on rimmed baking sheet, seam side down. Brush top with butter. Repeat with remaining breasts.

Bake in a preheated oven for 30 minutes or until golden brown. (If baking two sheets in one oven, rotate them halfway through the baking time.)

Prepare the Madeira Sauce while the chicken is baking. Melt butter in a medium saucepan. Add flour and cook, stirring until mixture is golden. Remove from the heat and whisk in Madeira and chicken broth. Cook, stirring just until mixture boils. Combine tomato paste, sour cream and a little of the hot Madeira sauce in a bowl, mix, and return to saucepan. Stir in chives, salt and pepper. If not serving immediately, place a piece of wax paper or plastic wrap directly on top to keep a skin from forming. Reheat before serving (do not boil), thinning with additional Madeira or cream if necessary.

Place chicken breasts on a serving platter and drizzle with some of the sauce. Pass the remaining sauce.

(For entertaining, the stuffing or phyllo-wrapped breasts may be refrigerated overnight or frozen up to 2 weeks. Bring chicken to room temperature before baking. The sauce may be held at room temperature for several hours or refrigerated overnight.)

Phyllo freezes beautifully. Place items on a baking sheet and freeze solid before wrapping. Small items may be frozen in plastic freezer bags; large items should be individually wrapped in plastic wrap and then foil. To defrost, unwrap items and place on a cookie sheet.

Roast Breast of Turkey with Corn Bread, Spinach and Pecans

Rinse and dry the turkey breast. Pound lightly to make as even as possible. Place in a shallow nonreactive pan.

Marinade: Mix together all marinade ingredients. Pour over turkey, turning breast to coat both sides. Cover and refrigerate overnight, turning occasionally.

Stuffing: Lightly toast the pecans. In a large frying pan, heat oil over moderate heat until hot. Sauté onions until tender, about 10 minutes. Stir in spinach and sauté until wilted. Remove to a large mixing bowl and stir in corn bread, pecans, mustard, broth and eggs.

Remove turkey from marinade. Dry well and place on a work surface, skinned side down. Pour marinade into a deep saucepan and set aside. Sprinkle meat with salt and pepper and spread with half the stuffing. Beginning with a short end, roll up like a jelly roll. (Do not be concerned about torn or uneven pieces of meat.) Tie with string at 1"/2½cm intervals. Sprinkle with salt and pepper.

Place turkey in a shallow roasting pan and add ½"/1¼cm of water. Roast 50 to 60 minutes in a preheated oven, or until a meat thermometer reaches 120°F/50°C. Baste breast with pan drippings every 15 minutes, adding more water to pan as needed.

Begin preparing the sauce while the turkey roasts. Pour wine and broth into remaining marinade and simmer over moderate heat until reduced by half. Set the sauce aside.

Remove turkey to a cutting board. Pour drippings into reserved sauce. Cut strings off turkey, brush top and sides with egg glaze and press remaining half of stuffing firmly over top and sides. Stir 1 tablespoon of the sauce into the honey and drizzle the corn bread topping with half the honey mixture. Return turkey to the oven and roast for another 15 minutes. Drizzle with remaining honey mixture and roast 15 minutes more or until brown and crusty and a thermometer inserted in the center reads 150°F/66°C. Remove

continued

---

1 whole turkey breast (see note)
salt
freshly ground pepper
1 egg white +1 tsp water (glaze)
¼ cup/60 ml honey

Marinade:
juice and grated peel of 3 oranges
⅔ cup/160 ml balsamic vinegar
¼ cup/60 ml olive oil
¼ cup/60 ml honey

Stuffing:
1½ cups/350 ml chopped pecans
1 tbsp olive oil
2 onions, chopped
2 cups/475 ml chopped fresh spinach
1½ cups/350 ml crumbled CORN BREAD *
1 tbsp mustard
¼ cup/60 ml chicken broth
2 large eggs, lightly beaten

Sauce:
reserved marinade
1 cup/240 ml dry red wine
¾ cup/175 ml chicken broth
1 tbsp cornstarch + 1 tbsp water
salt
freshly ground pepper

Oven Temp: 375°F/190°C
Yield: 8 - 12 servings

roast to a cutting board and let rest for 20 minutes before carving. (Turkey may be cooled to room temperature and then wrapped in foil and refrigerated overnight. To reheat, bring to room temperature, return to roasting pan, add ½"/1¼cm of broth or water, cover loosely with foil and roast at 375°F/190°C for 30 minutes or until heated through.)

Purchase a 6-7 lb/3 kg turkey breast with bones or a 4-5 lb/2 kg breast if boneless. Either way, ask the butcher to skin, bone, and butterfly the breast.

Deglaze the roasting pan over moderately high heat. Add a little of the sauce and bring to a boil, scraping the bottom of the pan and stirring constantly. Strain back into the remaining sauce in the saucepan. Remove sauce from heat and whisk in cornstarch mixture. Return to heat and cook, whisking, until sauce boils and thickens. Season to taste with salt and pepper, and more wine and/or honey, if needed. (Sauce may also be refrigerated overnight.)

Carve the roast into ⅜"/1cm slices and arrange, overlapping, on a platter. Drizzle with a little sauce. Pass the remaining sauce.

* As a time-saver, you may substitute dry corn bread stuffing mix for freshly baked corn bread.

> **Nothing is really work unless you would rather be doing something else.**
> Sir James M. Barrie

Poultry, Game and Meat

Wild Rice and Turkey Casserole

*I*n a large saucepan, gently sauté onion in butter; do not brown. Add flour, cook until bubbly and remove from heat. Whisk in chicken broth and half & half. Heat to boiling, whisking for 1 minute. Add turkey, mushrooms, rice, parsley, salt and pepper. Spoon into a 2 quart/liter buttered casserole dish, cover with a piece of buttered aluminium foil, and bake in a preheated oven for 1 hour. Uncover, sprinkle with almonds and bake for an additional 15 minutes.

½ cup/120 ml chopped onion
½ cup/115 g butter
¼ cup/35 g flour
2 cups/475 ml chicken broth
1½ cups/350 ml half & half (see index)
3 cups/700 ml cubed cooked turkey
6 oz/170 g mushrooms, sliced
1 cup/240 ml raw wild and white rice
2 tbsp parsley
1½ tsp salt
¼ tsp freshly ground pepper
½ cup/60 g slivered almonds

Oven Temp: 350°F/175°C
Yield: 6 - 8 servings

> "Can we ever have too much of a good thing?"
> Miguel de Cervantes

GAME

For those who love game, Belgium is truly paradise. In the fall, street markets, butcher shops and even the supermarkets display a wide variety of game birds and meats. Restaurants offer special game menus in celebration of the hunting season and there are hunt festivals and special game markets. What an opportunity to sample Belgium's bounty!

If you are interested in Venison/Venaison, look for either the smaller more tender Roe-Deer/Chevreuil or the larger Red Deer/Cerf. The female Red Deer/Biche, is also a good choice. Whatever you choose, the flavor of venison is rich and full. If you are roasting a saddle or tenderloin, cook it medium-rare. The less tender cuts impart robust flavor to stews and braised dishes. For the truly adventuresome try Young Wild Boar/Marcassin or Hare/Lièvre, both dark, richly flavored meats. Rabbit/Lapin is a lean, delicately flavored alternative to chicken.

Game birds are abundant in the fall as well. Look for Guinea Hen/Pintadeau, Pheasant/Faisan, Woodcock/Bécasse, Quail/Caille and Duck/Canard among others. Many "game birds" are farmed and have natural fat. If you have a wild bird, be sure to truss it tightly and cook with moist heat or, if roasting, cover the breast with bacon or sheets of pork fat. Baste often and cook just until it tests done (leg moves easily and juices run clear) to keep the meat juicy.

The stronger flavors of game go beautifully with red wine, garlic, mustard, juniper berries, bay leaves and the stronger tasting fall vegetables such as turnips, pearl onions and red cabbage.

Pintadeau à la Moutarde
(Roast Guinea Hen with Mustard)

Don't miss the opportunity to try this recipe in the fall when fresh guinea hens are widely available. Cornish game hens are an acceptable substitute, but you'll need one hen for each person.

1 guinea hen, trussed
3 tbsp/45 g butter
2 tbsp + 1 tsp Dijon mustard
½ tsp salt
¼ tsp freshly ground pepper
zest of 1 lemon, minced
1 cup/240 ml heavy cream

Béchamel Sauce:
1 tbsp/15 g butter
1 tbsp flour
½ cup/120 ml milk
salt
freshly ground pepper

Oven Temp: 400°F/200°C
Yield: 2 servings

Place the hen in a buttered roasting pan. Mix together 2 tablespoons of the butter, 1 tablespoon of the mustard, salt and pepper and spread over the hen. Roast in a preheated oven for about 1 hour, or until the juices run clear. Baste occasionally with the pan juices.

When using the zest of a lemon, lime or orange, be careful to use only the colored outside of the rind, avoiding the bitter white layer underneath.

While the hen is roasting, make the béchamel sauce. Melt butter in a small saucepan and stir in flour. Let cook a little but do not brown. Gradually add milk and cook, stirring constantly, until thick and smooth. Add salt and pepper to taste. Set aside, covered with plastic wrap.

In a small pan, cover lemon zest with water and bring to a boil. Simmer for 10 minutes, or until the water has nearly evaporated. Drain and reserve the rind.

When the hen is cooked, add the remaining mustard to the pan juices and cook, stirring. Add the béchamel sauce, cream and salt to taste. Just before serving, add the lemon zest, pepper and remaining 1 tablespoon butter to the sauce. Cut the hen in half, place on individual plates and pour the sauce on top. Serve immediately.

Poultry, Game and Meat

Pintadeau à la Bière de Framboise
In't Spinnekopke - Jean Rodriguez, Chef

Place the guinea hen in a buttered roasting pan. Place in a preheated 450°F/230°C oven and immediately reduce the temperature to 350°F/175°C. Roast 1 hour, or until juices run clear, basting frequently.

While the guinea hen is roasting, sauté the shallot in butter. Add the sugar and let caramelize. Pour in the raspberry beer and cook until reduced by half. Add the raspberries, cream, salt and pepper. Cut the guinea hen in half and serve on a pool of sauce.

1 guinea hen, trussed
1 shallot, minced
1 tbsp/15 g butter
1 tbsp granulated sugar
1 generous cup/250 ml raspberry beer
7 oz/200 g fresh raspberries
3½ oz/100 ml heavy cream
salt
freshly ground pepper

Oven Temp: 450°F/230°C
350°F/175°C
Yield: 2 servings

Magret de Canard à l'Orange

Try this nontraditional recipe for Duck à l'Orange. The orange marmalade creates a slightly different flavor.

1 orange
2 duck breasts
⅓ cup/80 ml white wine
4 tbsp orange marmalade
3 tbsp Dijon mustard
2 beef bouillon cubes
1½ cups/350 ml heavy cream
salt
pepper

Garnish:
orange zest strips
chopped fresh parsley

Yield: 2 servings

Cut long strips of orange zest using a zester or canneler and reserve for garnish. Squeeze the orange and set the juice aside.

Heat a frying pan over high heat. Score the duck fat and add the breasts to the pan, fat side down; sauté, without oil, for about 8 minutes. Turn the breasts and cook an additional 4 minutes. (The breasts should still be quite pink inside.) Set duck aside and keep warm. Pour off fat from pan, add wine and deglaze, scraping up the brown bits on the bottom. Add the juice from the orange, the marmalade and mustard, mixing well. Add the bouillon cubes and allow to dissolve. Reduce heat and add the cream, mixing well; let bubble for a few minutes until thickened. Season to taste with salt and pepper.

To serve, slice duck breasts into ¼"/½cm slices and arrange in an overlapping fan around the outside of each plate. Pour sauce over the slices and garnish with strips of orange zest and chopped parsley.

Magrets de canard, or duck breasts, are easily prepared. Score the skin, cutting through the fat but not all the way to the meat. Sprinkle the skin with salt and pepper and place, skin side down, in a very hot ungreased skillet. Sauté until brown and crisp, about 7 to 8 minutes. Turn and cook 2 to 4 minutes longer. Remove the duck from the pan and let it rest for 8 to 10 minutes before cutting into diagonal slices. For MAGRET DE CANARD À LA CRÈME, pour the fat from the pan and add chopped shallots. Sauté, scraping up the brown bits. Add heavy cream and cook until thickened. Pour the juices from around the duck breasts into the sauce and serve over the duck slices. On another occasion try duck breasts with PINK PEPPERCORN RASPBERRY SAUCE.

Lapin à la Moutarde

Rabbit and mustard is a perfect flavor combination, but don't pass up this recipe if rabbit isn't available. Dark meat chicken is an acceptable substitute.

1 (2½ lb/1¼ kg) rabbit, in 8 pieces
½ cup/120 ml Dijon mustard
salt
freshly ground black pepper
3 tbsp peanut oil
1 tbsp/15 g unsalted butter
1 (75 cl) bottle dry white wine
2 medium onions, minced
1 tbsp instant mix flour*
fresh thyme sprigs
1 bay leaf
chopped fresh parsley

Yield: 6 servings

Brush one side of each rabbit piece with some of the mustard. Season generously with salt and pepper. Heat oil and butter in a large frying pan over medium heat. When the fat is hot but not smoking, add several pieces of rabbit, mustard side down; do not crowd the pan. Cook until brown, about 10 minutes. Brush the second side with additional mustard. Season with salt and pepper. Turn the rabbit and cook until golden brown, another 10 minutes. Transfer the rabbit to a large platter and continue until all the rabbit is browned.

Add several tablespoons of wine to the skillet and scrape up any browned bits that stick to the pan. Add onions and cook, stirring, until golden brown, about 5 minutes. Remove the pan from the heat. Sprinkle flour over onions and stir to coat. Pour in remaining wine, the thyme, and bay leaf. Add the rabbit pieces. Return the skillet to medium heat and simmer until the rabbit is very tender and the sauce begins to thicken, about 1 hour.

Transfer the rabbit and sauce to a warmed platter and sprinkle with parsley. Serve immediately, over buttered fresh noodles or rice.

* In the United States, instant mix flour is called Wondra. In Belgium, use Maizena Express.

After the Hunt

Endive Salad with Roquefort and Walnuts

∞

Rich Venison and Beef Stew
Baking Powder Biscuits
Rosemary Roasted Potatoes
(Steamed Green Beans)

∞

Crème Caramel à la Crème de Marrons

> **"** An unadorned vegetable, a truly fresh vegetable, nicely steamed, is simply full of itself. **"**
> Laurie Colwin

Rich Venison and Beef Stew

You may certainly prepare this with all beef, but in the fall when game is widely available, don't miss the opportunity to sample local venison.

2 lb/900 g stewing venison
3 lb/1⅓ kg stewing beef
7 tbsp (or more) olive oil
3 stalks of celery, chopped
1 lb/450 g baby turnips, peeled, quartered
⅓ cup/45 g flour
2½ cups/600 ml beef stock
1 oz/30 g dried porcini mushrooms
2 (14 oz/400 g) cans artichoke hearts
5 oz/150 ml port
4 oz/115 g pitted black olives (optional)
salt
freshly ground pepper

Marinade:
1 lb/450 g onions, coarsely chopped
3 garlic cloves, sliced
1 (75 cl) bottle dry red wine
4 tbsp tomato paste
2 tbsp red wine vinegar
2 bay leaves
5 tbsp chopped fresh thyme
3 large sprigs rosemary
3 tbsp olive oil
grated rind and juice of 1 orange
salt
freshly ground pepper

Oven Temp: 325°F/165°C
Yield: 12 servings

Remove excess fat from meat, and cut into large chunks. Place the meat in a large bowl with all the marinade ingredients. Stir, cover and refrigerate overnight.

Soak the mushrooms in warm water to cover for 30 minutes. Lift out the mushrooms and strain the liquid through a sieve lined with moistened paper towels or a coffee filter. Set mushrooms and strained liquid aside.

Drain the liquid from the meat and onions, reserving the marinade. Discard the rosemary and bay leaves. Heat 6 tablespoons of the olive oil in a large flameproof casserole. Brown the meat and onions in batches, adding a little more oil if necessary. (Make sure the meat is well browned.) Remove with a slotted spoon.

Add 1 tablespoon olive oil to the casserole and lightly cook the celery and turnips until brown. Stir in the flour and cook for 1 minute. Pour in the stock, the liquid from soaking the mushrooms and the reserved marinade. Cut any large pieces of mushroom into smaller pieces and add. Return the meat to the casserole, season and bring to a boil. Cover tightly and cook in a preheated oven for 2 hours or until tender.

Drain and halve the artichoke hearts. Add to the casserole with port (and olives). Cover and simmer for 15 minutes, stirring occasionally. Add salt and pepper to taste.

San Jacinto Pork Fajitas

*M*ake these fajitas extra special with homemade SUPER GUACAMOLE.

4 lb/1⅘ kg pork loin, in 2"/5cm strips
olive oil
2 red bell peppers, julienned
2 yellow bell peppers, julienned
2 cups/475 ml sour cream
1 cup/240 ml honey mustard
flour tortillas
guacamole
salsa

Marinade:
2 onions, finely sliced
2 tbsp chopped garlic
juice of 4 limes
2 bottles dark beer
1 cup/240 ml red wine vinegar
2 jalapeños, seeded and diced
1 tbsp thyme
1 tsp oregano
2 tbsp Worcestershire sauce
salt
freshly ground pepper
fresh coriander (cilantro) to taste

Yield: 10 servings

Combine all marinade ingredients. Pour over the pork strips and refrigerate, covered, at least 24 hours.

Heat oil. Drain meat and sear pork and peppers in hot oil. Cook 4 to 6 minutes.

Mix sour cream with honey mustard. Serve meat in flour tortillas with honey mustard sauce, guacamole and salsa.

Fresh coriander (Chinese parsley or cilantro) is an essential ingredient in Mediterranean, Asian and Latin American cuisine. If you cannot find fresh, simply omit it from the recipe. Do not attempt to substitute dried since the leaves do not retain their flavor when dehydrated. Dried coriander is the seed of the herb.

Pork Tenderloin with Mustard Sauce

¼ cup/60 ml soy sauce
¼ cup/60 ml bourbon
2 tbsp brown sugar
3 lb/1⅓ kg pork tenderloin

Sauce:
⅓ cup/80 ml sour cream
⅓ cup/80 ml mayonnaise
1 tbsp minced green onions
1 tbsp dry mustard
salt
1½ tbsp vinegar

Oven Temp: 325°F/165°C
Yield: 5 - 6 servings

Combine soy sauce, bourbon and sugar. Pour over pork and marinate 2 to 3 hours, turning occasionally. Remove meat from marinade and place in a roasting pan. Bake in a preheated oven for 1 hour, basting occasionally with the marinade.

Combine the sauce ingredients and mix well. Carve the pork into thin diagonal slices and arrange on a serving platter. Pass the sauce.

> **Laughter is brightest where food is best.**
> Irish Proverb

Herb and Garlic Roast Pork

6 garlic cloves, peeled
¾ tsp salt
2 tbsp chopped fresh parsley
1 tbsp paprika
½ tsp oregano
¼ cup/60 ml olive oil
3 lb/1⅓ kg boneless pork loin
2 large baking potatoes

Oven Temp: 450°F/230°C
350°F/175°C
Yield: 6 servings

In a mortar, pound garlic and salt into a paste; add parsley. Stir in paprika and oregano. Gradually add oil to form a thick, rough paste. Rub some of the mixture all over the pork roast, reserving remaining marinade. Refrigerate pork and remaining marinade overnight (or up to 48 hours). Bring to room temperature before roasting.

To peel garlic, crush it slightly with the flat side of a broad knife. The peel will slip off easily. The finer garlic is chopped, the more juice will escape, increasing the pungency and strength of the flavor.

Cut potatoes in wedges and boil for 10 minutes; drain and set aside.

Place pork in a roasting pan and pour reserved marinade over the top. Roast in a preheated 450°F/230°C oven for 15 minutes. Reduce heat to 350°F/175°C. Add potato wedges and cook for 45 minutes or until pork juices run clear and potatoes are browned.

Transfer pork to a cutting board, cover loosely with foil and let rest for 10 minutes. Place potatoes around the edge of a serving platter. Slice the pork and arrange overlapping slices down the center of the platter.

Pork and Stilton Stroganoff

This unusual blue cheese and pork stroganoff is delicious served with brown rice or noodles.

1 tbsp vegetable oil
2 tbsp/30 g butter
2 lb/900 g pork tenderloin, in 2"/5cm strips
4 ribs celery, thinly sliced
4 carrots, peeled and julienned
16 pearl onions, peeled

Sauce:
15 oz/450 ml heavy cream
15 oz/450 ml chicken stock
3½ oz/100 g Stilton cheese
2 tbsp chopped fresh parsley
salt
freshly ground pepper

Yield: 6 - 8 servings

Melt the oil and butter in a large frying pan. In two batches, brown the pork for 4 or 5 minutes until cooked through. Remove with a slotted spoon and keep warm.

Steam the celery and carrots, 5 to 8 minutes, until cooked but still crisp. Set aside. Cook the onions in boiling water for about 15 minutes until tender. Drain and set aside.

To make the sauce, boil the cream and stock together in a pan. Reduce this mixture by half, about 10 minutes. Remove the rind and crumble the Stilton; add to the cream mixture. Whisk until the cheese has melted and the sauce is smooth. Add the parsley and season to taste. Add the pork and the vegetables to the sauce. Heat through and serve.

> *The perfect meal does not exist. It could well be a slice of toasted bread and some melted cheese, or fondue, shared with a friend. You cannot organize or anticipate good times or ideal meals. It's a question of simplicity, spontaneity, good times with friends.*
> Joël Robuchon

Herbed Pork Loin with Bourbon Gravy

Combine oil, thyme, oregano, caraway seeds, onion, garlic, and salt. Rub the mixture onto the pork loin. Chill the pork, covered, overnight.

2 tbsp vegetable oil
1 tsp thyme
1 tsp oregano
1 tbsp caraway seeds
1 small onion, minced
1 large garlic clove, minced
2 tsp coarse salt
4½ lb/2 kg boneless pork loin
1 tbsp bourbon
1 cup/240 ml chicken broth
½ cup/120 ml water
1 tbsp/15 g unsalted butter
2 tbsp all-purpose flour
½ cup/120 ml chopped green onions

Oven Temp: 350°F/175°C
Yield: 10 servings

Roast the pork in the middle of a preheated oven for 50 minutes to 1 hour, or until a meat thermometer registers 155°F/68°C. Remove the roast from the oven, transfer it to a cutting board and let stand, covered loosely with foil, for 10 minutes.

> **The kitchen makes everyone feel comfortable and warm.**
> Martha Stewart

Meanwhile, add the bourbon, broth and water to the pan juices. Boil the mixture for 1 minute, scraping up the brown bits, and then strain it through a sieve. In a heavy saucepan, melt the butter and add the flour. Cook over moderately low heat, whisking for a few minutes. Add the broth mixture in a stream, whisking. Bring the gravy to a boil, add the scallion greens and simmer for 1 minute. Cut the pork into slices and serve with the gravy.

Braised Veal Shanks with White Beans and Tomatoes

This unusual version of the classic Osso Buco is even heartier than the original.

5 tbsp olive oil
2 tbsp/30 g unsalted butter
6 (1½"/4cm thick) slices of veal shank
1½ cups/350 ml chopped onion
1 cup/240 ml chopped carrot
1 cup/240 ml chopped celery
2 garlic cloves, chopped
2 bay leaves
2 fresh thyme sprigs
3 tbsp chopped fresh parsley
2 (2"/5cm) strips lemon zest
1 (14 oz/400 g) can white beans
1 (28 oz/800 g) can plum tomatoes
1 cup/240 ml dry white wine
2 cups/475 ml chicken broth
salt
freshly ground black pepper

Gremolata:
¼ cup/60 ml minced fresh parsley
1 tbsp freshly grated lemon zest
1½ tsp minced garlic

Oven Temp: 350°F/175°C
Yield: 6 servings

In a large frying pan, heat 2 tablespoons of the oil and all the butter over moderately high heat. Brown the veal shanks and transfer them to a large baking dish just large enough to hold them in one layer. Remove the fat from the pan and add the remaining 3 tablespoons of oil. Add the onion, carrot, celery, garlic and bay leaves to the pan and sauté over moderate heat, stirring, until the vegetables are softened.

Thick slices of veal foreshank are often sold under the name Osso Buco. They are rich and tender when braised and are a common ingredient in meat stocks.

Add thyme, parsley, zest strips, beans, tomatoes, wine and 1½ cups/350 ml of the broth. Bring the liquid to a boil and add salt and pepper to taste. Pour the tomato mixture over the shanks.

Braise the veal in the middle of a preheated oven for 2 hours. With a slotted spoon, transfer the shanks to a serving dish. Cover and keep warm.

Discard the thyme sprigs and the bay leaves and purée the vegetable mixture. (If preferred, purée half the mixture and combine with the rest for a chunky sauce.) Reheat the sauce, thinning with the remaining chicken broth if the sauce is too thick.

Combine gremolata ingredients. Serve the veal shanks topped with sauce and sprinkled with gremolata.

Fresh herbs become mellow and add depth when they are cooked for a long time. For a fresh herb taste, add a little extra just before serving.

Blanquette de Veau

3 tbsp/45 g unsalted butter
2 lb/900 g boneless veal chunks
salt
freshly ground black pepper
4 garlic cloves, minced
2 tbsp flour
1 (75 cl) bottle dry white wine
2 bay leaves
1 tsp thyme
1 cup/240 ml peeled, sliced carrots
1 egg yolk
1 tbsp fresh lemon juice
2 tbsp heavy cream

Yield: 4 servings

Melt butter in a large deep frying pan. When the butter is hot but not smoking, add some veal and brown on all sides. (The meat should be browned in several batches, taking about 5 minutes to brown each batch.) As each batch is browned, remove the veal to a platter and season generously with salt and pepper.

When all the veal is browned, return it to the skillet. Add garlic and cook over moderately high heat for 2 to 3 minutes. Sprinkle the flour over the veal and stir with a wooden spoon to evenly coat the meat. Reduce the heat to medium and stir in 1 cup/240 ml of the wine, bay leaves, and thyme. Cover and bring just to a simmer; cook 5 minutes. Add 1 more cup/240 ml of wine. Simmer, covered, over medium heat for 1 hour.

Add the remaining wine and carrots. Cover and simmer 15 minutes longer. (The dish may be prepared up to this point and refrigerated up to 1 day; reheat very gently before proceeding.)

With a slotted spoon, remove the veal to a heated platter. Whisk together egg yolk, lemon juice, and cream in a small bowl. Off the heat, quickly whisk the egg yolk mixture into the wine sauce. Return to low heat and cook gently until the sauce is very smooth. (Do not allow the sauce to boil.) Pour the sauce over the veal and serve immediately.

Variation: Make BLANQUETTE D'AGNEAU *using lamb chunks, adding sautéed button mushrooms and pearl onions along with the carrots.*

Saltimbocca

This Roman dish literally means "leap into your mouth" (salta in bocca).

1 lb/450 g veal scallops (8)
freshly ground pepper
4 oz/115 g sliced prosciutto
8 fresh sage leaves
1 tbsp/15 g butter
1 tbsp olive oil
2 cups/475 ml dry white wine
freshly grated Parmesan cheese

Yield: 2 - 4 servings

Lightly pepper each veal scallop. Place a slice of prosciutto (cut to fit the veal scallop) on each and top with a sage leaf. Roll up each veal slice and secure each with a toothpick.

For especially tender veal, ask your butcher to cut scallops from the leg.

Brown the veal in butter and oil. Remove the veal rolls and add the wine to the pan. Boil until reduced by half. Return the rolls to the pan and continue reducing until sauce is dark brown and slightly thickened. Serve with a bowl of Parmesan cheese.

Variation: This would be equally delicious with basil leaves or minced rosemary instead of sage.

Escalope de Veau Normande

4 large veal scallops
salt
freshly ground pepper
¼ cup/35 g flour
4 tbsp/55 g butter
4 shallots, minced
2 apples, peeled and sliced
½ cup/120 ml French cider
⅔ cup/160 ml heavy cream
½ tsp cinnamon
¼ tsp glace de viande (see index)

Yield: 4 servings

Lightly pound the veal scallops between two sheets of wax paper or plastic wrap; sprinkle scallops with salt and pepper and dust with flour. Melt butter in a large sauté pan and quickly fry the scallops, 2 minutes per side. Remove scallops to a platter and keep warm.

Sauté the shallots and apples in the same pan for 3 minutes or until almost tender. Stir in cider, bring to a boil over high heat and reduce by half. Add the cream, cinnamon and glace de viande. Season with salt and pepper to taste. Cook over high heat until thickened.

Spoon apples around the veal and pour sauce on top.

FRENCH CIDER
French (or English) cider is totally unlike the pressed fresh apple cider available in America. Cider in Europe is an alcoholic beverage something like an "apple beer." It is dry and slightly fizzy with a bit of a sour apple taste. Look for dry (Brut) cider from Normandy. If French cider is not available, substitute unsweetened apple juice and a splash of Calvados.

Veal Marsala

Served with ITALIAN GREEN BEANS, *this is just perfect for a quick, delicious dinner.*

3 tbsp vegetable oil
1 lb/450 g veal scallops
¾ cup/100 g all-purpose flour
½ tsp salt
freshly ground pepper
½ cup/120 ml dry Marsala
3 tbsp/45 g butter

Yield: 4 servings

In a heavy frying pan, heat oil over moderately high heat until quite hot. Dip the veal scallops in flour, coating on both sides, and shake off any excess. Brown the scallops for 1 minute per side. Transfer the meat to a warm platter and season with salt and pepper. Repeat with remaining scallops, flouring them just before cooking.

Pour off most of the fat from the pan. Turn the heat to high, add the Marsala, and boil, scraping up any brown bits. Add butter and any juices that may have accumulated around the veal. When the sauce thickens, turn the heat down to low and return the veal to the pan, turning them and basting with the sauce. Transfer meat and sauce to a warm platter and serve immediately.

Lemon Braised Veal Chops

Succulent veal chops go perfectly with RICE PILAF *and a fresh green vegetable.*

4 veal chops
2 tbsp flour
salt
¼ tsp thyme
¼ tsp cayenne pepper
2 slices bacon, diced
1 garlic clove, minced
juice of 1 lemon
1 bay leaf
1 tsp Worcestershire sauce
½ cup/120 ml chicken broth
4 lemon slices

Yield: 2 - 4 servings

Lightly dredge the chops in a mixture of flour, salt, thyme and cayenne. Brown the bacon in a large frying pan. Add garlic and sauté (do not allow the garlic to brown). Remove the bacon and garlic and reserve. Add the veal chops to the pan and brown well on both sides. Return the bacon and garlic to the pan along with lemon juice, bay leaf, Worcestershire and chicken broth. Top each chop with a slice of lemon. Cover and simmer gently for 1 hour. Uncover, raise the heat and continue cooking for 5 minutes, or until the sauce is reduced and thickened. Remove bay leaf before serving.

Lamb Brochette

2 lb/900 g boneless leg of lamb
2 cups/475 ml red Burgundy wine
½ cup/120 ml minced onion
2 bay leaves
1 tbsp Worcestershire sauce
1 garlic clove, minced
1 tsp salt
freshly ground black pepper
2 cups/475 ml soft bread crumbs
olive oil
SHASHLIK SAUCE

Yield: 6 servings

Cut lamb into 1 ½"/4cm cubes. Combine wine, onion, bay leaves, Worcestershire, garlic, salt and pepper and marinate meat for 48 hours. Remove meat from marinade, dip in bread crumbs and thread on skewers. Sprinkle with oil and broil or barbecue for 20 minutes or until golden brown, turning frequently. Serve with SHASHLIK SAUCE or curried Greek yogurt.

Herbed Rack of Lamb

2 - 3 racks of lamb (12 - 16 chops)
2 garlic cloves, slivered
2 tbsp extra virgin olive oil
2 tbsp thyme
2 tbsp rosemary
2 tbsp coarsely ground black pepper

Oven Temp: 400°F/200°C
Yield: 4 servings

When the markets are bursting with a variety of fresh early vegetables, serve them with this tender young lamb for a lovely spring dinner.

Cut slits into the fleshy part of the lamb with the tip of a sharp knife and insert the garlic slivers into the slits. Brush the lamb with olive oil. Combine thyme, rosemary and pepper in a bowl and pat this mixture all over the lamb.

Place the lamb in a roasting pan and cook in a preheated oven for 25 minutes for medium-rare. Let rest 10 minutes, then carve the chops apart and serve immediately.

For an elegant preparation, have your butcher "French the bones" scraping away the thin strip of meat and fat from the ends to the eye, leaving bare bones. Or, for the family, you may prefer leaving these delicious bits of meat on the bones.

Lamb with Almonds

*A*bsolutely super with SPICED RICE - just omit the nuts from the rice and you'll have the perfect combination!

4 oz/115 g split blanched almonds
2⅓ lb/1 kg boneless leg or shoulder of lamb
3 tbsp vegetable oil
3 oz/85 ml red wine
1 tbsp Dijon mustard
¼ cup/60 ml beef broth
5 oz/150 ml heavy cream
1 large onion, minced
generous pinch of cayenne pepper
2 tsp peeled, minced ginger root
2 garlic cloves, minced
2 tbsp sour cream

Oven Temp: 325°F/165°C
Yield: 4 servings

Toast almonds in the oven until golden brown. Set aside.

Cut lamb into 1¼"/3cm cubes. Brown the lamb in 2 tablespoons of the oil in a large frying pan; remove it as it is browned to an oven-proof casserole with a cover. When all the lamb is browned, deglaze the pan with red wine. Add mustard, broth and heavy cream.

In a small frying pan, sauté onion in 1 tablespoon of oil just until soft. Add cayenne, ginger and garlic. Sauté 1 to 2 minutes. Add onion mixture and almonds to lamb. Cover the casserole and bake in a preheated oven for 1¼ hours or until the meat is tender.

Stir sour cream (and a little more broth if mixture seems dry) into the casserole. Cover and bake 10 to 15 minutes longer.

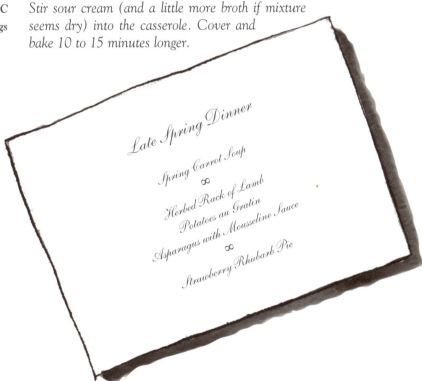

Late Spring Dinner

Spring Carrot Soup

∞

Herbed Rack of Lamb
Potatoes au Gratin
Asparagus with Mousseline Sauce

∞

Strawberry Rhubarb Pie

Gigot d'Agneau Farci en Croûte
(Stuffed Leg of Lamb in Puff Pastry)

1 (10 oz/280 g) jar sun-dried tomatoes
3 lb/1⅓ kg butterflied leg of lamb
salt
freshly ground pepper
herbes de Provence
2 garlic cloves, slivered
1 pkg pre-rolled puff pastry
1 egg, lightly beaten

Sauce:
7 oz/200 ml red wine
2 shallots, chopped
pinch of herbes de Provence
1¼ cups/300 ml veal stock
9 tbsp/100 g cold butter, diced

Oven Temp: 425°F/220°C
Yield: 8 servings

Drain the sun-dried tomatoes on paper towels. Lay the lamb flat and evenly distribute the tomatoes. Sprinkle with salt, pepper and herbes de Provence. Roll the roast lengthwise and tie it with kitchen string. Make small slits in the surface of the roast and insert the slivers of garlic. Sprinkle the roast with salt, pepper and herbes de Provence. Place in a shallow roasting pan and roast in a preheated oven for about 35 minutes (12 minutes per pound for medium, 10 minutes per pound for rare). Drain lamb on paper towels and reserve the roasting pan with the drippings. Allow lamb to cool completely.

To make herbes de Provence, mix equal quantities of dried thyme, rosemary, summer savory and lavender. If you prefer, you may also add crushed bay leaves, cloves and/or grated orange zest. Store in a tightly sealed jar away from light.

Place the cooled lamb, strings removed, in the center of the pastry. Completely wrap the meat, sealing all edges. Decorate the top with excess pastry and brush on beaten egg. Bake in a clean roasting pan in a preheated oven for 20 minutes. If the pastry is not golden brown, bake 5 minutes longer.

Sauce: Set the reserved roasting pan over medium heat. Deglaze the pan with the red wine. Add shallots and herbes de Provence. Reduce for a few minutes until syrupy; add veal stock and reduce again. Whisk in cold butter, a piece at a time, just before serving.

Variations: As a substitute for the sun-dried tomatoes, combine 2 cups/475 ml cooked and drained spinach, 8 oz/225 grams chèvre, salt, freshly ground pepper and 2 cloves of minced garlic. Spread on meat and roll. Continue as above. The lamb may also be served without the pastry. Cook 15 minutes per pound (450 grams) for medium and 12 minutes per pound (450 grams) for rare. Let the roast stand for 15 minutes. Slice and serve.

Carbonnade de Boeuf à la Gueuze
Aux Armes de Bruxelles - Jacques Veulemans, Chef

Heat the butter in a heavy flameproof casserole until it sizzles. Sear beef chunks until well browned. Add the diced onions and sugar. Deglaze the mixture with the vinegar and sprinkle the flour on top. Mix well. Pour in the gueuze and add salt and pepper. Spread mustard on a slice of bread and place in the casserole. Cover and cook over low heat for 1 hour or until the beef is tender, stirring occasionally with a wooden spoon. Taste and adjust seasonings.

4 tbsp/55 g butter or lard
2⅓ lb/1 kg spring beef, in chunks
2 large onions, diced
2 tbsp brown sugar
2 tbsp vinegar
⅓ cup/45 g flour
17 oz/500 ml gueuze beer
salt
freshly ground pepper
2 tbsp mustard
1 slice bread

Yield: 6 servings

" Belgians take enthusiastic, demonstrative relish in food. They talk about it, boast about it, devote long hours and a considerable portion of their budgets to consuming it, take extraordinary pains in preparing it, make celebrities out of chefs who excel at it. "
Arthur Frommer

Carbonnades Flamandes

Most Belgian households treasure an old family recipe for Carbonnades Flamandes. Here is one particularly delicious and authentic version.

4 tbsp/55 g butter
1¾ lb/¾ kg stewing beef, in cubes
1 slice bacon, chopped
9 oz/250 g onions, diced
bouquet garni* (see index)
salt
freshly ground pepper
½ bottle dark beer
2 sugar cubes
1 tbsp Dijon mustard
1 bread slice, crust removed

Yield: 4 servings

Melt the butter in a large flameproof casserole. Brown the meat, bacon and onions along with the bouquet garni, salt and pepper. Cover the meat with the beer and add the sugar cubes. Simmer for 1 hour, covered. Spread mustard on the slice of bread and add to the casserole. (The bread will dissolve and thicken the sauce.) Cover and simmer for ½ hour more. Serve with boiled potatoes, egg noodles or FRITES.

* thyme, bay leaf, parsley

> **But what never ceased to astound me is that the Belgian young, like their elders, love to eat and that Belgian husbands care passionately about their wives' cooking as if it were the only thing they married their wives for.**
> Nika Hazelton

Beef Burgundy

In a large flameproof casserole, fry bacon until crisp. Remove bacon and brown beef, in batches, in the bacon drippings. Remove beef and set aside. In the same pot, lightly brown carrots and sliced onion. Return bacon and beef to the pot and season with salt and pepper. Add wine, tomato paste, garlic, beef broth and herbs. Cover and simmer 3 hours.

Brown mushrooms and pearl onions in 2 tablespoons of the butter and add to stew. Cream flour with remaining 2 tablespoons of soft butter and add to the stew. Simmer until the sauce thickens.

6 slices bacon, chopped
3 lb/1⅓ kg stewing beef, in chunks
3 carrots, in chunks
1 medium onion, thinly sliced
1 tsp salt
¼ tsp freshly ground pepper
2 cups/475 ml Burgundy wine
2 tbsp tomato paste
2 garlic cloves, minced
2½ cups/600 ml condensed beef broth
½ tsp thyme
1 bay leaf
1 quart/liter small mushrooms
2 cups/475 ml pearl onions, cooked
4 tbsp/55 g butter
¼ cup/35 g flour

Yield: 8 servings

Belgian Evening

Crottin de Chavignol Salade

∞

Carbonnades Flamandes
Roasted Brussels Sprouts
Frites
(Belgian Beer)

∞

Tarte Tatin

Poultry, Game and Meat

MEAT

Shopping for food in Belgium is often an adventure, and shopping for meat is no exception. The cuts of meat are different from those available in the United States since European butchers separate the cuts along natural divisions rather than sawing them apart.

The local Belgian beef found in the supermarket is usually Blanc Bleu Belge, the result of crossbreeding between two breeds of Belgian cattle. It tends to have lean, dense meat that is not as flavorful as Angus beef. It is, however, a very healthy low-fat choice that is best braised, stewed or ground. Angus beef is rich, fatty and more tender. French beef, such as Charolais or Limousin, is also excellent. The butcher shops carry beef from various countries, including the United States, so shop around.

The popular American flank steak (Bavette) is rarely found in the supermarket but may be requested from a butcher. Ground beef comes in several grades. The top quality, lean ground beef suitable for cooking or eating raw as Steak Tartare is Filet Américain. Regular ground beef is called Haché Pur Boeuf or Haché Sans Epices. Steak Tartare and Haché Preparé are to be eaten raw and are already mixed with egg and spices. For stew, buy chunks of stewing beef cut from the shoulder called Carbonnade. For thin steaks to pan-fry, ask for "steak minute." For the best quality steaks, look for Rib-Eye Entrecôte, Contrefilet (a T-bone without the filet portion) or Filet Pur (a slice of

> " 'Tis not the meat,
> but 'tis the appetite
> makes eating a delight. "
> Sir John Suckling

...more on MEATS

the tenderloin). Since Belgian steaks are so lean, they become tough if cooked well done (bien cuit). For tender steaks, try very rare (bleu), rare (saignant) or medium-rare (à point).

If it's lamb you're looking for, leg of lamb (Gigot d'Agneau) and rack of lamb (Couronne d'Agneau) are the two most popular cuts for roasting. To get a butterflied leg of lamb ask for "désossé et non-roulé" or it will come rolled and tied. Lamb chops (Côtes d'Agneau) and tenderloin (Filet Pur d'Agneau) are also widely available. For stewing lamb, buy shoulder (Epaule d'Agneau) if you prefer a rich meat or boneless leg for leaner meat.

Pork loin roasts (Carré de Porc) come boned and then placed back on the bones for roasting. Loin chops (Côtes de Porc), shoulder chops (Basses Côtes de Porc) and tenderloin (Filet Pur de Porc) are easily found.

To get stewing veal, ask for Blanquette de Veau (chunks cut from the breast). For veal scallops buy Escalope or Brunir et Servir (large thin slices cut from the leg). Sauté de Veau is thicker and not appropriate for scaloppini. For Osso Buco you will need Jarret de Veau, thick cross sections of the shank. Veal chops (Côtes de Veau) are wonderful simply broiled or grilled.

Lasagne

An American family supper favorite. Serve this meat casserole with a tossed salad and garlic bread.

1½ lb/680 g ground beef
1 garlic clove, minced
1 tbsp basil
2½ tsp salt
1 lb/450 g can of plum tomatoes, chopped
6 oz/170 g can of tomato paste
8 lasagne noodles, cooked
2 eggs, beaten
2½ cups/600 ml ricotta*
¾ cup/175 ml grated Parmesan cheese
2 tbsp chopped fresh parsley
9 oz/250 g mozzarella cheese
½ tsp freshly ground pepper

Oven Temp: 375°F/190°C
Yield: 6 - 8 servings

Slowly brown meat and spoon off excess fat. Add garlic, basil, 1½ teaspoons of the salt, tomatoes and tomato paste. Simmer uncovered for 30 minutes. Combine eggs, ricotta, ½ cup/120 ml of the Parmesan cheese, parsley, 1 teaspoon salt and pepper. Mix well. Slice, dice or shred the mozzarella.

Layer in a 9"x13"/24 x 34cm baking dish half the noodles, half the ricotta mixture, half the meat mixture and all the mozzarella. Repeat with remaining noodles, ricotta and meat mixture and top with remaining ¼ cup/60ml of Parmesan. Bake in a preheated oven for 30 minutes. Let lasagne stand 10 to 15 minutes before serving.

* or cream-style cottage cheese

> **"** There are only two cuisines: good and bad. **"**
> André Guillot

Chili Con Carne

You can't miss with this family favorite. Add the chili powder gradually until it's "just right."

5 tbsp vegetable oil
1 cup/240 ml chopped onions
3 garlic cloves, minced
½ cup/120 ml diced green bell pepper
2 lb/900 g coarsely ground beef
4 cups/950 ml peeled, quartered tomatoes
4 cups/950 ml cooked kidney beans
1 tsp salt
1 tsp freshly ground black pepper
1 tsp cumin powder
4 tbsp chili powder

Yield: 8 servings

Heat oil in a Dutch oven and sauté onion, garlic and green pepper until onions are translucent. Add ground beef and brown. Mix in remaining ingredients. Cover and simmer at least 1 hour.

Variations: You may substitute ground turkey or veal for the ground beef. For a more authentic Mexican taste, add 1 tablespoon each of wine vinegar and brown sugar.

Store garlic at room temperature, in a dry place, out of the sunlight. It should keep for about one month.

" Community and family life are nourished by regularly sitting around our own tables with those we love. "
Barbara Kafka

Filet Mignon avec Sauce Béarnaise au Vin Rouge

Generously season all sides of the steaks with salt, pepper and herbes de Provence. Let rest at room temperature for 1 hour.

6 (8 oz/225 g) filet mignon steaks
salt
freshly ground pepper
4 tbsp herbes de Provence
3 tbsp olive oil

Red Wine Béarnaise Sauce:
3 shallots, minced
3 tbsp chopped fresh tarragon
3 tbsp red wine vinegar
½ cup/120 ml dry red wine
2 large egg yolks
¾ cup/170 g unsalted butter, melted and cooled to lukewarm

Yield: 6 servings

While the steaks are resting, make the sauce. Combine shallots, tarragon, vinegar, and wine in a small pan. Over moderately high heat, reduce the mixture until 2 tablespoons of liquid remain. Remove from heat and whisk in the egg yolks, one at a time. Gradually whisk in the melted butter, tablespoon by tablespoon, until all is absorbed and the sauce is thickened. Keep the sauce warm in a double boiler. (Be careful not to overheat or the mixture will separate.)

In a large frying pan, heat the olive oil until it is very hot. Add the steaks and cook until the bottoms are well browned, 3 to 4 minutes. Turn the steaks and brown the other side for 2 to 3 minutes. Reduce the heat to medium and continue cooking until the meat reaches the desired doneness (3 minutes more for rare). Transfer the steaks to serving plates and pour a generous amount of sauce over each one.

Ringing in the New Year

Smoked Salmon and Chèvre Canapés
(Champagne)
∞
Cream of Fennel Soup
∞
Filet Mignon
Sauce Béarnaise au Vin Rouge
Potatoes Anna
Green Beans with Walnuts
∞
White Chocolate Mousse
Raspberry Grand Marnier Sauce
∞
Chocolate Truffles
Coffee

Filet Mignon with Green Peppercorn Sauce

6 (8 oz/225 g) filet mignon steaks
salt
freshly ground pepper
2 tbsp vegetable oil
2 tbsp/30 g butter
6 shallots, minced
3½ oz/100 ml cognac
2 oz/55 g green peppercorns
1 tbsp glace de viande (see index)
1¼ cups/300 ml heavy cream
1 tbsp chopped fresh parsley

Yield: 6 servings

Serve with a big bowl of crisp FRITES *- another Belgian favorite!*

Season the steaks with salt and pepper. In a sauté pan, heat the oil and butter until it sizzles. Sauté the steaks until brown on one side. Turn and brown the other side. Remove the steaks to a platter and keep warm. Pour out all but 1 tablespoon of drippings from the pan.

Add the shallots to the pan and cook slowly until soft but not brown. Add the cognac, heat it gently and flame with a long match.

> *I soon learned that the best way to get attention was to cook something...*
> M.F.K. Fisher

Drain the green peppercorns and add them to the pan with the glace de viande and cream. Bring to a boil and simmer, stirring occasionally, until reduced and thickened. Add parsley, adjust seasoning and serve the steaks with the sauce.

PEPPER

Since pepper loses it's pungency soon after being ground, freshly ground pepper adds flavor and spice to food in a way that pre-ground pepper cannot. The size of the grind, as well as the type of pepper, will influence the flavor. A fine grind produces more heat while a crushed or cracked pepper produces a more assertive pepper flavor.

- Black peppercorns have a pungent heat and aromatic flavor.
- White peppercorns are hotter and less aromatic than black. They are often preferred for white sauces to avoid visible specks of pepper.
- Green peppercorns, unripe pepper berries, are available packed in brine or vinegar, or freeze-dried. Their pungent flavor is delicious in sauces to accompany meat.
- Pink pepper is not a genuine pepper, but the pungent berry of a South American poison ivy. It is aromatic, not very hot, and particularly pretty in terrines or sauces for fish or poultry.
- Cayenne pepper is dried, ground, hot red chili peppers.

Poultry, Game and Meat

Spicy BBQ Sauce

Use this flavorful sauce to perk up pork chops, ribs or chicken.

Heat butter in a large saucepan and sauté onion until light brown. Add the remaining ingredients and simmer for 20 minutes.

This chili sauce is similar to spiced ketchup, not hot chili sauce. In Belgium, Heinz Mexican Sauce may be substituted if Heinz Chili Sauce is not available.

2 tbsp/30 g butter
1 onion, thinly sliced
½ cup/120 ml water or white wine
½ cup/120 ml Heinz Chili Sauce
2 tbsp Worcestershire sauce
2 tbsp vinegar
1 tbsp horseradish
2 garlic cloves, minced
1 tsp salt
2 tbsp lemon juice
½ cup/120 ml ketchup
2 tbsp brown sugar
1 tsp freshly ground black pepper

Yield: 2 cups/475 ml

Shashlik Sauce

Combine all ingredients in a saucepan and mix well. Cook over low heat, stirring constantly, for 10 minutes.

2 cups/475 ml Heinz Chili Sauce
1 cup/240 ml ketchup
1 tbsp piccalilli relish
1 tbsp honey
1 tbsp horseradish
1 tbsp chopped chutney

Yeild: 3 cups/700 ml

> " The final goal is to nourish and nurture those who gather at your table. "
> Alice Waters

Pasta, Rice and Vegetables

Pasta, Rice and Vegetables

Broccoli Purée	223
Carrot Flans	217
Echalotes au Vin Rouge	228
Eggplant, Tomatoes and Chèvre	213
Endives et Jambon au Gratin	227
Frites	208
Fusilli Rustica	200
Green Beans with Roquefort and Walnuts	216
Horseradish Mashed Potatoes	212
Italian Green Beans	215
Leeks with Orange Ginger Sauce	220
Lemon and Garlic Pasta	193
Lemon Rice	207
Linguine with White Clam Sauce	192
Mushroom and Prosciutto Tortellini	195
Pappardelle Melanzane	198
Pasta with Prawns and Tomato Fondue	190
Pasta with Scallops and Bacon	193
Pasta with Shrimp and Asparagus	191
Pesto	201
Potatoes Anna	210
Potatoes au Gratin	209
Potatoes with Dijon Mustard	209
Rice Pilaf	204
Risotto with Dried Wild Mushrooms	203
Risotto with Parmesan Cheese	202
Roasted Brussels Sprouts	225
Rosemary Roasted Potatoes	212
Saffron Rice	205
Scampi and Tagliolini with Armoricaine Sauce	189
Sesame Broccoli Oriental	222
Shredded Brussels Sprouts with Prosciutto	224
Southwest Pasta	201
Spaghetti with Aubergine Sauce	199
Spaghettini with Fresh Basil and Tomato Sauce	194
Spiced Rice	206
Spinach Stuffed Pasta Shells Alfredo	197
Sunshine Glazed Carrots	219
Vegetable Terrine with Tomato Coulis	214
White Cabbage	228
Wild Rice with Walnuts	204
Zucchini au Gratin	221

SPECIAL TOPICS

Belgian Endive/Chicon	226
Frites	208
Onions	218
Pasta	196
Potatoes	211
Saffron	205

Scampi and Tagliolini with Armoricaine Sauce

2⅕ lb/1 kg large shrimp
6 tbsp olive oil
salt
freshly ground pepper
3 garlic cloves, minced
juice of ½ lemon
herbes de Provence
2 zucchini, cubed
1⅔ lb/750 g fresh tagliolini pasta

Sauce:
1 tbsp olive oil
shrimp shells
⅛ tsp saffron powder
⅛ tsp cayenne pepper
3 shallots, chopped
2 carrots, thinly sliced
2 celery stalks, minced
3⅓ cups/780 ml fish stock
14 oz/400 ml dry white wine
1 (5 oz/140 g) can tomato paste
2 tbsp cognac
7 oz/200 ml heavy cream
salt

Yield: 8 servings

Elegant and delicious! Prepare the sauce ahead and enjoy your guests.

Peel and clean shrimp, reserving the shells.

Marinate the shrimp in 3 tablespoons of the olive oil, salt, pepper, 2 of the minced garlic cloves, lemon juice and herbes de Provence (for about an hour).

To make the sauce, pour 1 tablespoon of olive oil into a deep pan and sauté the shrimp shells, saffron and cayenne for 2 minutes. Add the shallots, carrots and celery and cook a few more minutes. Add the fish stock, wine and tomato paste and simmer for 20 minutes. With a food processor or mixer, blend the sauce and strain through a fine sieve. Add cognac and cream. Let thicken. Adjust the seasoning.

Sauté the zucchini cubes and remaining garlic in 1 tablespoon olive oil until tender. Remove from heat. Peel and dice the tomatoes (see index) and add to zucchini.

Before serving, gently warm the zucchini and tomatoes. Sauté the shrimp in 2 tablespoons of olive oil just until pink and firm. Bring a large pot of water to a boil. Add salt and a dash of oil. Cook pasta for 3 minutes and drain.

To serve, put nests of pasta in the center of 8 heated plates. Top with the zucchini and tomato mixture. Surround the pasta nests with sauce and arrange the shrimp on top of the sauce.

Pasta with Prawns and Tomato Fondue
Castello Banfi - Ruane Breeda, Chef

To prepare the tomato fondue, sweat the sliced onions and garlic in oil over low heat. Remove the core from the tomatoes. Immerse tomatoes in boiling water for 10 seconds and immediately cool in a bowl of cold water. Peel and dice the tomatoes (see index) and add to the onions. Season with salt, pepper and sugar. Add basil and thyme and cook 5 to 10 minutes; remove from heat.

Shell and devein the prawns (see index); fry in 2 tablespoons of oil until pink. Add the artichokes, black olives and garlic; season to taste with salt and pepper. Add to the tomato fondue.

Bring a large pot of water to a boil. Add 2 teaspoons of salt and a dash of oil. Add the pasta and cook until al dente. Drain well and toss with butter.

Reheat prawns and tomato fondue. Divide the pasta among 4 plates and spoon the prawns and tomato fondue on top. Sprinkle with Parmesan cheese and garnish with herbs. Serve immediately.

14 oz/400 g prawns or shrimp
2 tbsp olive oil
3½ oz/100 g artichoke hearts, sliced
3½ oz/100 g pitted black olives, sliced
1 garlic clove, minced
salt
freshly ground pepper
18 oz/500 g tagliatelle
1 tbsp/15 g butter
2 oz/55 g Parmesan cheese, grated

Tomato Fondue:
4 oz/115 g sliced onions
1 garlic clove, crushed
1 tbsp olive oil
2 lb/900 g tomatoes
salt
freshly ground pepper
sugar to taste
1 tbsp chopped fresh basil
1 tbsp chopped fresh thyme

Garnish:
chopped fresh thyme
chopped fresh parsley
chopped fresh basil

Yield: 4 servings

Pasta with Shrimp and Asparagus

8 oz/225 g spaghetti
1 cup/240 ml packed fresh basil leaves
2 garlic cloves
¼ cup/60 ml fresh lemon juice
3 tbsp olive oil
¾ tsp salt
1 lb/450 g asparagus
¾ lb/340 g large shrimp, peeled
⅛ tsp hot red pepper flakes

Yield: 4 servings

Cook spaghetti al dente and drain well.

Meanwhile, purée basil, garlic, lemon juice, 1 tablespoon olive oil and ½ teaspoon salt until smooth.

Cut asparagus spears into 2"/5cm pieces. Heat remaining olive oil in a frying pan over moderately high heat. Cook asparagus, stirring frequently, until crisply tender, about 5 minutes. Add shrimp, red pepper and ¼ teaspoon salt. Cook, stirring frequently, just until the shrimp turn pink and are firm, about 4 to 5 minutes.

In a large serving bowl, toss the hot pasta with the basil mixture, asparagus and shrimp. Serve immediately.

To keep pasta warm, pour cooked pasta into a colander and drain well. Keep covered over a pot of hot water.
To reheat pasta, submerge the colander of pasta in a pot of boiling water for a few seconds. Drain and serve.

Linguine with White Clam Sauce

10 oz/280 g linguine
3 tbsp olive oil
1 medium onion, minced
8 garlic cloves, minced
2 tbsp flour
1 (6½ oz/185 g) can minced clams
1 cup/240 ml chicken broth
¼ cup/60 ml freshly grated Parmesan
2 tbsp minced parsley

Yield: 4 servings

Cook linguine al dente and drain well.

While pasta is cooking, heat olive oil in a large frying pan over moderate heat. Add onion and garlic and cook until onion is tender, about 5 minutes. Add flour and cook, stirring constantly, until blended. Add clams, with their juice, and chicken broth; cook 4 minutes. Stir in the Parmesan cheese.

Spoon linguine onto individual plates. Spoon clam sauce on top and sprinkle with parsley. Serve immediately.

Pasta with Scallops and Bacon

This rich, creamy sauce is so quick to prepare, you might want to warm the serving bowl before you begin!

Cook fettuccini al dente and drain well.

1 lb/450 g fettuccini
¼ cup/60 ml olive oil
½ lb/225 g lardons (see index)
1 lb/450 g scallops
¾ cup/175 ml chopped green onions
3 cups/700 ml heavy cream
2 tbsp chopped fresh thyme
¼ tsp hot red pepper flakes
2 tsp fresh lemon juice
freshly grated Parmesan cheese

Yield: 4 servings

While pasta is cooking, heat olive oil in a large frying pan and brown the lardons. Pour off all but ¼ cup/60 ml of the fat. Add the scallops and green onions and cook until scallops are barely firm. Add the cream and reduce by one-third. Return the bacon to the pan and add spices and lemon juice. Pour over the cooked pasta and sprinkle with grated Parmesan cheese.

Purchase scallops that are shiny and slightly translucent. Scallops that appear too opaquely white may have been soaked in water to increase their sale weight.

Lemon and Garlic Pasta

> *If you slurp them, so be it. Because the truly best way, the only classical and true way, to eat pasta is with gusto.*
> James Beard

Light and refreshing, this pasta dish is just right for a hot summer evening.

2 garlic cloves, minced
1 tsp olive oil
½ cup/120 ml dry white wine
¼ cup/60 ml fresh lemon juice
1 cup/240 ml chopped tomato
8 oz/225 g angel hair pasta
¼ cup/60 ml chopped fresh basil
2 tbsp freshly grated Parmesan
freshly grated black pepper

Yield: 4 servings

Sauté garlic in the oil until it begins to brown. Remove pan from heat and pour in the wine. Return pan to heat and cook for 1 to 2 minutes until heated through. Stir in lemon juice and tomato. Turn heat to low.

Cook pasta al dente, drain and turn into a warmed serving bowl. Add the basil, Parmesan cheese, pepper, and the tomato and wine mixture. Toss and serve immediately.

Spaghettini with Fresh Basil and Tomato Sauce

1 lb/450 g spaghettini
2 cups/475 ml chopped fresh basil
2 cups/475 ml drained, chopped canned plum tomatoes
5 garlic cloves, minced
⅓ cup/80 ml olive oil
1 tsp salt
freshly ground pepper

Yield: 4 servings

Cook the spaghettini al dente and drain well. Keep warm.

Meanwhile, combine basil, tomatoes, garlic, oil, salt and pepper in an uncovered saucepan. Cook over moderately high heat for 15 minutes. Taste and season with salt and pepper.

Transfer the pasta to a warm serving bowl. Toss with the sauce, adding extra drops of olive oil if desired. Serve immediately.

Variation: Stir in cubes of mozzarella and offer a bowl of freshly grated Parmesan cheese.

Pasta Sampler

Asparagus Salad Vinaigrette
∞
Pesto (with rotelle)
Mushroom and Prosciutto Tortellini
Spaghettini with Fresh Basil and Tomato Sauce
Chicken Piccata
(Italian Bread)
∞
Hazelnut Meringe Torte

Mushroom and Prosciutto Tortellini

A meal in itself! Serve with TOMATOES PROVENÇAL *or a simple green salad and French bread.*

18 oz/500 g cheese tortellini
3 tbsp olive oil
1 onion, chopped
6 oz/170 g prosciutto slices, chopped
1 tsp minced garlic
¼ tsp hot red pepper flakes
1 tsp freshly ground black pepper
1 cup/240 ml dry white wine
1 cup/240 ml sliced mushrooms
½ cup/120 ml chopped red bell pepper
1 cup/240 ml peas
1½ cups/350 ml heavy cream
¼ cup/60 ml chopped fresh parsley
1 cup/240 ml freshly grated Parmesan
salt

Yield: 4 servings

Cook tortellini in a large pot of boiling salted water until al dente; drain.

Heat oil in a large, heavy pan over high heat. Add onion, prosciutto, garlic, red pepper flakes and black pepper. Sauté until onion is golden brown, about 10 minutes. Add wine and bring to boil. Add mushrooms, bell pepper and peas and simmer until most of the liquid evaporates. Add cream and boil until sauce begins to thicken. Stir in tortellini, parsley and half the Parmesan cheese. Simmer briefly until the sauce coats the pasta. Season to taste with salt and pepper.

Transfer pasta and sauce to a large serving bowl and sprinkle remaining Parmesan on top.

Al dente is an Italian term meaning tender but still firm to the bite. It's literal translation is "to the teeth." For perfect pasta, drain and serve the moment it is cooked.

Pasta, Rice and Vegetables

PASTA

Pasta, usually a combination of wheat flour, liquid and often egg, is available fresh and dried and comes in a variety of shapes, sizes, and flavors. Fresh pasta is generally preferred for butter-based and cream-based sauces which coat the pasta. Dried pasta holds its shape better for oil-based, shellfish-based and heavy, chunky vegetable sauces.

Small pasta shapes such as acini di pepe, alphabet shapes, anelli (or rings), ditalini (thimbles) and orzo (rice-shaped pasta) are often added to soup. Larger shapes, such as elbow macaroni and conchigliette (small shells), are used for hearty soups such as minestrone because they hold their shape well.

Tubes, shells and spirals are well suited for meat sauces since the shapes trap pieces of meat in their ridges and hollows. Look for tubes such as bucatini, ziti, ditalie, rigatoni, penne/mastaccioli and macaroni. Shells (cavatelli and conchiglie), spirals (rotelle and rotini) and tubes are equally well suited for pasta salad as are farfalle (bow tie pasta) and ruote (wagon wheel pasta).

Long strand pasta, from thinnest to thickest, includes vermicelli, capelli d'angelo (angel hair), spaghettini, spaghetti, tagliolini or tagliarini, linguine, fusilli (twisted strands), fettucini, tagliatelle, mafalda and pappardelle (with a fluted edge). A general rule is, the lighter the sauce the thinner the pasta.

Some pastas come with fillings like agnolotti, ravioli and tortellini. Other pastas may be stuffed such as cannelloni, manicotti and lumache (large shells).

Lasagne noodles are available fresh, dried and pre-cooked and are used in casseroles. Layer with vegetables, cheeses, meat sauce and/or BÉCHAMEL SAUCE.

Spinach Stuffed Pasta Shells Alfredo

15 oz/425 g frozen chopped spinach
2 tbsp chopped onion
½ tsp seasoned salt
⅛ tsp black pepper
⅛ tsp cayenne pepper
½ cup/120 ml grated Swiss cheese
4 eggs
2 cups/475 ml heavy cream
1 tsp olive oil
24 jumbo pasta shells
6 tbsp/85 g unsalted butter
1 cup/240 ml grated Parmesan
½ tsp nutmeg

Oven Temp: 350°F/175°C
300°F/150°C
Yield: 4 - 6 servings

Thaw the spinach and drain well. Blend spinach, onion, salt, both peppers, Swiss cheese and eggs in a food processor until smooth. Add ½ cup/120 ml heavy cream. Pour mixture into a loaf pan and place in a bain marie (see index). Bake in a preheated 350°F/175°C oven for 50 to 60 minutes. Cool.

In a large pot, boil 3 quarts/liters water. Add 1 teaspoon olive oil and drop in pasta shells; cook 12 to 15 minutes. Remove with slotted spoon and cool.

Melt butter and add 1½ cups/350 ml heavy cream; bring to a simmer. Remove from heat. Add Parmesan cheese and nutmeg, stirring constantly.

Stuff pasta shells with spinach mixture. Place in a greased baking dish just large enough to hold the shells in one layer. Ladle cream sauce over the shells and cover with foil. Bake in a preheated 300°F/150°C oven for 15 minutes or until heated through.

...more on PASTA

Cook pasta in rapidly boiling, salted water with a dash of oil added to prevent sticking. Use at least 4 quarts/liters of water to 1 pound/450 grams of pasta. Cook pasta al dente, keeping in mind that flat fresh pasta is usually cooked within seconds of the water returning to a boil. Stuffed fresh pasta takes a bit longer, but still much less time than dried pasta. Drain immediately in a colander. If serving warm, pour into a warm serving bowl. Spoon sauce on top or toss with pasta. If using pasta cold, for instance in salad, pour cold water over the drained pasta to stop the cooking and drain thoroughly.

Pappardelle Melanzane
Il Carpaccio - Mauro Cinti, Chef

Cook pasta al dente and drain.

Meanwhile, prepare the sauce. Brown the carrots, onions, celery, garlic and basil in hot oil for 10 minutes. Add tomatoes and continue cooking for 15 minutes. Press the sauce through a fine strainer. Add salt and pepper to taste.

Sauté diced eggplant in olive oil in a nonstick frying pan. Season to taste with salt and pepper.

Mix pasta, eggplant and Neapolitan Sauce in a large dish and serve covered with grated Parmesan cheese.

Melanzane, eggplant to Americans and aubergine to the French and British, lend substance to many Italian dishes. Choose firm, shiny eggplants with flat bottoms, designating they are male. These have fewer seeds and are likely to be less bitter. Eggplant absorbs oil when fried. Use a nonstick pan to reduce the amount of oil required.

14 oz/400 g pappardelle pasta
2 eggplants, diced
4 tbsp (or more) olive oil
salt
freshly ground pepper
freshly grated Parmesan cheese

Neapolitan Sauce:
2 carrots, minced
2 onions, minced
1 celery stalk, minced
5 garlic cloves, minced
fresh basil
2 tbsp olive oil
2⅓ lb/1 kg ripe tomatoes, diced
salt
freshly ground pepper

Yield: 4 servings

Spaghetti with Aubergine Sauce

This delicious spaghetti sauce makes a hearty vegetarian main dish.

To make the sauce, peel the eggplant and cut into ½"/1¼cm cubes. Mix eggplant cubes with some salt and drain in a colander for 1 hour. Pat dry.

Heat oil in a large pot over moderately high heat. Add eggplant, onion, garlic and mushrooms and sauté until tender, about 5 minutes. Add parsley, tomatoes with juice, tomato sauce, tomato paste, wine, spices, salt and sugar. Cook 1½ to 2 hours at a low simmer. (If the sauce appears to be too thick, cover for part of the cooking time.) Before serving, mash eggplant cubes with a potato masher if a more uniform texture is desired. Adjust seasoning.

Serve with spaghetti and a bowl of grated Parmesan cheese.

1 lb/450 g spaghetti, cooked, drained
freshly grated Parmesan cheese

Aubergine Sauce:
1 large eggplant
¼ cup/60 ml olive oil
1 medium onion, chopped
4 garlic cloves, minced
6 oz/170 g mushrooms, sliced
2 tbsp chopped fresh parsley
1 (32 oz/900 g) can plum tomatoes
1 (8 oz/225 g) can tomato sauce
1 (6 oz/170 g) can tomato paste
½ cup/120 ml dry red wine
1 tsp oregano
1 tsp basil
¼ tsp hot red pepper flakes
½ tsp salt
1 tsp sugar

Yield: 6 - 8 servings

Pasta, Rice and Vegetables

Fusilli Rustica

Remove the skin of the pepper with a vegetable peeler. Remove the core and seeds and cut the flesh into strips. Peel and dice the tomatoes. Slice the olives into rings.

Heat the oil in a large frying pan. Over moderately low heat, sauté the onion, garlic, pancetta and parsley, stirring occasionally, until the onion is tender, but not brown. Add the bell pepper, stirring occasionally, and cook until tender. Add the salt to taste. Increase the heat to high and add the tomatoes. Cook for 5 minutes, stirring frequently, until most of the moisture has evaporated. Add oregano, olives, capers, red pepper flakes and basil. Stir and keep warm over low heat.

Drop the fusilli into a large pot of boiling salted water and cook al dente. Drain immediately and turn into a warm bowl. Toss with the sauce, add the grated cheese and toss again. Serve immediately.

* Pancetta is an Italian variety of unsmoked peppered bacon.

1 large bell pepper
1 lb/450 g plum tomatoes
½ cup/120 ml pitted green or black olives
½ cup/120 ml olive oil
3 cups/700 ml thinly sliced onion
4 large garlic cloves, thinly sliced
3 oz/85 g pancetta, in thin strips*
2 tbsp chopped fresh parsley
salt
½ tsp oregano
2 tbsp tiny capers
1 tsp hot red pepper flakes
8 fresh basil leaves, torn in pieces
1 lb/450 g fusilli pasta
½ cup/120 ml freshly grated Romano

Yield: 4 - 6 servings

Romano can be quite a sharp cheese. If you cannot find a mellow Romano (such as Pecorino Romano), or if you prefer a milder taste, replace the full amount of Romano with 3 tablespoons Romano mixed with 5 tablespoons Parmesan.

Autumn at the Market

Warm Chèvre with Red Bell Pepper Sauce

∞

Risotto with Dried Wild Mushrooms

∞

Tarte Provençale
(Mixed Greens with) Herbed Vinaigrette
(French Bread)

∞

Bavarian Apple Tart

Southwest Pasta

Add some spice to a casual dinner for two!

Combine tomatoes, oil, garlic, jalapeño, fresh coriander, lime juice, chili powder, salt and pepper. Set aside for 1 hour.

Cook pasta al dente and drain. Immediately add the tomato mixture and goat cheese and toss. Serve sprinkled with pine nuts.

3 small tomatoes, chopped
2 tbsp olive oil
3 garlic cloves, minced
1 jalapeño, seeded and minced
3 tbsp chopped fresh coriander (cilantro)
1 tbsp lime juice
½ tsp chili powder
¼ tsp salt
¼ tsp freshly ground pepper
4 oz/115 g penne pasta
4 oz/115 g goat cheese, cubed
2 tbsp pine nuts, toasted

Yield: 2 servings

Pesto

To enjoy the taste of summer all year, make lots of pesto when fresh basil is abundant. It's great on baked potatoes, bread or pasta.

In a mortar or food processor, purée basil, olive oil, pine nuts, garlic and salt. Stir in the grated cheeses and butter by hand. Keep refrigerated, covered with a thin layer of additional olive oil.

When serving over pasta, add 1 tablespoon of boiling water from the pasta to the pesto just before serving.

2 cups/475 ml fresh basil leaves
½ cup/120 ml olive oil
2 tbsp pine nuts
2 garlic cloves, minced
1 tsp salt
½ cup/120 ml freshly grated Parmesan
2 tbsp freshly grated Pecorino Romano
3 tbsp/45 g butter, softened

Yield: 1 cup/240 ml

Pesto may be made in large quantities. Make the basil purée and freeze. Stir in the cheeses and butter after defrosting.

Variation: Substitute goat cheese for the Parmesan and Romano.

Risotto with Parmesan Cheese

*T*his basic risotto deserves the very finest imported Parmigiano-Reggiano, freshly grated of course!

Bring the broth to a slow, steady simmer.

5 cups/1⅓ liters quality broth
2 tbsp minced shallot or onion
3 tbsp/45 g butter
2 tbsp vegetable oil
1½ cups/350 ml Arborio rice
½ cup/120 ml freshly grated Parmesan
salt
additional grated Parmesan

Yield: 4 servings

In a large heavy frying pan, sauté shallots in 2 tablespoons of butter and all the oil. Cook over moderately high heat until translucent but not browned.

Add the rice and stir until it is well coated. Sauté lightly, then add a ladle of simmering broth. Cook, stirring constantly. As the rice absorbs the liquid, continue adding more, a little at a time, always adding broth when the rice just begins to stick. Adjust the heat so the liquid simmers, but does not fully boil.

When you estimate that the rice is about 5 minutes away from being done (it takes 20 to 25 minutes), add ½ cup/120 ml grated Parmesan and the remaining tablespoon of butter. Mix well. Continue cooking, adding broth little by little, just until the rice is tender all the way through but still chewy. The risotto should be creamy but not runny. Taste and correct for salt. Serve immediately, with a bowl of grated Parmesan cheese.

Variations: Use this basic recipe to make any flavor risotto - add seafood with fish broth, sautéed bacon and onion with meat broth, vegetables with vegetable broth. Add saffron or chopped fresh herbs. For a special occasion, serve the basic Parmesan risotto topped with freshly grated slivers of white truffle (see index).

" Not everyone in Italy may know how to cook, but nearly everyone knows how to eat. "
Marcella Hazan

Risotto with Dried Wild Mushrooms

1 oz/30 g dried wild mushrooms
2 cups/475 ml warm water
1 quart/liter quality meat broth
2 tbsp minced shallot or onion
4 tbsp/55 g butter
3 tbsp vegetable oil
2 cups/475 ml Arborio rice
¼ cup/60 ml freshly grated Parmesan
salt
freshly ground pepper
additional grated Parmesan

Yield: 6 servings

Soak the mushrooms in 2 cups/475 ml of lukewarm water until the liquid turns very dark, at least 30 minutes. Lift out the mushrooms and strain the liquid through a sieve lined with moistened paper towels (or use a coffee filter) and set the liquid aside. If necessary, rinse the mushrooms until they are thoroughly free of soil and sand.

Bring the broth to a slow, steady simmer.

In a large heavy or nonstick frying pan, sauté the shallots or onions in half the butter and all the oil. Cook over moderately high heat until translucent. Add the rice and stir until well coated. Sauté briefly and then add a ladle of the simmering broth. Cook, stirring constantly. As the rice absorbs the liquid, continue adding more, a little at a time, always adding more broth as the rice just begins to stick. Adjust the heat so the liquid simmers but does not fully boil. When the rice has cooked for 10 to 12 minutes, add the mushrooms and ½ cup/120 ml of the strained mushroom liquid. As it absorbs, add more of the mushroom liquid, ½ cup/120 ml at a time. When all the mushroom liquid has been used, continue cooking the rice with hot broth. The total cooking time should be 20 to 25 minutes. Taste the rice near the end of the cooking time. It should be creamy and cooked, but still firm to the bite.

Arborio rice, a short-grained Italian specialty, is essential for a perfectly creamy, chewy risotto.

When the rice is cooked, turn off the heat and mix in the grated Parmesan and remaining butter. Taste and add salt if necessary. Add a few twists of pepper and mix. Spoon the risotto into individual shallow bowls and serve immediately with a bowl of freshly grated Parmesan on the side.

Rice Pilaf

A special accompaniment to a simple chicken dish.

4 tbsp/55 g butter
½ cup/120 ml vermicelli pasta
1 cup/240 ml rice
4 green onions, chopped
2 cups/475 ml chicken broth
½ tsp oregano (optional)
½ tsp parsley (optional)
salt
freshly ground pepper

Yield: 4 servings

Melt the butter in a medium saucepan. Add vermicelli and sauté until light brown. Add rice and sauté until coated with butter. Add green onions, chicken broth (and herbs) and bring to a boil. Add salt and pepper to taste. Cover and reduce heat to low. Simmer for 20 minutes or until all the liquid is absorbed.

Variations: Substitute orzo (rice-shaped pasta) for the vermicelli, but sauté the orzo and rice without browning. Just before serving, stir cooked peas and/or sautéed mushrooms into either the vermicelli or orzo version.

Wild Rice with Walnuts

Wild rice is a natural accompaniment to any game preparation, and this recipe is particularly delicious.

1½ quarts/liters water
2 cups/475 ml wild rice
1 tbsp/15 g unsalted butter
1 tbsp walnut oil
3 oz/85 g walnuts, coarsely chopped
small bunch of parsley, chopped

Yield: 8 servings

In a large saucepan, heat water and rice to boiling. Reduce to low, cover and simmer for 45 minutes. Drain excess liquid from rice.

In a sauté pan, melt the butter with walnut oil. Add walnuts and toast lightly. Mix walnuts and parsley into wild rice.

Saffron Rice

Saffron rice is excellent with chicken or fish. Use the bouillon flavor that complements your main dish.

4 tbsp/55 g butter
½ cup/120 ml slivered almonds
1 cup/240 ml rice
2¼ cups/530 ml water
¼ tsp saffron threads
½ cup/120 ml mushrooms, sliced
¼ tsp freshly ground black pepper
2 bouillon cubes

Yield: 6 servings

Melt the butter in a sauté pan and add the almonds and rice. Cook over low heat, stirring, until rice is delicately browned. Add the remaining ingredients, cover and bring to a boil. Reduce heat and simmer 20 to 25 minutes. Remove from heat and keep covered until ready to serve.

SAFFRON

Saffron comes from the reddish-orange stigma of a species of crocus. It is the world's most expensive spice because each blossom yields only three stigmas and they must be picked by hand. Fortunately, a little saffron goes a long way, lending a bright yellow color and exotic flavor and aroma to food preparations.

Saffron is available in both thread and powdered form. Since powder can quickly lose its pungency and sometimes be adulterated with cheaper powders, threads are often preferred. Both powder and threads may be purchased in loose packets or, in Belgium, in small "thimble" doses (equivalent to ⅛ teaspoon of saffron powder).

Saffron must be heated in liquid to release its color and flavor. Threads should be crushed between fingers and then dropped into boiling liquid during recipe preparation. Saffron may also be steeped in a small amount of hot liquid for 2 to 5 minutes and then added to the dish. For the strongest flavor, add saffron near the end of the cooking time.

Spiced Rice

The perfect accompaniment to LAMB WITH ALMONDS *- just omit the pine nuts.*

1 cup/240 ml rice
1"/2½cm ginger root, peeled
2 cups/475 ml boiling salted water
¼ cup/60 ml seedless raisins
¼ cup/60 ml dried currants
¼ cup/60 ml chopped dried apricots
freshly ground black pepper
½ tsp ground nutmeg
2 tsp minced shallots
1 tbsp fresh lemon juice
½ tsp ground coriander seed
1 tbsp olive oil
½ cup/120 ml pine nuts, toasted

Yield: 6 servings

Add rice and ginger to boiling salted water. Reduce heat to low and simmer, covered, for 20 minutes or until all the liquid is absorbed. Meanwhile, soak raisins, currants, and apricots in hot water; drain well when plump. Remove ginger from cooked rice and place rice in a warm serving dish. Add pepper, nutmeg, shallots, lemon juice, coriander and olive oil to rice. Gently fold in plumped raisins, currants and apricots. Serve sprinkled with pine nuts.

> **They had best not stir the rice, though it sticks to the pot.**
> Miguel de Cervantes

Lemon Rice

Melt the butter in a saucepan. Add rice and cook over medium heat, stirring, for 3 to 4 minutes. Add zest and continue cooking until rice is slightly translucent, about 1 to 2 minutes. Add broth and salt; cover and simmer 20 minutes or until liquid is absorbed. Stir in lemon juice. Season with pepper to taste.

To serve, turn into a serving bowl and dust the top with paprika.

Variations: For a richer version, cook the rice with 3 cups/700 ml of chicken broth. Stir in the lemon juice and then add 1 cup/240 ml heavy cream; cook an additional 5 minutes or until cream is absorbed.

½ cup/115 g unsalted butter
2 cups/475 ml rice
grated zest of 2 lemons
4 cups/950 ml chicken broth
salt
2 tbsp fresh lemon juice
freshly ground pepper
paprika

Yield: 8 - 10 servings

" *... for me the kitchen is the center of the household...* "
Barbara Kafka

Pasta, Rice and Vegetables

Frites

To be truly Belgian, serve with fluffy, homemade MAYONNAISE.

6 large potatoes, peeled
cooking oil
salt

Yield: 4 servings

Cut potatoes into sticks the size of a small finger. Dry them thoroughly in a cloth towel. Heat oil in a deep-fat fryer until a bread cube immediately rises to the surface and starts browning. Carefully add the potatoes to the hot oil and cook until golden. (It may be necessary to fry the potatoes in several batches.) Remove and drain well on absorbent paper. Fry the potatoes a second time until they are puffed and brown (this should only take a few minutes). Drain again on absorbent paper. Serve piping hot, sprinkled with salt.

After the first frying, the drained potatoes may be frozen; thaw and complete cooking at another time.

 Take it with a grain of salt…

FRITES

Frites, erroneously called "French" fries, were created last century in a Belgian village near Dinant. It was an annual tradition for the inhabitants to catch small fish to deep-fry and eat together by the river banks. One year, however, the winter was particularly severe and the river froze. Since fishing was unsuccessful, one of the fishermen cut potatoes into the shape of little fish to deep-fry. The following year, they did not even bother to fish.

The Belgian frite has become a favorite snack food as well as a side dish. Frite stands seem to be on every street corner, serving up big paper cones of crisp, hot frites topped with the Belgian favorite, mayonnaise, or any of a host of other flavors of sauce.

The Belgian "twice-fried" method of cooking produces a crisper, more tender frite. The first frying may be done in advance, but delay the second frying until just before serving. Use older potatoes to make the very best frites.

Potatoes au Gratin

For relaxed entertaining, prepare these delicious potatoes several hours in advance. Sprinkle with cheese and bake just before serving.

2 1/5 lb/1 kg potatoes, peeled and sliced
1 cup/240 ml heavy cream
7 oz/200 ml whole milk
5 oz/150 ml sour cream
3 garlic cloves, minced
1 cup/240 ml shredded Gruyère cheese
1 tsp salt
freshly ground pepper

Oven Temp: 400°F/200°C
Yield: 4 servings

In a large pot over very low heat, gently cook potatoes, cream, milk, sour cream and garlic until they are partially softened, about 45 minutes. Stir frequently to prevent potatoes from sticking. Mix in half the cheese and the salt and pepper. Pour into a greased 9"/24cm square pan. Sprinkle the remaining cheese on top. Bake in a preheated oven for 35 to 45 minutes or until potatoes feel soft when pierced with a knife.

Potatoes with Dijon Mustard

> *Pray for peace and grace and spiritual food, for wisdom and guidance, for all these things are good, but don't forget the potatoes.*
> John Tyler Pettee

Peel the potatoes and slice thinly. Rinse with warm water and dry thoroughly. Melt the butter in a large frying pan and cook potatoes over moderately high heat, turning frequently, until well browned. Sprinkle with salt and pepper to taste. Reduce heat to low, cover and cook for 15 minutes, or until potatoes are soft.

1 1/2 lb/ 680 g potatoes
6 tbsp/85 g butter
salt
freshly ground pepper
1/2 cup/120 ml crème fraîche épaisse*
1 tbsp Dijon mustard
1 bunch chervil or parsley, chopped
1 bunch chives, chopped

Yield: 4 servings

In a small bowl, stir together the crème fraîche, mustard and herbs. Pour the mixture over the potatoes and stir to coat. Simmer gently, stirring occasionally, about 5 minutes.

Variation: For a lighter version, brown the potatoes in half the butter and then cook covered, for 15 minutes, with 1/2 cup/120 ml chicken broth. Mix only 2 tablespoons of crème fraîche with the mustard and herbs, stir into potatoes and cook briefly before serving.

* see index

Potatoes Anna

This rich potato cake is one of the classic dishes of French cuisine - be sure to try the delicious variations.

Peel the potatoes and cut into very thin slices.

3 lb/1⅓ kg potatoes
4 tbsp/55 g unsalted butter
2 tbsp oil
salt
freshly ground pepper

Oven Temp: 350°F/175°C
Yield: 8 servings

In a large, heavy skillet with an oven-proof handle, melt the butter with the oil. Pour three-quarters of the fat into a bowl, leaving the rest in the pan. Arrange a layer of overlapping potato slices in a spiral design, covering the bottom and partly up the sides of the pan. (This design will show when the potato cake is turned over.) Do not season the first layer of potatoes as the salt may cause them to stick to the bottom of the pan. Drizzle a little of the oil and butter mixture over the potatoes. Add another layer of potatoes, season with salt and pepper and drizzle with some of the oil and butter. Continue layering with remaining ingredients.

Cook the potatoes over moderately low heat, without stirring, until the bottom is crisp and golden brown, about 30 to 40 minutes. Cover with an oven-proof plate and bake in a preheated oven for 25 minutes or until the potatoes are tender when pierced with a knife. Using a spatula, loosen the potatoes from the sides of the pan. Turn the potatoes onto a platter and cut into wedges before serving.

Variations: For garlic potatoes, add 4 minced garlic cloves to the melted butter and oil before pouring over the potato layers. For Parmesan potatoes, mince 5 shallots and stir into the melted butter and oil along with ¼ cup/60 ml of freshly grated Parmesan cheese.

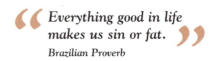

"Everything good in life makes us sin or fat."
Brazilian Proverb

POTATOES

For those used to only three or four kinds of potatoes to choose from, the wide variety of potatoes available in Belgium can be confusing. The potato packaging and grocery shelf offer some help as to which potato is suitable for which method of preparation. At the market or green grocers, it is often best to ask.

The specific types of potatoes available vary depending on the time of year. The following guidelines may help in potato selection.

The equivalent to the American "baking potato" does not exist in Belgium, but the Bintje is the local all-purpose potato. This potato may be puréed, baked, boiled or used in a gratin or salad. It is also a good potato for FRITES. For something closer to a baking potato, look for Maris Piper potatoes imported from England.

For steaming or boiling, buy smaller potatoes with thin smooth skins. Cook them in the skins and then peel them if you prefer serving them without the skin. Nicola, Charlotte and Cornes de Gatte are excellent boiling potatoes. Nicola potatoes, in particular, are firm and waxy, making them the perfect choice for potato salad. Red-skinned potatoes, such as Rosa, are also an excellent choice for salad.

New potatoes, tiny little potatoes with fragile skins, are best simply boiled in their skins and served with butter and parsley. Ratte and Grenaille are two possibilities, but many others are available.

The choice is vast. Sample the exciting variety of potatoes available from the grocery store, neighborhood street market, green grocer, or even a local farmer and find your own personal favorites.

Rosemary Roasted Potatoes

2 lb/900 g new potatoes, quartered
3 tbsp olive oil
2 tbsp chopped fresh rosemary
2 tsp thyme
1 tsp freshly ground pepper
1 tsp coarsely ground salt

Oven Temp: 350°F/175°C
Yield: 4 - 6 servings

In a shallow roasting pan, toss together potatoes and olive oil and bake in a preheated oven for 20 minutes. Remove potatoes from oven and add remaining ingredients, mixing well. Continue to bake, turning occasionally, until they are crisp and browned on the outside and tender in the center, about 40 to 50 minutes longer.

Variation: Whole cloves of unpeeled garlic may be roasted with the potatoes.

Horseradish Mashed Potatoes

6 medium potatoes, peeled
4½ oz/130 ml warm milk
4½ tbsp/60 g butter
3 tbsp prepared horseradish
salt
freshly ground pepper

Yield: 6 servings

Cut the potatoes into chunks. Cook in a large pot of boiling salted water until tender, about 20 minutes. Drain. Place potatoes in a large bowl and add milk, butter and horseradish. Using an electric mixer, beat potatoes until creamy. Season to taste with salt and pepper.

The potatoes may be prepared 2 hours in advance. Cover and let stand at room temperature. Rewarm over low heat, stirring constantly; thin with additional milk if necessary.

" *Potatoes, like wives, should never be taken for granted.* "
Peter Pirbright

Pasta, Rice and Vegetables

Eggplant, Tomatoes and Chèvre

Try the eggplant by itself - it's delicious cooked under the broiler or on an outdoor grill.

Peel eggplant and slice crosswise into ½"/1¼cm rounds. Place the eggplant on paper towels and sprinkle lightly on both sides with salt. Cover with another paper towel and let sit for 30 minutes.

Slice tomatoes ⅓"/¾cm thick and put in a large baking dish. (You should have the same number of tomato slices as eggplant rounds.) Brush tops lightly with olive oil or garlic butter and sprinkle lightly with salt, pepper, basil and oregano. Slice chèvre in ¼"/½cm thick rounds. Place a slice of chèvre on each tomato slice and sprinkle bread crumbs on top. Lightly brush both sides of eggplant with olive oil and place on a baking sheet. Broil eggplant and tomatoes, turning eggplant slices over after 5 minutes. When eggplants and tomatoes are tender, remove from oven and layer tomato and chèvre on top of each eggplant slice.

2 large eggplants
6 tomatoes
olive oil or melted garlic butter
salt
freshly ground pepper
1½ tsp basil
1 tsp oregano
10½ oz/300 g log of mild chèvre
4 tbsp bread crumbs

Yield: 6 - 8 servings

The flavor of fresh herbs may be preserved by drying, freezing or infusing them into oils or vinegars (see index). Hang bunches of fresh herbs upside down in a cool, dry, airy location until well dried. You may also dry herbs on a rack in a very low slow oven (below 90°F/32°C); a convection oven is best. Herbs dried this way will be slightly less potent than those which have been hung. Be sure the herbs are completely dry and brittle before packing into light-proof jars. Herbs such as chives or rosemary may be snipped and frozen. Soft-leaf herbs such as oregano, basil, or thyme can be puréed with a little water and frozen in ice cube trays. Store the cubes in plastic bags for use in sauces, stews or soups.

Vegetable Terrine with Tomato Coulis
La Maison du Boeuf, Hilton Hotel - Michel Theurel, Chef

Clean and trim the vegetables. Cut the zucchini (and carrots if they are large) into long julienne the diameter of the asparagus. Boil the vegetables, one type at a time, in salted water until tender. Blanch the leek leaves until soft and lay crosswise across a 12"/30cm long terrine to cover bottom and sides. Fill the terrine with vegetables (laying the green beans, carrots and zucchini lengthwise) in the following order: green beans, cauliflower, carrots, asparagus, corn and zucchini. Top with basil leaves.

5½ oz/150 g green beans
5½ oz/150 g cauliflower florets
5½ oz/150 g young carrots
5½ oz/150 g thin green asparagus
5½ oz/150 g young corn
5½ oz/150 g zucchini
2 leeks (green leaves only)
fresh basil leaves
17 gelatin sheets (see index)
1 quart + 2 oz/1 liter white chicken broth

Tomato Coulis:
2⅓ lb/1 kg plum tomatoes
½ bunch fresh basil
1 cup/240 ml olive oil
3½ oz/100 ml balsamic vinegar
salt
freshly ground pepper

Yield: 12 servings

Cover the gelatin sheets with cold water to soften. Heat the stock, melt the drained gelatin sheets in the stock and let cool until it becomes syrupy. Pour the gelatin mixture over the vegetables and refrigerate overnight.

To make the tomato coulis, blend all ingredients in a food processor and press through a fine strainer. Refrigerate.

To serve, spoon a pool of tomato coulis on individual serving dishes and place a slice of terrine on top.

Pasta, Rice and Vegetables

Italian Green Beans

An assertive, flavorful vegetable guaranteed to perk up any simple main dish.

1 lb/450 g green beans
1¼ cups/300 ml chicken broth
2 garlic cloves, minced
pinch of hot red pepper flakes
4 sun-dried tomatoes, chopped
4 pitted black olives, sliced
1 tbsp balsamic vinegar
freshly ground pepper
7 fresh basil leaves, shredded

Yield: 4 servings

Steam the beans until crisply tender. Rinse under cold water, drain well and set aside.

Pour the broth into a large frying pan. Add garlic, red pepper, sun-dried tomatoes, olives and balsamic vinegar. Boil until reduced by half. Add the beans, toss and cook for 2 to 3 minutes. Season with pepper and stir in basil. Cook, stirring, 4 minutes longer. Serve warm or at room temperature.

> *Tear all but the tiniest leaves into two or more pieces. Be gentle, so as not to crush the basil... and waste the first, fresh droplets of juice.*
> Marcella Hazan

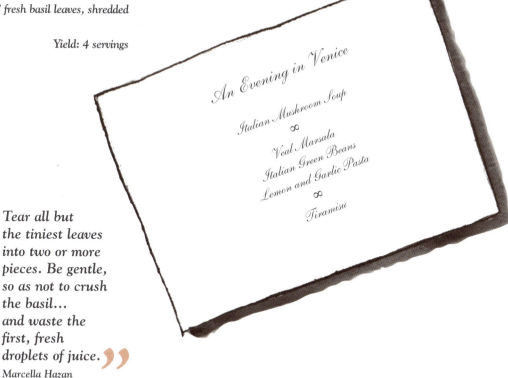

An Evening in Venice

Italian Mushroom Soup
∞
Veal Marsala
Italian Green Beans
Lemon and Garlic Pasta
∞
Tiramisu

Pasta, Rice and Vegetables

Green Beans with Roquefort and Walnuts

Bring a saucepan of water to a boil and add the beans. Simmer until crisply tender. Drain, rinse under cold water and drain again. Set aside.

2 lb/900 g fresh green beans
8 thick bacon strips
8 oz/225 g Roquefort cheese, crumbled
1½ cups/350 ml walnut halves, toasted
freshly ground pepper

Yield: 8 servings

Cut the bacon into ¼"/½cm wide strips. In a large frying pan, fry bacon until crisp. Remove bacon with a slotted spoon and drain on paper towels. Add green beans to the bacon drippings and heat for 2 minutes. Add the Roquefort, tossing until the cheese just begins to melt, about 30 seconds. Sprinkle with walnuts and lots of pepper; serve immediately.

Variation: For a simple Green Beans with Walnuts, *melt 3 tablespoons butter with 1 tablespoon walnut oil and toss with hot cooked and drained beans. Add ⅓ cup/80 ml chopped toasted walnuts.*

Carrot Flans

Versatile and delicious, this impressive side dish may be made with almost any vegetable that's in season. If prepared ahead, reheat in a bain marie.

14 oz/400 g carrots (7 small)
2 tbsp/30g unsalted butter, softened
2 large eggs
½ cup/120 ml milk
3 tbsp heavy cream
½ tsp freshly grated nutmeg
½ tsp salt
freshly ground pepper

Garnish:
parsley sprigs

Oven Temp: 350°F/175°C
Yield: 6 servings

Peel the carrots and cut into 1"/2½cm pieces. Cook the carrots until soft, drain well and pat dry. Purée carrots and butter until smooth. Add remaining ingredients, except parsley, and blend well. Adjust seasoning.

Divide the mixture among 6 buttered (⅓ cup/80 ml) soufflé dishes. Place in a bain marie (see index) in the center of a preheated oven. Bake until firm, about 30 minutes. Remove flans from water and let cool on a rack for 5 minutes. To serve, loosen gently with a knife, invert onto a serving platter and garnish with parsley.

Variations: Substitute cauliflower and 3 oz/85 grams grated Gruyère cheese, broccoli florets or peeled parsnips for the carrots.

"Food is an important part of a balanced diet."
Fran Lebowitz

ONIONS

Onions, members of the lily family, are a basic ingredient in most cuisines. In the United States, as in Europe, there are a variety of onions available and each has specific uses.

- ◆ Yellow Onions/Oignons Jaunes are medium-sized onions with brownish, papery skin. They are most often used for general cooking.
- ◆ Green Onions, Scallions or Spring Onion/Ciboule or Jeunes Oignons have a small white bulb with long green shoots and are used raw in salads, as a garnish, sautéed, or as a crudité.
- ◆ Shallots/Echalotes are used to flavor sauces and add delicate onion flavor with a hint of garlic to dishes which do not require long cooking. The bulb grows in several cloves, similar to garlic, and gets its name from Ascalon, an ancient Palestinian port. They blend particularly well with sauces containing wine or vinegar and are excellent minced and added to vinaigrette dressing.
- ◆ Red Onions/Oignons Rouges are used raw since they lose taste and texture after cooking. They are excellent in salad, briefly grilled or used as a garnish.
- ◆ White Onions/Oignons Blancs are large, round and sweet with a mild flavor. They are delicious cooked or raw and are ideal to stuff.
- ◆ Chives/Ciboulettes are slender shoots with a fresh, mild onion flavor. Their green color enhances the appearance of a dish and the slender leaves are often used whole or chopped as a garnish.
- ◆ Pearl Onions/Grelot de Printemps are tiny white onions that are generally boiled and then glazed or served in a cream sauce as an accompaniment to a strongly flavored dish. They are often part of a traditional American Thanksgiving menu. Blanch for 1 minute and cool before peeling.
- ◆ Leeks/Poireau resemble over-sized scallions. They have a mild, sweet taste that enhances the flavor of soups, stocks and stews. They are also excellent sautéed in butter. In the spring, you will find slender, pencil-thin roots which may be eaten raw or lightly cooked. The remainder of the year, they are thicker. Avoid those larger than 1½"/4cm wide since they become tough and stringy. The mild white stalk is used much like any onion, while the tender light green stalk is finely sliced and added to soups, stews, stocks or sauces.

Sunshine Glazed Carrots

Diagonally slice carrots, about ½"/1¼cm thick. Steam until just tender.

In a saucepan, combine sugar, cornstarch, ginger and salt. Add the orange juice. Cook, stirring constantly, until thickened and bubbly. Boil 1 minute. Remove from heat and stir in the butter. Pour the glaze over the hot carrots, tossing to coat. Garnish with an orange twist.

8 large carrots
1 tbsp sugar
1 tsp cornstarch
¼ tsp powdered ginger
¼ tsp salt
¼ cup/60 ml fresh orange juice
2 tbsp/30 g butter

Garnish:
twist of orange peel

Yield: 4 servings

Leeks with Orange Ginger Sauce

12 medium leeks
6 tbsp/85 g unsalted butter
5 tbsp peeled, grated ginger root
1 tsp ground ginger
1 cup/240 ml fresh orange juice
2 tbsp grated orange zest

Yield: 6 servings

Trim, soak and rinse leeks (see index), leaving them whole.

Fill a large pot with water and bring to a boil. Add the leeks, reduce heat and simmer until tender, 5 to 7 minutes. Drain the leeks and pat dry.

Over low heat, melt the butter in a large frying pan. Add the fresh ginger and ground ginger and cook for 1 minute, stirring. Add the leeks and raise the heat to medium. Cook until they are lightly browned on all sides, turning occasionally, for 5 to 7 minutes. Transfer to a warm serving dish.

Add the orange juice and 1 tablespoon of zest to the pan. Raise the heat and whisk the sauce until it thickens slightly. Spoon sauce over the leeks and sprinkle with the remaining 1 tablespoon orange zest. Serve immediately.

To preserve fresh ginger root, peel and pack into a glass jar and cover with dry sherry. Refrigerated, the ginger will stay fresh and juicy to be used when needed. Use the perfumed sherry for oriental stir-fried dishes.

" *Imagine that a fierce pestilence strikes the earth and obliterates forever a single crop - ginger. The consequences would be appalling: no more gingerbread for school kids, no more gingersnaps to dunk into milk... No one would handle a delicate task "gingerly." And lively red-haired women would answer to some other spicy name.* "
Barbara Hansen

Zucchini au Gratin

1½ lb/680 g zucchini
4 tbsp olive oil
½ tsp minced garlic
½ cup/120 ml chopped onion
1 cup/240 ml canned plum tomatoes
⅛ tsp marjoram
1 tbsp chopped fresh parsley
salt
freshly ground pepper
2 tbsp freshly grated Parmesan

Oven Temp: 400°F/220°C
Yield: 6 servings

Cut the zucchini into very thin slices.

In a sauté pan, heat 2 tablespoons of the olive oil. Add the garlic and zucchini slices and cook, stirring occasionally, until limp.

Put the chopped onion and remaining olive oil in a small saucepan and cook until onion is translucent. Chop the tomatoes and add them along with their juice. Add marjoram and continue to cook for 15 to 20 minutes. Stir in the parsley and add salt and pepper to taste.

Oil the bottom of an oven-proof casserole.

> La Cuisine commence au marché...

Spread half the zucchini in an even layer on the bottom. Cover with half of the sauce and sprinkle with a tablespoon of Parmesan. Cover with remaining zucchini, the rest of the sauce and the remaining cheese.

Bake on the top rack of a preheated oven for 20 minutes. Let rest for 10 minutes before serving. (If made earlier in the day, do not refrigerate. Reheat before serving.)

Sesame Broccoli Oriental

This easy broccoli recipe is the perfect accompaniment to broiled fish.

Blanch broccoli in boiling, salted water for 1 minute; plunge into ice water, drain and pat dry.

Heat a wok or frying pan over high heat. Pour in oil and heat until it smokes. Put broccoli and sugar in the pan and stir-fry for 2 minutes. Add garlic and ginger root and stir-fry another minute. Add soy sauce, sesame oil, sesame seeds, salt and pepper to taste. Toss and serve immediately.

2 quarts/liters broccoli florets
3 tbsp vegetable oil
½ tsp sugar
2 garlic cloves, minced
1½ tsp peeled, minced ginger root
1½ tbsp soy sauce
2 tbsp oriental sesame oil
3 tbsp toasted sesame seeds
salt
freshly ground pepper

Yield: 6 servings

Oriental sesame oil is a strong-tasting oil made from toasted sesame seeds. It is used in small amounts as a flavoring and is not suitable as a cooking oil.

Broccoli Purée

3 large bunches broccoli
1 small onion, chopped
1 tsp olive oil
3 cups/600 ml chicken broth
⅓ cup/80 ml freshly grated Parmesan
¼ cup/60 ml heavy cream
pinch of nutmeg
salt
freshly ground pepper

Yield: 10 - 12 servings

Chop the broccoli, saving 8 small whole florets for garnish.

In a large saucepan, sauté the onion in olive oil. Add the broccoli and chicken broth and simmer until soft, approximately 5 to 8 minutes. Drain and purée the broccoli mixture. Add Parmesan cheese, cream, and nutmeg and season to taste with salt and pepper. The purée may be prepared in advance; keep warm and garnish with florets just before serving.

Variations: Use the same method with other vegetables. The purée may also be used to stuff vegetables such as large mushroom caps, parboiled onion shells, partially baked zucchini boats, or baked winter squash halves. Fill with purée and top with a sprinkling of grated cheese and freshly buttered bread crumbs. Bake until the vegetables are cooked and the crumbs are crisp and brown.

> *Ingredients are to recipes as words are to sentences. We can combine and recombine them in many different ways.*
> Michael Roberts

Pasta, Rice and Vegetables

Shredded Brussels Sprouts with Prosciutto

4 oz/115 g prosciutto slices
½ cup/115 g unsalted butter
6 garlic cloves, minced
2 lb/900 g Brussels sprouts, trimmed
3 tbsp flour
1½ cups/350 ml heavy cream
1 cup/240 ml light cream
¼ cup/60 ml sweet Marsala wine
1 tsp grated nutmeg
salt
freshly ground black pepper
1½ cups/350 ml freshly grated Parmesan

Oven Temp: 350°F/175°C
Yield: 10 - 12 servings

Cut the prosciutto into thin slivers. Over moderately high heat, melt the butter in a large sauté pan. Add prosciutto and garlic and cook, stirring, for 4 minutes.

Cut the Brussels sprouts into thin slices. Add to the pan and continue to cook, stirring constantly, for 4 minutes. Stir in the flour and toss to coat the Brussels sprouts.

Gradually stir in heavy cream, light cream and Marsala. Reduce heat and simmer until the Brussels sprouts are barely tender, about 5 minutes. Add nutmeg and season to taste with salt and pepper. Stir in 1 cup/240 ml of the Parmesan cheese and cook just until cheese melts.

Transfer mixture to a shallow gratin dish. Top with remaining Parmesan cheese. Bake in a preheated oven until bubbly and slightly browned, about 20 minutes. Serve hot.

> *Meals epitomize the mutual moment of relaxation in a stressful world, the time when people gather to share, to seduce, to console, to shape their children's characters and culture, to argue, to enjoy themselves.*
> Catharine Reynolds

Roasted Brussels Sprouts

2 lb/900 g Brussels sprouts, trimmed
1 tsp salt
½ tsp freshly ground pepper
2 tbsp balsamic vinegar
⅓ cup/80 ml extra virgin olive oil

Oven Temp: 375°F/190°C
Yield: 6 - 8 servings

Put the sprouts into a baking dish just large enough to hold them in one layer.

Combine salt, pepper and vinegar in a bowl and whisk until the salt has dissolved. Slowly beat in the olive oil and pour the mixture over the sprouts, stirring until they are well coated.

Bake the sprouts in a preheated oven for 45 minutes to 1 hour. Every 15 minutes or so, turn the sprouts with a metal spatula. Be careful that the sprouts are thoroughly loosened from the pan before you turn them, or they will tear. The sprouts are done when they are very dark brown and glazed and give no resistance when pierced with a fork. The sprouts may be set aside at room temperature for several hours and reheated just before serving.

To prepare Brussels sprouts, wash and trim stem ends and remove wilted or discolored leaves. Cut an "X" in the base for faster, more even cooking.

> **Properly cooked vegetables are a sheer delight.**
> Craig Claiborne

Belgian Endive/Chicon

Perhaps the most popular of all the vegetables found in Belgium, the Belgian endive may be considered the "national vegetable." The method of growing them in the dark was discovered by a gardener at the old Brussels Botanical Garden who noticed endives growing in the cellars with no light, only heat and moisture. He introduced them to others and the Belgian endive quickly became a favorite winter vegetable. Endives are sold wrapped with dark blue paper to keep out the light and protect their delicate color and flavor.

Endives may be stuffed, cooked, or cut raw into salad, but one of the most popular recipes is for BRAISED ENDIVES. Trim the stem ends of the endive to cut away any browned rims. Snugly place 8 endives in one layer in a sauté pan with a tight-fitting cover. Add 4 teaspoons butter, 1 teaspoon sugar, the juice of 1 lemon, 1 cup/240 ml water, salt and pepper. Cover and bring to a boil. Cook about 30 to 45 minutes or until the endives are tender and the liquid has evaporated. Watch carefully that the cooking liquid does not boil away. If absolutely necessary, add a little more water to prevent sticking and burning. Toward the end of the cooking time, uncover and brown lightly on all sides, or until the outer leaves turn a caramel color. Drain well before serving, squeezing out any extra moisture. Adjust seasoning and sprinkle with nutmeg if desired.

Endives et Jambon au Gratin

Place the ham slices on a flat surface. Place a well-drained braised endive, crosswise, in the center of each slice. Roll the ham slices to enclose the endives.

8 thin slices cooked ham
8 whole BRAISED ENDIVES, drained
3 tbsp/45 g butter
¼ cup/35 g flour
2½ cups/600 ml milk
salt
white pepper
freshly grated nutmeg
cayenne pepper
4 oz/115 g Gruyère cheese, grated
2 egg yolks

Oven Temp: 425°F/220°C
Yield: 4 - 6 servings

Melt the butter in a saucepan and add the flour, stirring with a whisk. When blended, gradually add the milk, whisking constantly. Cook, stirring constantly, until the sauce thickens. Add salt, white pepper, nutmeg and cayenne to taste.

Add two-thirds of the cheese and stir until melted. Add the yolks, stirring rapidly with the whisk. Bring to just below a boil, stirring, and remove from heat.

Lightly butter a 9"x13"/24 x 34cm baking dish. Arrange the ham rolls in the baking dish and pour the sauce on top. Sprinkle with the remaining grated cheese.

Bake 10 minutes in a preheated oven or until piping hot, bubbling and browned. If the top is not uniformly brown, run the dish briefly under the broiler.

Pasta, Rice and Vegetables

White Cabbage

*S*erve this with your favorite grilled sausage or pork roast. Use the drippings to make the cabbage.

6 tbsp/85 g butter or bacon drippings
1 onion, chopped
2 tart apples, peeled and chopped
2⅓ lb/1 kg white cabbage, shredded
½ tsp vinegar
salt
freshly ground pepper
caraway seeds
1 cup/240 ml water
1 potato, peeled and grated
1 tbsp granulated sugar

Yield: 6 servings

Melt the butter in a large frying pan and gently sauté the onion and apples. Add the cabbage and vinegar and season with salt, pepper and caraway seeds to taste. Add water and cover. Bring to a boil and simmer for 30 minutes. Add the potato and simmer until it melts into the cabbage. Add sugar to taste.

> *In Belgium…the cuisine has evolved to warm the body, as the hospitality has evolved to warm the spirit. Generosity is everywhere in a country where quantity and quality meet.*
> Lynn Rossetto Kasper

Echalotes au Vin Rouge

*M*elt 2 tablespoons of butter in a large saucepan and add the shallots. Sauté until they are a light, golden brown, about 10 minutes. Add the chicken broth, sugar and thyme.

4 tbsp/55 g butter
1 lb/450 g shallots, peeled
¾ cup/175 ml chicken broth
1 tsp sugar
1 sprig of fresh thyme
1 cup/240 ml red wine

Yield: 4 - 6 servings

Over high heat, cook the shallots until the cooking liquid has almost evaporated. (Watch carefully so the butter does not burn.) Add the wine and boil until reduced to a few tablespoons. Remove pan from heat and add the remaining butter. Stir gently to combine and coat shallots. Serve with a little sauce spooned on top.

Select shallots that are firm and uniform in size so that they bake evenly.

Bread and Brunch

Bread and Brunch

Apple Compote	256
Baking Powder Biscuits	246
Banana Bread	231
Basic Savory Tart Pastry	272
Bran Muffins	243
Breakfast Corn Muffins	242
Breakfast Pancakes	259
Cheese Soufflé	263
Chèvre Spread	237
Chocolate Muffins	244
Cinnamon Apple Cake	254
Cornmeal Pancakes	260
Crab Quiche	271
Crêpes	258
Crusty Yeast Rolls	245
Curried Chicken Cheesecake	265
Date Nut Bread	237
English Cream Scones	248
English Muffin Bread	241
Hot Spinach Cheesecake	266
Lemon Blueberry Bread	235
Lemon Sauce	234
Mango Tea Bread	236
Oatmeal Bread	240
Overnight Crunch Coffee Cake	252
Pâte Brisée au Fromage	268
Pecan and Almond Coffee Cake	251
Popovers	243
Poppy Seed Bread	238
Pumpkin Bread	233
Quiche au Saumon	270
Raised Waffles	261
Raspberry Cream Cheese Coffee Cake	253
Red Currant Jelly	255
Sally Lunn	250
Sausage and Cheese Strata	264
Shirred Eggs	262
Soft Gingerbread	234
Sticky Buns	247
Sticky Toffee Puddings with Pecan Toffee Sauce	257
Sweet Roll Dough	248
Tarte Provençale	268
Texas Corn Bread	249
Tomato and Onion Quiche	269
Vegetable Frittata	267
Zucchini Bread	232

SPECIAL TOPICS

Belgian Bread	239
Buttermilk	
Substitution for	249
Substituting with	242
Fresh Currants	256
Proofing Yeast	245

Banana Bread

Great for brunch or as an afternoon snack when the kids get home from school.

½ cup/115 g vegetable shortening
1 cup/200 g granulated sugar
2 large eggs
2 cups/260 g flour
¾ tsp baking soda
¼ tsp baking powder
½ tsp salt
1 cup/240 ml mashed ripe bananas
¼ cup/60 ml soured milk (see index)
1 tsp vanilla extract

Oven Temp: 350°F/175°C
Yield: 1 large or 3 small loaves

Cream shortening and sugar. Add eggs and beat until fluffy. Stir together flour, baking soda, baking powder and salt. Combine bananas, soured milk and vanilla. Gradually add the flour mixture to the creamed mixture, alternating with the banana mixture. (Begin and end with flour.)

Pour into 1 large or 3 small greased loaf pan(s). Bake for 55 minutes for a large loaf or 40 to 45 minutes for small loaves.

Over-ripe bananas are the secret to moist, flavorful banana bread. If you can't make the bread when the bananas are soft, either freeze the banana purée or simply peel the bananas and freeze them in a plastic bag for use at a later time.

Zucchini Bread

1 cup/240 ml dark raisins
4 large eggs
2¼ cups/450 g granulated sugar
1 cup/240 ml vegetable oil
3 tsp vanilla extract
3½ cups/450 g all-purpose or wheat flour
1½ tsp baking soda
1½ tsp salt
¾ tsp baking powder
1 tsp cinnamon
2 cups/475 ml grated zucchini
1 cup/240 ml chopped nuts

Oven Temp: 350°F/175°C
Yield: 2 loaves

Cover raisins with boiling water and let stand to plump the raisins.

Beat the eggs well. Gradually beat in sugar, oil and vanilla. Combine the dry ingredients and gradually add to the creamed mixture, alternating with the zucchini. Drain the raisins. Stir raisins and nuts into the batter.

Spoon the batter into 2 greased and floured loaf pans. Bake on the lowest oven rack for 55 minutes, or until done. Let stand 10 minutes. Turn out onto a rack to cool.

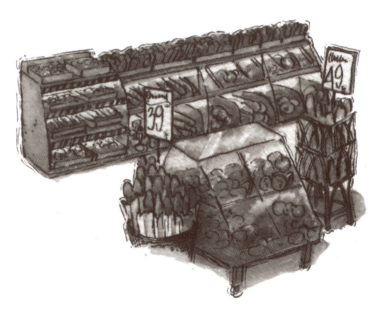

Pumpkin Bread

This healthy bread is moist and delicious without using any butter or shortening.

3⅓ cups/435 g flour
2⅔ cups/530 g granulated sugar
½ tsp baking powder
2 tsp baking soda
1 tsp salt
1 tsp cinnamon
1 tsp cloves
1 tsp ginger
2 cups/475 ml cooked, mashed pumpkin
⅔ cup/160 ml water
4 large eggs, beaten
⅔ cup/160 ml golden raisins
⅔ cup/160 ml chopped nuts

Oven Temp: 350°F/175°C
Yield: 2 loaves

Combine the flour, sugar, baking powder, baking soda, salt, cinnamon, cloves and ginger. Blend in pumpkin, water and eggs. Stir in raisins and nuts.

Pour into 2 greased and floured loaf pans. Bake in a preheated oven for 50 to 55 minutes.

If you run out of baking powder, mix together 2 teaspoons of cream of tartar, 1 teaspoon of baking soda and ½ teaspoon salt for every 1 cup/130 grams of flour in the recipe. Use immediately as it will lose potency rapidly. To test the effectiveness of baking powder, mix 1 teaspoon of the powder with ⅓ cup/80 ml of hot water. Use only if it bubbles vigorously.

> *The smells in the kitchen and the smiles on the faces of friends and family are my rewards.*
> Barbara Kafka

Bread and Brunch

Soft Gingerbread

2½ cups/325 g all-purpose flour
1 tsp cinnamon
2 tsp ground ginger
1 tsp ground cloves
½ cup/115 g butter, softened
½ cup/100 g granulated sugar
1 cup/240 ml dark molasses
2 tsp baking soda
1 cup/240 ml boiling water
2 large eggs, slightly beaten

Oven Temp: 350°F/175°C
Yield: 9 servings

Sauce:
½ cup/100 g granulated sugar
1 tbsp cornstarch
1 cup/240 ml boiling water
2 tbsp/30 g butter
4½ tsp fresh lemon juice
pinch of salt

Yield: 1 cup/240 ml

Sift together the flour, cinnamon, ginger and cloves. Set aside.

In a large mixing bowl, beat the butter until it is smooth and creamy. Add the sugar and molasses and continue beating until well blended. Combine the baking soda and boiling water and pour it into the creamed mixture, beating well. Add the flour mixture and beat until the batter is smooth. Beat in the eggs.

Pour into a greased and floured 8"/20cm square baking pan and bake in a preheated oven for 45 to 55 minutes, or until a toothpick inserted in the center of the cake comes out clean. Remove from the oven and let cool in the pan for 5 minutes. Turn out onto a rack. Serve plain or with LEMON SAUCE.

The flavor of ground ginger fades after about nine months. For perfect gingerbread, buy a fresh jar - you'll taste the difference!

Lemon Sauce

In a small saucepan, mix together the sugar and cornstarch. Add the boiling water, stirring constantly, and boil for 5 minutes. Remove from the heat and stir in the butter, lemon juice and salt.

> *Soon they found themselves in a small field, where they saw the most amazing house. The house was made of gingerbread, with a roof of icing.*
> Grimm's Hansel and Gretel

Lemon Blueberry Bread

*G*rate the lemon rind and squeeze the juice of the lemon. To make the glaze, combine lemon juice, ¼ cup/50 grams sugar and all but 1 teaspoon of the lemon rind. Set aside.

1 lemon
1¼ cups/250 g granulated sugar
6 tbsp/85 g butter
2 large eggs
1½ cups/200 g pastry flour
1¼ tsp baking powder
½ tsp salt
½ cup/120 ml milk
¾ cup/175 ml fresh blueberries

Oven Temp: 350°F/175°C
325°F/165°C
Yield: 1 loaf

Cream the butter with an electric mixer. Add 1 cup/200 grams of sugar and the eggs and beat until creamy. Mix together the flour, baking powder and salt. Gradually add to the creamed mixture, alternating with the milk, beginning and ending with flour. Blend until smooth. Add the reserved 1 teaspoon of lemon rind and gently fold in the blueberries.

Line a loaf pan with wax paper. (Be sure the paper comes over the edge of the pan.) Spoon batter into the pan and bake at 350°F/175°C for 15 minutes. Reduce oven temperature to 325°F/165°C and bake for 30 to 45 minutes more.

Remove bread from the oven and pour the lemon juice glaze over the bread while still hot. Let the bread cool in the pan (for a moist bread) or remove it after 10 to 15 minutes.

Mango Tea Bread

If you love the taste of mangos, add a little more!

Sift together the flour, baking soda, cinnamon and salt and set aside.

2¼ cups/290 g flour
2 tsp baking soda
2 tsp ground cinnamon
½ tsp salt
½ cup/115 g butter, softened
3 large eggs, room temperature
1½ cups/300 g granulated sugar
½ cup/120 ml vegetable oil
1 large ripe mango, peeled and chopped
½ cup/120 ml raisins
1 cup/240 ml shredded coconut

Cream the butter with an electric mixer. Beat in the eggs and sugar until light and fluffy; beat in the oil. Slowly fold the dry ingredients into the creamed mixture. Fold in the mango, raisins and two-thirds of the coconut.

Line the bottoms of 2 greased loaf pans with baking paper and grease the paper. Spoon the batter evenly into the pans. Sprinkle the remaining coconut over the loaves and bake for 50 to 60 minutes, or until a skewer inserted into the middle comes out clean. Let the loaves stand for 10 minutes before turning out onto wire racks. Cool completely before serving.

Oven Temp: 350°F/175°C
Yield: 2 loaves

Entertaining Weekend Guests

(Grapefruit Halves)

∞

Vegetable Frittata
Country Sausage (Patties)
English Muffin Bread
(Butter)

∞

Coffee
Juice

Date Nut Bread

¾ cup/175 ml chopped walnuts
1 cup/240 ml pitted dates
1 tsp baking soda
½ tsp salt
3 tbsp/45 g butter
¾ cup/175 ml boiling water
2 large eggs
1 tsp vanilla extract
1 cup/200 g granulated sugar
1½ cup/200 g sifted flour

Oven Temp: 350°F/175°C
Yield: 1 loaf

Spread:
4 oz/115 g cream cheese, room temperature
4 oz/115 g chèvre, room temperature
½ cup/115 g unsalted butter, softened

Yield: 1 cup/240 ml

Mix together walnuts, dates, baking soda and salt. Add butter and water and let stand for 20 minutes. Beat together eggs, vanilla and sugar; add flour and mix well. Blend in the date mixture. Pour into a buttered loaf pan and bake approximately 1 hour and 5 minutes. Cool. Serve with cream cheese or CHÈVRE SPREAD.

Chèvre Spread
Combine all ingredients until smooth. Pack into a crock to serve.

> *Keep things simple, and use only the best ingredients.*
> André Soltner

Bread and Brunch

Poppy Seed Bread

Beat all the cake ingredients together for 2 minutes. Pour into 2 large greased loaf pans or 5 mini-loaf pans.

Bake in a preheated oven for 50 to 60 minutes for large pans or approximately 30 minutes for small pans.

Mix all the topping ingredients together. Pour over the bread while it is still hot from the oven. Remove the breads from the pans after 20 minutes. When cool, wrap in plastic wrap. (Best made a day or two ahead.)

3 cups/400 g flour
1½ tsp salt
1½ tsp baking powder
2½ cups/500 g granulated sugar
3 large eggs
1½ cups/350 ml milk
1 cup/240 ml vegetable oil
3 tbsp poppy seeds
1½ tsp vanilla extract
1½ tsp almond extract

Topping:
½ tsp vanilla extract
½ tsp butter extract
¾ cup/150 g granulated sugar
½ tsp almond extract
¼ cup/60 ml orange juice

Oven Temp: 350°F/175°C
Yield: 2 large or 5 small loaves

BELGIAN BREAD

Bread, purchased fresh and warm from the local boulangerie, is one of Belgium's many delights. Tuck a familiar crusty baguette under your arm, or try some of the many other delicious possibilities.

Two loaves which are similar to the Baguette are Bâtard (a wider version) and Ficelle (a narrow baguette). Pain de Mie/Pain Carré Blanc is the Belgian equivalent to a loaf of basic white bread. It has a firm, even "crumb" which makes it a good choice for toasted sandwiches, stratas and croutons. Pain de Campagne, Boulot and Pain Galette Blanc are among the various country-style white breads. For whole-grain breads, look for Pain Complet or Pain Gris. Rye bread is Pain de Seigle. Ciabatta, a chewy Italian loaf, comes either white or with nuts.

If you are looking for soft rolls, the Sandwich comes with or without sugar or raisins and in white or wheat.

For crusty rolls, look for Piccolo (oval) or Pistolet (round). Croissants, Couque au Beurre and Pain au Chocolat (croissant dough baked with chocolate inside) are all sweet and flaky. Brioche are high in eggs, giving them a distinctive yellow color. They are sweet and very soft, almost like a cake.

Pain aux Noix (nut bread) and Cramique (raisin bread) are delicious toasted. Craquelin, a bread baked with pearl sugar throughout, is a Belgian specialty.

If these breads don't entice you, visit the local bakery shops and sample the wide variety. Remember that Belgian breads are made without preservatives. Eat them while they are fresh or wrap tightly and freeze.

> *Good bread is the most fundamentally satisfying of all foods.*
> James Beard

Oatmeal Bread

2 cups/475 ml milk, scalded
2 cups/475 ml quick oats
½ cup/110 g light brown sugar
2 tbsp/30 g butter, softened
1 tsp salt
1 pkg dry yeast
¼ cup/60 ml warm water
4 cups/520 g (or more) flour

Oven Temp: 400°F/200°C
375°F/190°C
Yield: 2 loaves

Place milk, oats, brown sugar, butter and salt in a mixing bowl and stir. Cool to lukewarm.

Dissolve the yeast in warm water (110°F/43°C). Pour into the oat mixture. Beat in 1½ cups/200 grams of flour. Let stand until light and bubbly, approximately 15 minutes.

Gradually add 2½ cups/320 grams of flour, adding more if necessary so that the dough is soft and does not stick to sides of bowl. Knead dough on a lightly floured surface until smooth, about 5 minutes. Place dough in a greased bowl, turn to coat on all sides and cover with a damp towel. Let rise in a warm place for 1 to 1½ hours.

> "…the smell of yeast, the crunch of crisp crust and the still warm taste of freshly baked bread…"
> Shaun Hill

Punch down the dough. Divide in half and shape into loaves. Place in greased loaf pans, cover with a damp towel and let rise until dough doubles in bulk, about 30 to 40 minutes.

Bake in a preheated 400°F/200°C oven for 10 minutes. Reduce heat to 375°F/190°C and bake an additional 30 to 40 minutes.

To scald milk, bring it just to the point of boiling. The surface will barely ripple and a "skin" will form on top.

English Muffin Bread

Slice and toast for a breakfast treat!

5½ cups/715 g (or more) flour
2 pkg dry yeast
1 tbsp granulated sugar
2 tsp salt
¼ tsp baking soda
2 cups/475 ml milk
½ cup/120 ml water
cornmeal

Oven Temp: 400°F/200°C
Yield: 2 loaves

Combine 3 cups/400 grams flour, yeast, sugar, salt and baking soda. Heat milk and water until very warm. Add to dry mixture and beat well. Stir in enough additional flour to make a stiff batter. Spoon into 2 loaf pans that have been greased and sprinkled with cornmeal. Sprinkle tops with cornmeal. Cover and let rise in a warm place for 45 minutes.

Bake for 25 minutes in a preheated oven. Remove the loaves from the pans immediately. Cool on a rack.

" *Nobody, my darling,
could call me a fussy man -
BUT I do like
a little bit of butter to my bread!* "
A.A. Milne

Bread and Brunch

Breakfast Corn Muffins

Combine cornmeal, flour, sugar, baking powder and salt in a large bowl. Cut in the butter until the mixture resembles coarse crumbs. Beat in egg. Stir together milk and vanilla and add to the cornmeal mixture, stirring just enough to moisten.

Grease 12 muffin cups and fill with batter. Bake in a preheated oven for 20 to 25 minutes until golden. Carefully remove from muffin cups and cool on a rack.

2 cups/475 ml cornmeal
1 cup/130 g flour
½ cup/100 g granulated sugar
1 tbsp baking powder
pinch of salt
1 cup/225 g butter
1 large egg
1¼ cups/300 ml milk
1 tsp vanilla extract

Oven Temp: 350°F/175°C
Yield: 12 muffins

SUBSTITUTING WITH BUTTERMILK

The fermentation in Buttermilk/Lait Battu helps the batter rise higher and makes the finished product fluffier and more flavorful. Buttermilk may be substituted for the liquid in your favorite recipe provided baking powder is used for the leavening. You will need to adjust the recipe, however, adding baking soda to neutralize the acid in the buttermilk.

For every ½ cup/120 ml of buttermilk used, add ¼ teaspoon of baking soda and eliminate 1 teaspoon of the baking powder. If in doubt, it is better to use a bit too little rather than a bit too much baking soda. Mix the baking soda with the dry ingredients before adding the liquid.

Bran Muffins

3 cups/700 ml All-Bran cereal
1½ cups/350 ml boiling water
2 large eggs, slightly beaten
⅔ cup/160 ml buttermilk (see index)
⅓ cup/80 ml vegetable oil
⅓ cup/80 ml dark molasses
¼ cup/60 ml honey
1⅓ cups/175 ml whole-wheat flour
2½ tsp baking soda
1 cup/240 ml raisins

Oven Temp: 425°F/220°C
Yield: 24 muffins

Pour boiling water over cereal. Stir well and let cool. Add eggs, buttermilk, oil, molasses and honey to the cooled cereal and mix well. Combine flour and baking soda and add, mixing just until dry ingredients are combined with the wet ingredients. Stir in raisins.

Grease muffin tins and fill two-thirds full with batter. Bake in a preheated oven for 12 to 15 minutes or until the muffins pull away from the sides of the pans. Turn out onto a rack. Serve warm with butter and jam.

For tender, light muffins, mix the batter just until the dry ingredients are moistened. Over mixing makes the batter tough and the muffins chewy and heavy. For crustier muffins, preheat the oven 50°F/25°C higher than called for. As soon as the muffins are in the oven, lower the temperature to what is stated in the recipe.

Popovers

2 large eggs
1 cup/130 g flour
½ tsp salt
1 cup/240 ml milk
1 tbsp/15 g melted butter

Oven Temp: 400°F/200°C
350°F/175°C
Yield: 10

A crackling fire and the smell of freshly baked popovers - the perfect antidote to a rainy Belgian day.

Beat eggs slightly. Sift together flour and salt and add to eggs, alternating with milk. Add butter and beat the batter with an egg beater until smooth and full of bubbles. Grease 10 muffin tins and heat in the oven until very hot. Fill the hot muffin tins one-half full of batter. Bake in a preheated 400°F/200°C oven for 20 minutes. Lower heat to 350°F/175°C and bake 10 minutes more, or until brown and puffed.

Chocolate Muffins

Melt the chocolate and butter together in a small pan over low heat. Set aside to cool.

5 oz/140 g semi-sweet chocolate
½ cup/115 g butter
2 cups/260 g flour
1 tsp baking powder
½ tsp baking soda
1 tsp salt
½ cup/100 g granulated sugar
2 eggs, slightly beaten
1 cup/240 ml milk
1 tsp vanilla extract
½ cup/120 ml chocolate pieces (optional)

Oven Temp: 350°F/175°C
Yield: 12 large muffins

Stir together the flour, baking powder, baking soda and salt. Combine the sugar, eggs, milk and vanilla in a large mixing bowl, beating well until blended. Add the dry ingredients and the chocolate mixture and beat until the batter is smooth. (Stir in the chocolate pieces.)

Spoon batter into greased or paper-lined muffin cups and bake in a preheated oven for 35 minutes or until a toothpick comes out clean. Serve slightly warm.

In Belgium, baked goods are an integral part of Sunday morning. People queue outside their favorite Pâtisserie/Boulangerie for traditional Belgian favorites. Crusty baguettes, earthy grain breads, buttery croissants, glistening fruit tarts, and delicate cookies are purchased for the eager family members waiting at home.

Crusty Yeast Rolls

Soften yeast in warm water with a pinch of the sugar and set aside to proof.

1 pkg active dry yeast
¼ cup/60 ml warm water
¾ cup/175 ml boiling water
1 tbsp granulated sugar
2 tbsp/30 g butter
1½ tsp salt
3 cups/400 g (or more) flour*
2 large egg whites, slightly beaten

Oven Temp: 450°F/230°C
Yield: 18 rolls

Combine boiling water, remaining sugar, butter and salt. Stir until butter melts and cools to lukewarm. Add 1 cup/130 grams flour and beat well. Stir in the egg whites and the yeast mixture. Add enough flour to make a soft dough. Knead with a bread hook on an electric mixer or turn out onto a lightly floured surface and knead by hand, adding flour as needed, until dough is no longer sticky. Knead for 10 minutes or until smooth and elastic. Place in a lightly greased bowl, turn once to grease the surface, cover, and let rise until dough doubles in bulk, about 1 hour.

Punch dough down, cover and let rest 10 minutes. Shape into 18 round rolls. Place about 2"/5cm apart on a greased baking sheet. Cover and let rise until double, about 45 minutes. Place a large shallow pan on the bottom oven rack and fill with boiling water. Bake rolls, on the rack above, in a preheated hot oven for 10 to 12 minutes.

*The amount of flour you need will depend on what kind you use. Yeast doughs absorb a greater quantity of all-purpose flour than bread flour.

When baking yeast breads, butter makes a richer, tastier roll. You may use vegetable shortening if you prefer a fluffier product.

PROOFING YEAST

Yeast is a live organism which must be fresh to be effective. To be certain that dry yeast is active, it must be proofed. Sprinkle one package of dry yeast over ¼ cup/60 ml of warm water (from the recipe). The water must be around 110°F/43°C to activate, but not kill, the yeast. Add a pinch of sugar to encourage the yeast, but do not add any salt or too much sugar or the yeast will be inhibited. If the yeast is active, it will begin to foam and increase in size within a few minutes. The yeast may then be incorporated into the other ingredients. If using fresh compressed yeast, you may test the freshness by creaming a small amount with an equal amount of sugar. It should become liquid at once.

Bread and Brunch

Baking Powder Biscuits

*P*erfect with BEEF BURGUNDY or baked country ham - they're even great for breakfast!

2 cups/260 g all-purpose flour
4 tsp baking powder
½ tsp salt
½ tsp cream of tartar
2 tsp granulated sugar
½ cup/115 g butter
⅔ cup/160 g milk

Oven Temp: 425°F/220°C
Yield: 12

Combine all the dry ingredients. Cut in the butter until the mixture resembles coarse crumbs. Add the milk all at once. Stir until the dough clings together.

Turn out onto a lightly floured surface. Knead gently for 30 seconds. (The less you handle the dough, the more tender the biscuits.) Pat or roll to ½"/1¼cm thick. Cut into biscuits with a 2½"/6¼cm round cutter.

Bake on an ungreased cookie sheet in a preheated oven, 10 to 12 minutes.

Variations: Roll out into a ¼"/½cm thick rectangle and spread with one of the following fillings: For CINNAMON PINWHEEL BISCUITS, cream 4 tablespoons/55 grams butter with ⅓ cup/70 grams brown sugar and ⅓ cup/65 grams granulated sugar. Add 2 tablespoons all-purpose flour and 1½ teaspoons cinnamon. (If you desire, add ½ cup/120 ml chopped nuts.) Spread the mixture on the dough and roll up into a cylinder. Cut into ¾"/2cm thick slices. Place close together in a baking pan, cut side down. Brush with melted butter, sprinkle with more nuts, if desired, and bake. Cool and drizzle with a simple icing of confectioners' sugar, milk and a drop or two of vanilla extract. For CHEESE PINWHEEL BISCUITS, sprinkle the dough with 4 oz/115 g grated cheese (cheddar or Parmesan). Roll and cut as above. For ORANGE MARMALADE PINWHEEL BISCUITS, spread the dough with orange marmalade. Roll and cut as above.

> "Cooking is…intuitive, and recipes are only blueprints."
> André Guillot

Sticky Buns

To make the glaze, beat the softened butter, brown sugar, and corn syrup together until thoroughly combined. Butter the bottoms of 3 (8"/20cm) round cake or pie pans. Pour the glaze into the pans and spread evenly. Set aside.

Caramel Glaze:
¾ cup/170 g butter, softened
1½ cups/325 g brown sugar
3 tbsp dark corn syrup

Dough and Filling:
1 recipe SWEET ROLL DOUGH
6 tbsp/85 g butter, melted
1 cup/215 g brown sugar
½ cup/120 ml chopped nuts
½ cup/120 ml raisins or dried currants

Oven Temp: 375°F/190°C
Yield: 24

After the dough has risen once, roll it on a floured surface to form a rectangle about 12"x32"/30 x 81cm and ⅓"/¾cm thick. Brush the surface with melted butter. Combine brown sugar, nuts and raisins. Sprinkle evenly over the buttered dough, and press in gently with your fingers. Beginning with a long end, roll the dough up like a jelly roll. Cut into 24 slices about 1¼"/3cm thick.

Place 8 pieces, cut side down, in each of the prepared pans, putting 7 around the edge and 1 in the middle. Press them down gently so they just touch. Cover and let rise until puffy and doubled in bulk.

Place pans of rolls on cookie sheets or foil to catch any drips. Bake in a preheated oven for about 25 minutes, or until golden brown on top. Remove from the oven and let cool in the pans for 5 minutes so the glaze will set, then invert onto serving boards or platters. (Some of the glaze will dribble over the sides.) Serve warm.

Variation: For CINNAMON STICKY BUNS, omit the Caramel Glaze and add 1 tbsp cinnamon to the filling. Arrange filled slices in buttered cake pans.

Sweet Roll Dough

2 pkgs dry yeast
¼ cup/60 ml warm water
1 cup/240 ml milk, warmed
½ cup/100 g granulated sugar
2 tsp salt
½ cup/115 g butter, softened
3 large eggs, room temperature
5 cups/650 g (or more) all-purpose flour

Sprinkle the yeast over the warm water in a small bowl; stir and let stand for 5 minutes to proof (see index). Combine the milk, sugar, salt, butter and eggs in a large mixing bowl, and beat well. Stir in the dissolved yeast. Add 2½ cups/325 grams of the flour and beat until smooth. Add 2½ cups/325 grams more flour and beat until the dough holds together. Turn out onto a floured board and knead until smooth and elastic, adding only as much flour as needed to keep the dough from sticking. Place dough in a large, greased bowl and turn so the greased side is up. Cover and let rise in a warm place until doubled in bulk, about 1½ hours. Punch down and shape as desired. (See STICKY BUNS for baking instructions.)

English Cream Scones

2 cups/260 g flour
2 tsp baking powder
2 tsp granulated sugar
½ tsp salt
4 tbsp/55 g butter
2 large eggs
½ cup/120 ml heavy cream

Oven Temp: 450°F/230°C
Yield: 8 - 10 scones

On a sunny afternoon, Belgians love to sit outside a favorite pâtisserie shop or local café for a good strong cup of coffee and a special pastry.

Sift flour, baking powder, sugar and salt into a mixing bowl. Using a fork or pastry blender, cut in the butter. Break the eggs into another bowl, reserving a small amount of the egg white for the topping. Beat the eggs until light and add to the flour mixture along with the cream. Add a little more cream, if needed, to make the dough just firm enough to handle, but still soft.

Turn out onto a floured board and knead for 30 seconds. Pat and roll out the dough ¾"/2cm thick. Cut into scones using a 3"/7½cm round cookie cutter. Brush with the reserved egg white diluted with a small amount of water. Sprinkle with granulated white or brown sugar. Place on a baking sheet and bake in a preheated oven for 15 to 20 minutes.

Variation: Add 1 medium cooking apple (peeled, cored and finely chopped) to the dough. Roll and cut as above. Brush tops with milk and sprinkle with light brown sugar.

Texas Corn Bread

This very dense, moist corn bread is wonderful for a hearty breakfast or with your favorite Southwestern cuisine.

1 cup/240 ml yellow cornmeal
½ cup/65 g flour
1 tsp salt
1 cup/240 ml buttermilk
½ cup/120 ml milk
1 large egg
1 tbsp baking powder
½ tsp baking soda
¼ cup/60 ml melted shortening

Oven Temp: 450°F/230°C
Yield: 8 servings

Grease an iron skillet, muffin tins or cornstick pans and heat in a preheated oven.

Mix the cornmeal, flour and salt. Add the remaining ingredients and stir well. Pour the mixture into hot pan(s). Bake until done (approximately 20 minutes for an iron skillet). The bread will be moist and browned on the bottom.

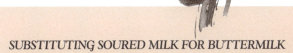

SUBSTITUTING SOURED MILK FOR BUTTERMILK
To make soured milk as a substitute for buttermilk, put 1 tablespoon lemon juice or distilled white vinegar in a measuring cup. Fill the cup with room temperature milk to the 1 cup/240 ml line. Stir and let stand 5 minutes to thicken. Although soured milk is a perfectly acceptable replacement, it does not have the thickness or full rich tanginess of buttermilk.

Sally Lunn

To retain its shape, this delicate loaf, when fresh, should be torn apart with forks rather than cut. After cooling, it may be sliced and toasted.

1 pkg active dry yeast
⅓ cup/65 g granulated sugar
½ cup/120 ml warm water*
½ cup/120 ml lukewarm milk
½ cup/115 g butter, diced
1 tsp salt
3 large eggs, lightly beaten
3½ cups/450 g (or more) flour

Oven Temp: 375°F/190°C
Yield: 1 loaf

Combine the yeast, sugar and warm water in a large mixing bowl and allow to proof (see index).

Heat milk to warm. Add butter and salt and stir until the butter melts. Add to the yeast mixture. Add the eggs and stir in well with a wooden spoon. Add the flour in small amounts, beating well with a wooden spoon after each addition. Make a stiff but workable batter using more flour if necessary. Cover the bowl and let the batter rise slowly in a rather cool spot until doubled in bulk. Beat the batter down with a wooden spoon. Scrape into a well-buttered tube pan and let the batter rise, this time to the top of the pan.

Bake in a preheated oven for 45 to 50 minutes or until the bread is dark and golden on top and sounds hollow when rapped with your knuckles. Turn out onto a rack. Serve warm with sweet butter.

*110°F/43°C

> *Go eat your bread with enjoyment,
> and drink your wine with a merry heart.*
> Ecclesiastes 9:7

Pecan and Almond Coffee Cake

Cream together butter and 1½ cups/300 grams of the sugar. Add the eggs, blending well. Then add the yogurt and vanilla. Sift together the flour, baking powder and salt. Fold dry ingredients into creamed mixture and beat until just blended.

In a separate bowl, mix remaining sugar with nuts and cinnamon. Pour half the batter into a buttered and floured 10"/24cm bundt pan. Sprinkle with half the nut mixture, add remaining batter and top with remaining nut mixture. Press nuts into the batter so they do not fall off after baking. Bake in a preheated oven for 60 minutes or until a cake tester comes out clean. Serve warm.

1 cup/225 g unsalted butter, softened
2 cups/400 g ultrafine sugar
2 large eggs, beaten
2 cups/475 ml plain yogurt
1 tbsp vanilla extract
2 cups/260 g all-purpose flour
1 tbsp baking powder
¼ tsp salt
1 cup/240 ml chopped almonds
1 cup/240 ml chopped pecans
1 tbsp cinnamon

Oven Temp: 350°F/175°C
Yield: 10 servings

" A pâtissier sells a little happiness... "
Albert and Michel Roux

Overnight Crunch Coffee Cake

Since this delicious coffee cake is prepared the night before, it is a perfect breakfast treat when you have houseguests.

2 cups/230 g sifted flour
1 tsp baking powder
1 tsp baking soda
1 tsp cinnamon
½ tsp salt
⅔ cup/150 g butter
1 cup/200 g granulated sugar
½ cup/110 g packed brown sugar
2 large eggs
1 cup/240 ml buttermilk (see index)

Topping:
½ cup/110 g packed brown sugar
½ cup/120 ml chopped nuts
½ tsp cinnamon
¼ tsp nutmeg

Oven Temp: 350°F/175°C
Yield: 16 servings

In a medium bowl, stir together flour, baking powder, baking soda, cinnamon and salt. Cream together butter and sugars until light and fluffy. Add eggs, one at a time, beating well after each. Add dry ingredients, alternating with buttermilk, beating well after each addition.

Spread batter into a greased and floured 9"x13"/24 x 34cm baking pan. Combine all topping ingredients and mix well. Sprinkle over batter.

Cover and refrigerate 8 hours or overnight. Bake in a preheated oven for 45 minutes or until it tests done. Cut into squares and serve warm.

Neighborhood Coffee

Overnight Crunch Coffee Cake
∞
Lemon Blueberry Bread
∞
*Bran Muffins
(Cream Cheese)*
∞
(Fresh Fruit Salad)
∞
*Coffee and Tea
Orange Juice*

Raspberry Cream Cheese Coffee Cake

2¼ cups/300 g flour
1 cup/200 g granulated sugar
¾ cup/170 g butter
½ tsp baking powder
½ tsp baking soda
¼ tsp salt
¾ cup/175 ml sour cream
1 tsp almond extract
2 large eggs
8 oz/225 g cream cheese, softened
½ cup/120 ml raspberry preserves
½ cup/120 ml sliced almonds

Oven Temp: 350°F/175°C
Yield: 16 - 20 servings

In a large bowl, combine flour and ¾ cup/150 grams of the sugar. Using a pastry blender or fork, cut in the butter until the mixture resembles coarse crumbs. Reserve 1 cup/240 ml of the crumb mixture. To the remaining mixture, add baking powder, baking soda, salt, sour cream, almond extract and 1 egg, blending well. Spread over the bottom and 2"/5cm up the sides of a greased and floured 9" or 10"/24cm springform pan.

In a small bowl, combine cream cheese, ¼ cup/50 grams of sugar and the remaining egg, blending well. Pour evenly into the pastry-lined pan. Carefully spoon preserves over cream cheese mixture. Combine reserved crumb mixture with sliced almonds and sprinkle over preserves.

> **Several times every day, food offers each of us the promise of short-term happiness.**
> Patricia Wells

Bake in a preheated oven for 45 to 55 minutes or until the cream cheese filling is set and the crust is a deep golden brown. Cool for 15 minutes. Remove sides of pan, cut the coffee cake into wedges and serve barely warm. Leftover coffee cake must be refrigerated.

Cinnamon Apple Cake

Lightly grease the bottom and sides of an 8"/20cm round cake pan. Line the bottom with baking paper and grease again.

2 cups/260 g self-rising flour
½ tsp ground cloves
1 tsp ground cinnamon
½ cup/115 g butter, diced
¾ cup/150 g fine granulated sugar
1 lb/450 g tart cooking apples
2 large eggs, beaten

Garnish:
granulated sugar
whipped cream

Oven Temp: 325°F/165°C
Yield: 8 servings

Sift the flour, cloves and cinnamon into a mixing bowl. Gently rub the butter into the flour mixture with your fingers until the mixture resembles fine bread crumbs. Stir in the sugar. Peel, core and chop the apples and add to the mixture along with the beaten eggs. Mix together with a wooden spoon, beating until soft and smooth.

> There is something very elemental and satisfying about our relationship with food.
> Raymond Blanc

Pour the mixture into the pan and smooth the top. Bake for 1 to 1¼ hours, or until the cake springs back when it is gently pressed in the center. Remove from the oven and cool the cake in the pan for 5 minutes. Turn the cake onto a wire rack. Sprinkle the top with granulated sugar. Serve fresh and warm with unsweetened whipped cream.

254   Bread and Brunch

Red Currant Jelly

4½ lb/2 kg fresh red currants
2⅕ lb/1 kg ultrafine sugar*
paraffin wax

Yield: 1 quart/liter of jelly

Wash the currants. (You may leave them on the stems.) In a big pot, heat the berries over low heat until they start to give off their juice. Then raise the heat to moderate and cook until the berries are soft and have lost their color. Strain through cheesecloth. Do not squeeze. This should give you approximately 4 cups/1 kilo of juice. (If you have more juice, keep it for a second batch.)

Before cooking the jelly, fill jelly glasses three-fourths full with water and place well apart in a kettle partially filled with water. Simmer 15 to 20 minutes and keep hot.

Carefully measure 4 cups/1 kilo juice back into a clean pot and bring it to a boil. After 4 to 5 minutes, remove the pot from the heat. Add the same amount of sugar as juice, little by little, to the pan, stirring constantly. Be sure all the sugar dissolves. Put back on the heat and boil to 220°F/104°C (or slightly over the boiling point of water depending on where you live.) When ready, the slightly cooled jelly should "sheet" off a spoon (or place a little on a saucer and refrigerate a minute or two. The jelly should "wrinkle" when pushed with a finger.) Remove from heat.

When ready to use, remove the jars from the water, empty them and place upright on a rack. Pour the hot jelly into the jars while they are still hot, but dry. (If you use tongs and a funnel, be sure they are sterilized too.) Fill to ½"/1¼cm of the top. Wipe any drips clean and cover with melted wax.

Let jars stand until completely cool, then label, date and cover with pretty squares of fabric, secured with ribbon or a rubber band. Store in a cool, dark, dry place.

It is best to make batches no larger than this. If you have extra juice, make a small batch with the same proportion of sugar. Melt the wax over hot water just until liquid. (If it is too hot, it tends to pull away from the sides of the jar.) The jars and the paraffin wax can be recycled each year.

> **Mountains and fountains
> Rain down on me
> Buried in berries
> What a jam jamboree!**
> Bruce Degen

* This is an approximate measurement since the sugar is proportionate to the quantity of juice.

Apple Compote

An old-fashioned side dish to complement a rich pork roast, or serve with BREAKFAST PANCAKES or RAISED WAFFLES.

6 Granny Smith apples
¼ cup/60 ml water
1 tbsp lemon juice
¼ tsp cinnamon
¾ cup/165 g brown sugar
¼ tsp salt
¼ cup/35 g flour
4 tbsp/55 g butter

Oven Temp: 350°F/175°C
Yield: 4 servings

Peel and core apples. Slice each apple into 12 pieces. Toss apples with water and lemon juice and put in a lightly greased baking dish. Mix together cinnamon, brown sugar, salt and flour. Sprinkle mixture over apples and dot with pieces of butter. Bake in a preheated oven for 40 minutes.

FRESH CURRANTS

Tiny, fresh currants come with red, black or white berries and appear all over Belgium in mid-summer. These beautiful, translucent berries make a lovely garnish on dessert and game dishes, but they are probably most prized for making jelly. Because of their high pectin content, currants are the perfect choice to combine with low pectin fruits such as strawberries or raspberries. If used alone to make pure RED CURRANT JELLY, the bright red color and sweet/tart flavor of the jelly make it a favorite to brush on fresh fruit tarts for a rosy, glistening glaze. A spoonful served along side or added to rich game sauces provides a complementary touch.

To freeze currants for use as a garnish in the winter, place stems with berries attached flat on a cookie sheet. Freeze until solid and then pack in plastic bags. Use frozen since they become mushy after defrosting.

Sticky Toffee Puddings with Pecan Toffee Sauce

If the meal isn't complete without something sweet, serve this at your next brunch.

Puddings:
- ¾ cup/175 ml boiling water
- 1 cup/240 ml chopped dates
- ½ tsp vanilla extract
- 2 tsp very strong coffee
- ¾ tsp baking soda
- 6 tbsp/85 g butter, softened
- ⅔ cup/130 g granulated sugar
- 2 large eggs, beaten
- 1¼ cups/165 g self-rising flour

Pecan Toffee Sauce:
- ¾ cup/165 g soft brown sugar
- ½ cup/115 g butter
- 6 tbsp heavy cream
- ⅓ cup/80 ml chopped pecans

additional heavy cream

Oven Temp: 350°F/175°C
Yield: 8 - 12 servings

Pour boiling water over the dates. Add vanilla, coffee and baking soda and set aside.

With an electric mixer, cream the butter and sugar until the mixture is pale and fluffy. Gradually add the beaten eggs, a little at a time, beating well after each addition. Carefully fold in the flour and then the date mixture, including the liquid. (The mixture will look quite wet and loose.)

Thoroughly butter 12 muffin tins or 8 pudding molds. Divide the mixture equally among the tins or molds and bake in the center of a preheated oven for 25 minutes. Remove from the oven and let cool for 5 minutes. Then run a knife around the sides and lift the puddings out.

To make the sauce, combine all the ingredients in a saucepan and heat very gently until the sugar has melted and all the crystals have dissolved.

Before serving, preheat the broiler. Place the puddings on a foil-lined cookie sheet and pour the sauce on top. Place the pan under the broiler so the tops of the puddings are about 5"/13cm from the heat. Let them heat through for about 5 to 8 minutes, or until bubbly and browned. Serve with chilled unsweetened cream.

> "Whenever I think of Brueghel...
> I see his roly-poly peasants
> dipping their plump fingers into bowls..."
> Lynn Rossetto Kasper

Crêpes

The perfect versatile basic crêpe! Sprinkle warm crêpes with sugar and cinnamon for a quick breakfast or stuff with savory fillings for brunch.

1 cup/130 g all-purpose flour
½ tbsp granulated sugar
¼ tsp salt
1 cup/240 ml milk
⅓ cup/80 ml water
3 large eggs
3 tbsp/45 g unsalted butter, melted

Yield: 16 - 18 crêpes

Combine the flour, sugar, and salt in a food processor and process briefly. With the motor running, add the milk, water, eggs and butter. Process until smooth. (A blender or a mixer may also be used.)

Heat a heavy 7"/18cm nonstick skillet until quite hot. Pour in 3 tablespoons of batter, then quickly pick the pan off the heat and tilt it so the batter spreads evenly, forming a crêpe.

Cook until the crêpe is set and the edges begin to curl, about 30 to 45 seconds. Flip it over and cook 15 seconds longer. (One side will appear to have much better color than the other.)

Let the batter sit for about ½ hour before making the crêpes. This resting time will allow the flour molecules time to swell, giving the finished crêpes a better consistency.

Repeat until all the batter is used. As you finish the crêpes, stack them between sheets of wax paper or plastic wrap to prevent them from sticking together. (Crêpes will keep in a plastic bag in the refrigerator for 2 days.)

Variations: Increase the sugar for dessert recipes. For savory fillings, eliminate the sugar and/or add herbs to the crêpe recipe. Top filled savory crêpes with BÉCHAMEL SAUCE and a sprinkling of grated cheese. Lightly broil before serving.

> **Master the basics - be patient and learn them all.**
> André Soltner

Breakfast Pancakes

For a quick and easy Sunday breakfast, make the batter the night before. It's even better after a night in the refrigerator!

¾ cup/175 ml milk, room temperature
2 tbsp/30 g butter, melted
1 large egg
1 tsp vanilla extract
1 cup + 1 tbsp/140 g flour
2 tsp baking powder
2 tbsp granulated sugar
½ tsp salt

Yield: 12 - 16 pancakes

Lightly beat the milk, butter, egg and vanilla in a mixing bowl. In another bowl, mix together the flour, baking powder, sugar and salt. Add the dry ingredients to the liquid mixture and stir just enough to moisten the flour.

Butter a griddle or frying pan and place over moderately high heat. When the surface is hot, spoon batter on the griddle. Allow the pancakes to cook until the top is covered with bubbles and the bottom is lightly browned. (If the bottom becomes too dark before the top is full of bubbles, turn down the heat.) Turn the pancakes with a spatula and brown the other side.

Keep the pancakes warm in the oven until ready to serve.

Variations: For BLUEBERRY PANCAKES, add ½ cup/120 ml of fresh blueberries. Reduce or eliminate the vanilla extract. For APPLE PANCAKES, add 1 peeled and diced tart apple. Reduce or eliminate the vanilla extract. For CINNAMON PANCAKES, substitute ½ tsp of cinnamon for the vanilla extract. For WHOLE-WHEAT PANCAKES, use one-third whole-wheat flour and two-thirds all-purpose flour. Sweeten the pancakes with 2 tablespoons of molasses or honey, instead of the sugar. For BUTTERMILK PANCAKES, use buttermilk, soured milk or yogurt instead of milk, and substitute ½ teaspoon of baking soda for the 2 teaspoons of baking powder.

Bread and Brunch

Cornmeal Pancakes

An alternative to the standard pancake, these are fluffy on the inside and crunchy on the outside.

½ cup/120 ml yellow cornmeal
½ cup/120 ml boiling water
½ cup/65 g all-purpose flour
½ tsp salt
1 tbsp granulated sugar
1 tbsp baking powder
1 egg, beaten
4 tbsp/55 g butter, melted
⅓ cup/80 ml milk

Yield: 24 (3"/5cm) pancakes

Put the cornmeal in a mixing bowl and pour in the boiling water, stirring briskly until well blended. Add the flour, salt, sugar, baking powder, egg, butter and milk. Beat the batter until it is thoroughly mixed.

Heat a griddle over moderately high heat. (Do not cook these pancakes over as high a heat as you would normally use for pancakes.) Grease the griddle when it is hot. Using 2 tablespoons of batter for each pancake, spoon the batter onto the griddle and cook the pancakes until bubbles break on top. Turn them over and cook another few minutes, or until the bottoms of the pancakes are lightly browned and set. Serve hot.

Raised Waffles

Make the batter the night before - your family will awaken to the aroma of fresh waffles.

½ cup/120 ml warm water
1 pkg dry yeast
2 cups/475 ml milk, warmed
½ cup/115 g butter, melted
1 tsp salt
1 tsp granulated sugar
2 cups/260 g all-purpose flour
2 large eggs
¼ tsp baking soda

Yield: 8 waffles

Put water in a large mixing bowl and sprinkle with the yeast. Let stand for 5 minutes to proof (see index).

Add milk, butter, salt, sugar, and flour to the yeast mixture and beat until smooth and blended. Cover the bowl with plastic wrap and let stand overnight at room temperature. (The batter will rise to double its original volume.)

Just before cooking the waffles, beat in the eggs, add the baking soda, and stir until well mixed. (The batter will be very thin.) Pour about ½ cup/120 ml of batter per waffle into a very hot waffle iron. Bake the waffles until they are crisp and golden.

If you have any waffles left over, wrap them tightly and refrigerate. Pop them into the toaster the next morning for a quick breakfast.

Shirred Eggs

An easy egg dish to serve to a crowd - and elegant too!

8 tbsp heavy cream
4 tsp/20 g butter
8 eggs
salt
freshly ground pepper

Oven Temp: 350°F/175°C
Yield: 4 servings

Into each of 4 shirred egg dishes (shallow individual oven-proof casseroles) place 2 tablespoons of heavy cream and 1 teaspoon of butter. Place in a preheated oven until the butter is melted and the cream is hot.

Remove the dishes from the oven and break 2 eggs into each dish. Season with salt and pepper to taste. Return to the oven and bake for 10 minutes or until the whites are set.

Place the hot dishes on individual plates and serve immediately.

Variation: After heating the cream, place a thin slice of ham and/or Swiss cheese on the bottom of the baking dish. Carefully break the eggs on top and sprinkle with a little grated Swiss cheese or Parmesan cheese. Bake as above.

Cheese Soufflé

4 tbsp/55 g butter
4 tbsp flour
1 cup/240 ml milk
1 tsp Dijon mustard
4 eggs, separated
1 egg white
¼ tsp white pepper
pinch of cayenne pepper
cream of tartar
1 cup/240 ml freshly grated Parmesan
1 cup/240 ml grated Gruyère cheese

Oven Temp: 400°F/200°C
Yield: 4 - 6 servings

Melt the butter in a large saucepan and stir in the flour. Cook for a minute without letting it brown. Gradually add the milk and cook, stirring, until sauce is smooth and very thick. Remove from the heat and stir in the mustard. In a separate bowl, lightly beat the egg yolks with a fork. Add a spoonful of the hot sauce to the yolks and stir. Pour the yolks back into the sauce, stirring vigorously, until well combined. Season with white pepper and cayenne pepper.

Beat the 5 egg whites with a pinch of cream of tartar until stiff peaks just begin to form. Do not overbeat. Fold the cheeses into the sauce along with a large spoonful of the beaten whites. Gently fold in the remaining whites.

Butter a 7"/18cm round soufflé dish and sprinkle it with additional grated Parmesan. Wrap a buttered strip of foil around the soufflé dish and fasten it with a straight pin to form a collar. Gently spoon in the soufflé mixture. Bake in a preheated oven for 30 minutes, or until the soufflé has risen and is golden on top. Serve immediately.

Variations: Try experimenting with other types of cheese, such as chèvre or cheddar, or with a combination of cheeses. Fold in crisp, crumbled bacon and spoon the soufflé mixture over poached eggs or creamed spinach.

You may safely prepare a soufflé an hour or two in advance. After filling the soufflé dish, cover with plastic wrap and put out of the way, in a draft-free place, until ready to bake.

Sausage and Cheese Strata

Wonderful for those hungry brunch guests and easy for the hostess since it is prepared the night before. Omit the sausage for a lighter vegetarian version.

½ lb/225 g sausage meat (see note)
8 slices firm white bread
½ lb/225 g cheddar cheese, grated
½ lb/225 g Emmentaler cheese, grated
4 large eggs, lightly beaten
1½ cups/350 ml milk
½ tsp salt
1 tsp Dijon mustard
pinch of cayenne pepper
½ tsp Worcestershire sauce
3 tbsp/45 g unsalted butter, melted and cooled

Oven Temp: 350°F/175°C
Yield: 4 servings

In a skillet, brown the sausage over moderately high heat, breaking it up with a fork as it cooks. With a slotted spoon, transfer the sausage to a paper towel to drain.

Brush a 1 quart/liter soufflé dish with some of the fat remaining in the skillet. Remove crusts from bread and cut into ½"/1¼cm cubes. Combine the two cheeses. Arrange one-third of the bread cubes in the bottom of the dish, and sprinkle with one-third of the cheese. Top the cheese with all the sausage, then half the remaining bread and half the remaining cheese. Top the strata with the remaining bread and gently press the layers together.

In a bowl, whisk together the eggs, milk, salt, mustard, cayenne and Worcestershire. Pour the mixture over the strata and sprinkle the top with the remaining cheese. Drizzle with melted butter and chill, covered, for at least 1 hour or overnight.

Remove the strata from the refrigerator and let stand at room temperature for 45 minutes. Place the soufflé dish in a bain marie (see index) and bake in a preheated oven for 1 hour, or until puffed and golden brown.

For homemade COUNTRY SAUSAGE, mix together 1½ lb/680 grams finely ground pork (or pork and veal) with the following seasonings: ½ teaspoon each thyme, pepper and marjoram; 1 teaspoon salt; 1 tablespoon minced parsley; 2 tablespoons minced onion. Optional seasonings are ¼ teaspoon each powdered bay leaf and/or sage, minced garlic and hot red pepper flakes. To make sausage patties, add 1 egg and 3 tablespoons of fresh or dried bread crumbs to the mixture. Form into patties and pan-fry until browned and cooked through.

Curried Chicken Cheesecake

Sinfully rich - an unusual main dish cheesecake.

Combine cracker crumbs and butter; press on bottom and 1"/2½cm up the sides of a 9"/24cm springform pan.

With a mixer, beat cream cheese at high speed until light and fluffy. Add eggs, one at a time, beating well after each addition. Add bouillon, sour cream, onion, celery, flour and salt. Beat at low speed until well blended. Stir in chicken, almonds and raisins.

Pour mixture into prepared pan. Bake in a preheated oven for 45 minutes or until set. Turn off oven, partially prop open the oven door and let the cheesecake remain in the oven for 1 hour. Remove cheesecake from oven and let cool completely on a wire rack. Cover and chill.

Combine all sauce ingredients, stirring well. Cover and chill.

When ready to serve, unmold onto a platter lined with lettuce. Garnish with condiments and serve with the sauce.

1½ cups/350 ml buttery cracker crumbs
¼ cup/60 ml melted butter
1 lb, 10 oz/720 g cream cheese
3 eggs
½ cup/120 ml bouillon
8 oz/225 g sour cream
3 tbsp grated onion
3 tbsp minced celery
1 tbsp flour
¼ tsp salt
1½ cups/350 ml chopped cooked chicken
¼ cup/60 ml chopped almonds, toasted
⅓ cup/80 ml raisins

Curried Sour Cream Sauce:
8 oz/225 g sour cream
1½ tsp curry powder
⅛ tsp ground ginger

Condiments:
flaked coconut
chutney
chopped green or red bell pepper
toasted almonds
raisins
crisp bacon

Oven Temp: 300°F/150°C
Yield: 8 - 10 servings

Bread and Brunch

Hot Spinach Cheesecake

Similar to a quiche, this recipe is perfect for brunch.

4 tbsp/55 g butter
1 cup/240 ml crushed cheese crackers
1 lb/450 g frozen chopped spinach
3 bacon slices, chopped
1 medium onion, chopped
6 tbsp grated Parmesan cheese
9 oz/250 g cream cheese
4½ oz/125 g feta cheese
1¼ oz/300 ml sour cream
4 eggs, lightly beaten

Oven Temp: 325°F/165°C
Yield: 8 - 10 servings

Melt the butter in a saucepan, add cracker crumbs and press the mixture evenly over the base of a 8"/20 cm springform pan. Refrigerate 30 minutes.

Defrost the spinach and drain, pressing out excess liquid. Fry the bacon and onion, stirring frequently, until the onion is soft. Beat 4 tablespoons Parmesan cheese, cream cheese and feta cheese together until smooth. Add sour cream and eggs and beat until combined. Stir in the spinach and bacon mixture.

Pour the filling over the crumb base and bake in a preheated oven for 1¼ hours or until golden brown and set. Sprinkle with remaining 2 tablespoons of Parmesan and allow to stand for 10 minutes before cutting.

Biscotti crushed in a food processor, make a very tasty crumb base.

Vegetable Frittata

3 medium summer squash*
3 medium zucchini
1 red bell pepper
1 yellow bell pepper
1 green bell pepper
3 tbsp olive oil
1 large Spanish onion, thinly sliced
3 garlic cloves, minced
8 oz/225 g mushrooms, sliced
6 large eggs
¼ cup/60 ml heavy cream
2 tsp salt
2 tsp freshly ground pepper
2 cups/475 ml stale French bread cubes
8 oz/225 g cream cheese, cubed
2 cups/475 ml grated Swiss cheese

Oven Temp: 350°F/175°C
Yield: 8 servings

Cut the summer squash, zucchini, and seeded bell peppers into ¼"/½cm slices.

Heat the oil in a large pot over moderately high heat. Add the onion, garlic, summer squash, zucchini, peppers and mushrooms. Sauté, stirring and tossing the vegetables occasionally, until crisply tender, drain excess liquid.

While the vegetables are cooking, whisk the eggs and cream together in a large mixing bowl. Season with salt and pepper. Stir in the bread, cream cheese and Swiss cheese.

Add the sautéed vegetables to the egg mixture and stir until well combined. Pour into a greased 10"/24cm springform pan. Place the pan on a baking sheet. Bake the frittata in a preheated oven until firm to the touch, puffed and golden brown, about 1 hour. (If the top of the frittata is getting too brown, cover with a sheet of aluminum foil.) Remove from the oven and let stand at least 10 minutes before serving (or let cool to room temperature).

* If summer squash is unavailable, increase the quantity of the other vegetables in the frittata or substitute another lightly cooked vegetable.

Tarte Provençale

10"/24cm Pâte Brisée au Fromage shell, partially baked

2 tbsp Dijon mustard
2 small eggplants, thinly sliced
2 tbsp olive oil
salt
white pepper
3 egg yolks
1½ cups/350 ml fromage blanc or sour cream
2 garlic cloves, minced
6 oz/170 g Gruyère or cheddar, grated
3 large tomatoes
½ green or red bell pepper
chopped fresh herbs*
8 pitted black olives, sliced

Oven Temp: 400°F/200°C
Yield: 6 - 8 servings

Brush Dijon mustard on the bottom of the partially baked shell and chill.

Place eggplant slices in a single layer on one or more oiled baking sheets. Brush eggplant with olive oil and season with salt and white pepper. Bake in a preheated oven for 10 minutes. Turn slices and bake 10 minutes on the other side. Drain well between two layers of paper towels.

Cut tomatoes into thick slices, remove the seeds and drain on paper towels, patting them dry.

> *So many simple ingredients can appear exotic merely by being dressed up in a pastry crust.*
> Julia Child

To make the filling, combine egg yolks, fromage blanc, garlic and Gruyère. Pour filling into the pastry shell. Arrange the tomato slices in a single layer on top of the filling; follow with a layer of eggplant. Cut bell pepper into thin slices and sprinkle over the eggplant.

Place on a baking sheet and bake in a preheated oven for 30 minutes. Sprinkle with fresh herbs and olives and bake an additional 10 minutes. Let stand 15 minutes to set before cutting. Serve warm or room temperature.

* Use rosemary, a combination of oregano and basil or other fresh herbs.

Pâte Brisée au Fromage

The perfect crust for the Tarte Provençale, but don't be afraid to try it with any other savory filling.

Crust:
1¾ cups/225 g flour
1 tsp paprika
pinch of salt
½ cup/115 g butter
2 oz/55 g Gruyère cheese, grated
6 tbsp (or more) ice water

Oven Temp: 400°F/200°C
Yield: 1 crust

Mix flour, paprika and salt in a large bowl. Cut in butter until pea-sized pieces are formed. Stir in the Gruyère and gradually add ice water, mixing with a fork, until dough can be formed into a ball.

On a well-floured surface, roll pastry to a 12"/30cm circle. Press dough into a 10"/24cm tart pan and trim excess pastry. Line the pastry with foil and fill with beans or pie weights. Bake in a preheated oven for 15 minutes. Remove weights and foil; bake 5 minutes longer for a partially baked shell and 10 to 15 minutes longer, or until light brown, for a fully baked shell.

Tomato and Onion Quiche

For the nicest presentation, bake this quiche in a tart pan with a removable bottom.

10"/24cm prebaked BASIC TART PASTRY shell

¼ cup/55 g butter
2½ tbsp olive oil
1 lb/450 g onions, thinly sliced
2 lb/900 g ripe tomatoes
2 large garlic cloves
½ bay leaf
1½ tsp herbes de Provence
3 tbsp chopped fresh parsley
salt
freshly ground pepper
2 large eggs, lightly beaten
¾ cup/175 ml heavy cream
½ cup/120 ml grated Swiss cheese

Oven Temp: 400°F/200°C
Yield: 6 servings

Heat butter and 2 tablespoons of oil in a heavy frying pan. Add the onions and cook slowly over very low heat until they are golden and tender, about 45 minutes, stirring occasionally.

Peel and seed tomatoes (see index) and chop coarsely. Heat remaining ½ tablespoon oil and add tomatoes, garlic and bay leaf. Cook slowly, stirring occasionally for 20 minutes or until liquid is gone. Remove bay leaf. Combine tomato and onion mixture, herbes de Provence and parsley. Highly season with salt and pepper before stirring in eggs and cream.

When ready to bake, fill the tart shell and sprinkle with cheese. Bake 18 minutes or until the filling is set and the top is nicely browned. Cool to lukewarm and serve.

Sunday Brunch Buffet

(Mimosas)
Petites Gougères
∞
Sausage and Cheese Strata
Tomato and Onion Quiche
Orange Avocado Salad
∞
Popovers
Red Currant Jelly
Pecan and Almond Coffee Cake
∞
Coffee

Quiche au Saumon
Vallauris - Christian Lapicoré, Chef

Crust (for 2 shells):
10½ oz/300 g flour
½ tsp salt
⅞ cup/200 g butter
1 large egg
3½ oz/100 ml milk

Filling:
14 oz/400 g Belgian endive
4 tbsp/55 g butter
14 oz/400 g smoked salmon
4 large eggs
1¼ cups/300 ml milk
1¼ cups/300 ml heavy cream
½ tsp nutmeg
salt
freshly ground pepper

Oven Temp: 350°F/175°C
400°F/200°C
Yield: 2 quiches

Put flour and salt in a bowl. Dice the butter, add to the flour and work in with fingertips until soft. Make a well in the center and add the egg. Beating with a fork, drizzle in milk, drawing in flour until a dough forms. Divide in half and press the pastry into 2 quiche pans. Line with foil, fill with beans or pie weights and bake for 15 minutes in a preheated 350°F/175°C oven. Remove weights and foil and set aside.

Chop the endives and sauté in butter until just tender. Cut the salmon into small slices. Mix together the eggs, milk, cream and nutmeg. Add salt and pepper to taste. Distribute the endives and salmon evenly into the two crusts and pour in the egg mixture.

Bake in a preheated oven for 15 minutes.

Variation: You may substitute broccoli for the Belgian endive.

Crab Quiche

To make the crust, sift flour, measure, and sift again into a bowl. Make a hole in the center and add all ingredients except the ice water. Stir with a fork to form a paste, working in the flour. Sprinkle in the ice water and toss with a fork. Press firmly and evenly on the bottom and sides of a 12"/30cm quiche pan. Bake for 5 to 8 minutes at 450°F/230°C. Cool and freeze for 1 hour or longer.

Combine all filling ingredients and pour into the prepared shell. Bake in a preheated 450°F/230°C oven for 15 minutes. Reduce heat to 300°F/150°C and bake for an additional 30 minutes. Cool for 10 minutes before serving.

Crust:
1¼ cups/145 g sifted flour
½ cup/115 g butter, softened
1 egg yolk
1 tsp salt
½ tsp dry mustard
1 tsp paprika
1 tbsp ice water

Filling:
2 cups/475 ml light cream
2 tbsp minced onion
1 (6 oz/170 g) can crab meat
1 cup/240 ml grated Swiss cheese
2 tbsp chopped fresh parsley
⅛ tsp cayenne pepper
4 eggs, beaten
½ tsp salt

Oven Temp: 450°F/230°C
300°F/150°C
Yield: 6 - 8 servings

Bread and Brunch

Basic Savory Tart Pastry

1½ cups/200 g pastry flour
½ tsp salt
1 - 2 tsp herbs (optional)
pinch of spice* (optional)
¼ cup/60 ml grated Gruyère or cheddar (optional)
½ cup/115 g unsalted butter, diced
2 - 3 tbsp (or more) ice water

Oven Temp: 375°F/190°C
Yield: 1 Crust

Combine the flour and salt in a mixing bowl. (Add herbs, spices and/or cheese.) Add butter and, using a pastry blender or your fingertips, quickly work it in until the mixture resembles coarse crumbs.

Sprinkle the ice water over the mixture, a little at a time, tossing after each addition until you can gather the dough into a ball. Flatten the dough slightly, wrap in wax paper or a plastic bag and refrigerate for 30 minutes to 1 hour. (You may freeze the dough wrapped in plastic wrap.)

To prebake a crust: Roll out chilled dough on a lightly floured surface to form a circle. Transfer the pastry to a tart pan and press into the bottom and sides. Trim the edge and line with aluminum foil, shiny side down. Fill with beans or pie weights and bake the pastry for 8 minutes. Remove the foil and beans and return the pastry to the oven. Bake until golden brown, 10 to 13 minutes. Set aside to cool.

If the filling is not runny, prick the pastry shell with a fork before lining with foil to help prevent shrinking and bubbling.

To partially bake a crust: Follow steps above through removing the beans and foil. Return it to the oven for 5 minutes more. Remove from oven and set aside until ready to be filled.

* Try paprika, chili powder, curry powder or any other spice that complements the filling.

Desserts

Desserts

Almond Macaroons	321
Apple Cranberry Crisp	296
Apple Pie	277
Apple Tart with Caramel Sauce	283
Apricot and Almond Tart	280
Apricot Soufflé	297
Bavarian Apple Tart	285
Carrot Cake	309
Cheesecake Supreme	312
Chocolate Birthday Cake	306
Chocolate Chestnut Torte	293
Chocolate Crackles	317
Chocolate Layered Torte	294
Chocolate Mousse	298
Chocolate Sauce	322
Chocolate Sheet Cake	305
Chocolate Tart Gourmandise	282
Chocolate Truffles	321
Clafoutis aux Cerises	296
Cold Lemon Soufflé	298
Cookie Crumb Crust	325
Cranberry Cake	308
Crème Brûlée	301
Crème au Café	300
Crème Caramel à la Crème de Marrons	302
Embassy Brownies	314
Galette des Rois	311
Gâteau aux Framboises	307
Gaufres Liègoises	324
Ginger and Spice Sugar Cookies	318
Hazelnut Meringue Torte	292
Molasses Spice Cookies	317
Pâte Brisée	326
Pâte Sablée	327
Pâte Sucrée	326

SPECIAL TOPICS

Apples	285
Cheese	276
Chocolate	322
Cream	303
Flour	308
Gelatin	299
Pears	281
Sugar	315

Peach Crumb Pie	278
Plum and Almond Cobbler	295
Pumpkin Pie	289
Pumpkin Tart	288
Raspberry Meringue Torte	290
Raspberry Sauce	313
Red Currant Meringue Pie	291
Reina Nobile, La	310
Sour Cream Pound Cake	304
Speculoos	319
Spitzbuben	320
Strawberry Rhubarb Pie	279
Strawberry Tart	287
Sugar Cookies	316
Summer Fruit Compote	313
Tarte Amandine aux Poires et au Chocolat	281
Tarte au Sucre	286
Tarte Tatin	284
Tiramisu	304
Ultimate Chocolate Chip Cookies	315
White Chocolate Mousse with Raspberry Grand Marnier Sauce	299

Flours vary according to type of wheat, country of origin and intended use. Please refer to specific information before preparing recipes using flour (see page 308).

CHEESE

One of the great pleasures of being in Belgium is the variety of cheese available. Your local fromagerie can help you in your cheese selection. Europeans traditionally eat cheese as a separate course preceding dessert. A typical cheese selection might include a soft cheese (Brie de Meaux or Camembert), a chèvre (Montrachet or Boucheron), a blue-veined cheese (Roquefort, Gorgonzola and Stilton are the three great ones), a semi-firm cheese (Double Gloucester, Cheshire or Aged Gouda are good choices) and a triple cream cheese (Brillat-Savarin, Explorateur, or St. André). Reblochon and Vacherin Mont d'Or* are also marvelous choices. If you enjoy experimenting with the wide variety of cheese available in Belgium, be sure you offer guests some recognizable old favorites in your selection.

Serve the cheeses on a flat tray with whole-grain crackers, water biscuits and pieces of French bread. A selection of fruits and special wines enhance the cheese course. Pears and port go particularly well with the blue cheeses. Apples and port or an old Bordeaux are wonderful with the semi-firm cheeses. Grapes and figs are the perfect match with soft cheeses and chèvre.

A lovely nutty Parmigiano-Reggiano is superb with an excellent champagne and ripe pears before sitting down for dinner.

One should consider seasonality, compatibility with the meal, and variety when selecting cheese. Always remove cheese from the refrigerator and its wrapper one hour before serving.

* Vacherin Mont d'Or is a white wine basted seasonal cheese available in late fall.

> *Comment peut-on gouverner un pays où il y a plus de quatre cent variétés de fromages?*
> Charles de Gaulle

Apple Pie

A spicier version of the traditional apple pie.

Crust:
- 2 cups/260 g unsifted flour
- 1 tsp salt
- 1 cup/190 g vegetable shortening, chilled
- ½ cup cold water

Filling:
- 3 lb/1⅓ kg Granny Smith apples
- ½ cup/100 g granulated sugar
- 2 tbsp fresh lemon juice
- 2 tbsp/30 g butter, melted
- ½ cup/110 g packed light brown sugar
- ¼ cup/30 g all-purpose flour
- 1 tsp ground cinnamon
- ½ tsp ground nutmeg
- ½ tsp grated lemon peel
- ¼ tsp ground mace
- ¼ tsp ground cloves
- ¼ tsp ground allspice

Oven Temp: 400°F/200°C
Yield: 8 - 10 servings

Crust: Put flour and salt in a mixing bowl. Add shortening and cut in with pastry cutter or fork until small lumps form. Add water all at once and mix only enough to moisten and form a ball. Place on a lightly floured surface and knead 2 or 3 times. Divide in half.

Filling: Core and peel apples and cut into ¼"/½cm thick slices. Toss the prepared apples in a large bowl with lemon juice and granulated sugar. Let sit for 20 minutes. Drain and discard the liquid from the apples. In a bowl, toss the drained apples with butter, brown sugar, flour, cinnamon, nutmeg, lemon peel, mace, cloves and allspice.

Brushing the top crust with a little cream and sprinkling it with sugar will brown it nicely.

Roll out half the pastry on a lightly floured surface to a 12"/30cm diameter round. Transfer to a 9"/24cm deep-dish pie plate. Trim dough overhang to approximately ½"/1¼cm. Mound apple mixture in crust. Roll out other half of dough to a 12"/30cm round. Place on apples. Trim dough overhang to 1"/2½cm. Fold top crust edge under bottom crust edge, pressing to seal. Crimp edge decoratively. Cut several slits in crust to allow steam to escape.

Place pie on a baking sheet in the lower third of a preheated oven. Bake until crust is golden brown and juices bubble, covering crust edges with aluminum foil if they brown too quickly, about 1 hour, 10 minutes. Transfer pie to rack and cool.

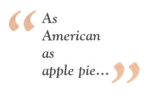

" As American as apple pie… "

Peach Crumb Pie

Crust: Mix flour and salt together. Cut in shortening until the dough resembles fresh bread crumbs. Add water, a tablespoon at a time, until dough holds together. Form a ball. Roll out on a lightly floured surface and place in a 9"/24cm pie pan.

Crumb mixture: Mix together flour, brown sugar and salt. Cut in butter until mixture is very crumbly. Set aside.

Filling: Toss peaches with flour, sugar, cinnamon, and rum. Place in a dough-lined pie pan. Dot with butter. Bake in a preheated oven, 15 minutes. Remove from oven and top with crumb mixture. Bake 15 to 20 minutes longer, or until crumbs are crisp and browned.

Crust:
1½ cups/200 g flour
¼ tsp salt
½ cup/100 g vegetable shortening
3 tbsp (or more) cold water

Crumb mixture:
1 cup/130 g flour
½ cup/110 g packed light brown sugar
pinch of salt
5 tbsp/75 g butter

Filling:
5 cups/1¼ liters yellow peaches, peeled and sliced (10)
2 tbsp flour
½ cup/100 g granulated sugar
½ tsp cinnamon
2 tbsp rum
2 tbsp/30 g butter, cubed

Oven Temp: 425°F/220°C
Yield: 8 servings

Strawberry Rhubarb Pie

Great for late spring/early summer. As Belgian rhubarb tends to be green, the strawberries give the pie its traditional lovely red color.

Crust:
2¼ cups/290 g flour
½ tsp salt
¾ cup/150 g vegetable shortening
6 tbsp/90 ml (or more) cold water

Crust: Toss the flour and salt together. Cut in, or blend in the shortening with your fingertips, until the mixture looks crumbly. Add the water and mix until dough holds together. Form 2 balls, one slightly smaller. Roll out and line a 9"/24cm pie pan with larger ball; reserve the smaller ball for the top crust.

Filling:
1½ cups/300 g granulated sugar
⅓ cup/45 g flour
⅛ tsp salt
3 cups/700 ml rhubarb, in small pieces
2 cups/½ liter strawberries, hulled, sliced
2 tbsp orange liqueur*
2 tbsp/30 g butter

Filling: Combine the sugar, flour and salt in a bowl. Add the rhubarb, strawberries and orange liqueur and mix well. Pile the filling into the pie shell and dot with butter. Roll out the top crust. Cover the filling, trim and crimp the edges and cut vents in the top to let steam escape. (If you prefer, cut the pastry into strips for a lattice-top crust.)

Oven Temp: 450°F/230°C
350°F/175°C
Yield: 8 servings

Bake the pie in a preheated 450°F/230°C oven for 15 minutes; reduce the heat to 350°F/175°C and continue baking for about 30 to 40 minutes. Serve warm with vanilla ice cream.

* Grand Marnier or Cointreau

Peel rhubarb if the outer layer is fibrous. Peeling is not necessary if rhubarb is young and tender.

Apricot and Almond Tart

Lovely for a late summer dessert when apricots are at their best.

10"/24cm Pâte Brisée tart shell, pre-baked and cooled

¼ cup/40 g whole blanched almonds
5 tbsp/60 g granulated sugar
1 large egg, lightly beaten
⅛ tsp almond extract
¾ cup/180 ml crème fraîche épaisse*
1 lb/450 g fresh apricots (approx. 10)
½ cup/120 ml fresh cherries, halved and pitted (optional)
⅓ cup/80 ml apricot jam

Garnish:
sweetened whipped cream

Oven Temp: 375°F/190°C
Yield: 8 servings

In a food processor, grind the almonds with 1 tablespoon of the sugar until fine. Add the remaining sugar, the egg, almond extract and cream and blend until smooth.

Peel, pit, and halve the apricots. Spread the almond mixture in the tart shell. Arrange the apricots, cut side down, on top of the mixture. (If you are using cherries, fill in the spaces with the cherry halves, cut side down.)

Place the tart in the center of a preheated oven and bake until the cream filling is set and the tart shell is nicely browned, about 35 minutes. While the tart is baking, heat the apricot jam until melted. Strain.

Lightly glaze the apricots with the jam. Serve warm or at room temperature with heavy cream, sweetened and lightly whipped.

* see index

Afternoon Tea

Egg Spread Tea Sandwiches
Shrimp Spread Tea Sandwiches
∞
Date Nut Bread with Chèvre Spread
English Cream Scones (with Clotted Cream and Strawberry Jam)
∞
Ginger and Spice Sugar Cookies
Strawberry Tart (lets)
La Reina Nobile

Tarte Amandine aux Poires et au Chocolat
(Almond Tart with Pears and Chocolate)

1 recipe Pâte Sablée

1¾ cups/200 g confectioners' sugar
2 cups/200 g ground almonds
2 large eggs
2 large egg yolks
7 tbsp/100 g butter, softened
2 tbsp rum or a few drops of rum extract
3 ripe pears
3½ oz/100 g dark chocolate
1 tbsp peanut oil

Garnish:
slivered almonds or walnuts

Oven Temp: 375°F/190°C
Yield: 8 servings

Place pastry in a 9"/24cm tart pan with a removable bottom. Prick the pastry, line with foil and fill with dried beans or pie weights. Bake in a preheated oven for 8 minutes. Remove foil and beans and bake for 2 minutes more. Remove from oven, maintaining oven temperature.

Mix the sugar and the almonds. Add the whole eggs and the yolks, the butter and the rum. Combine well.

Peel the pears and cut into thin slices. Arrange the slices in the bottom of the pastry shell and cover with the almond mixture. Bake for 25 to 30 minutes. Let the tart cool, then remove from the pan.

Melt the chocolate over hot water. Add the oil and mix well. Pour the chocolate mixture into the center of the tart and spread evenly to the edge. Decorate the edge with almonds or walnuts.

PEARS

In general, firm textured, slightly granular, tart pears are best for cooking. In Belgium, Coing is a cooking pear. Beurre Hardy and Durondeau are considered good cooking and good eating pears. Juicy, fragrant, tender pears are best for eating raw. Among these are Conference, Passe-Crassane, and William (the Bartlett pear in the United States). Doyenne de Comice, considered by many to be the best pear, is fine for cooking if not fully ripened and a delicious eating pear when perfectly ripened.

Chocolate Tart Gourmandise

A decadently fudgy chocolate tart.

Crust:
1 cup/130 g all-purpose flour
¼ cup/30 g confectioners' sugar
6 tbsp/85 g unsalted butter, chilled
1 tbsp heavy cream, chilled

Filling:
½ cup/120 ml heavy cream
¼ cup/60 ml milk
10 oz/280 g bittersweet or semi-sweet chocolate, chopped
1 large egg

Oven Temp: 350°F/175°C
Yield: 8 - 10 servings

Crust: Blend flour and sugar. Cut in butter until mixture is crumbly. Add cream and stir with a fork until moist clumps form. Gather into a ball and flatten into disk. Wrap dough in plastic wrap and refrigerate 15 minutes.

Roll out pastry on a lightly floured surface to an 11"/28cm round. Transfer to a 9"/24cm tart pan with removable bottom. Press gently into place. Fold edges over to form double-thick sides. Line crust with aluminum foil. Fill with dried beans or pie weights. Bake in a preheated oven for 20 minutes. Remove beans and foil. Bake crust until golden brown, about 20 minutes, watching carefully. Transfer to rack and cool. Maintain oven temperature.

Filling: Bring heavy cream and milk to a simmer in a heavy saucepan. Reduce heat to low, add chocolate and stir until smooth. Beat egg in a medium bowl. Gradually whisk one-fourth of the hot chocolate mixture into egg. Whisk in remaining chocolate mixture. Pour filling into the baked crust. Bake until set, about 15 minutes. Transfer to a rack and cool.

> "Belgium is the home of gourmandise. Achieving an elegant and pleasurable balance between eating and pleasure is part of the raison de vivre. At times, this holy rite becomes the quintessence of pleasure."
> Rosine De Dijn

Apple Tart with Caramel Sauce

10"/24cm tart pastry shell, prebaked and cooled

3 lb/1⅓ kg tart cooking apples
½ cup/115 g unsalted butter
¾ cup/150 g granulated sugar
1 tsp freshly grated nutmeg
1 tbsp all-purpose flour
pinch of salt
¼ cup/30 g sliced almonds, toasted

Oven Temp: 350°F/175°C
Yield: 8 servings

Sauce:
1 cup/200 g granulated sugar
4 tbsp/60 ml water
1 cup/240 ml heavy cream

Yield: 1½ cups/350 ml sauce

*P*eel and core apples and cut into ¾"/2cm wedges.

In a large saucepan, melt butter over moderate heat. Stir in sugar and nutmeg. Add apples and cook until softened, 15 to 20 minutes. Stir flour and salt into apple mixture.

Spoon into shell and bake in the middle of a preheated oven until the apple wedges on top are golden brown, 45 minutes to 1 hour. Cool tart slightly on a rack. Sprinkle with toasted almonds just before serving.

Serve tart warm or at room temperature with the sauce.

Caramel Sauce

In a large heavy saucepan stir together sugar and water and bring to a boil (washing down any sugar crystals clinging to the side of the pan with a brush dipped in cold water) until sugar is dissolved. Boil mixture, without stirring, until a deep golden caramel, 30 to 45 minutes. Remove pan from heat and set in sink.

Meanwhile, in another saucepan, heat cream over moderate heat until warm. Gradually pour cream into caramel (mixture will bubble up), stirring until sauce is smooth. Let cool.

Tarte Tatin

This delicious caramelized apple tart was made famous by two sisters named Tatin who ran a hotel restaurant in France in the early 1900's.

8 - 10 tart cooking apples
juice of 1 lemon
1½ cups/300 g granulated sugar
1 tsp cinnamon (optional)
¼ tsp nutmeg (optional)
6 tbsp/85 g unsalted butter
1 recipe Pâte Brisée*
1 egg beaten with 1 tsp water for glaze
1 - 2 tsp granulated sugar

Oven Temp: 425°F/220°C
Yield: 8 servings

Peel and core the apples, then cut into eighths. Toss in a bowl with the lemon juice and ½ cup/100 grams sugar, (cinnamon and nutmeg) and let stand for 20 minutes. Drain.

Set a heavy oven-proof 9"/24cm frying pan over moderately high heat. Melt butter and blend in the remaining sugar. Stir until the syrup turns a bubbly caramel brown.

Toss the apples into the caramel mixture. Continue cooking, stirring occasionally until the apples are softened and the juices are thick and syrupy. Do not overcook. Remove the apples with a slotted spoon and reduce the juices to a syrupy consistency if necessary. Arrange the apples in the frying pan in a spiral and set aside to cool slightly.

Place rolled out pastry over the apples. Press the edges of the pastry down between the apples and the inside of the pan. Cut four steam holes, brush with the egg glaze and sprinkle with granulated sugar.

Bake in a preheated oven for 20 minutes, or until the pastry has browned and crisped. Tilt the pan, and if the juices are runny rather than a thick syrup, boil down rapidly on top of the stove, being sure not to evaporate them completely or the apples will stick to the pan.

To serve, invert the pan onto a serving plate. Serve warm or cold with whipped cream or ice cream.

Variation: You may use firm peaches or pears instead of apples.
* or pâte feuilletée (puff pastry)

Bavarian Apple Tart

Crust:
½ cup/115 g butter, softened
⅓ cup/65 g granulated sugar
¼ tsp vanilla extract
1 cup/130 g flour

Filling:
12 oz/340 g cream cheese, softened
¼ cup/50 g granulated sugar
1 large egg
1 tsp vanilla extract

Topping:
⅓ cup/65 g granulated sugar
½ tsp cinnamon
4 cups/1 liter peeled, sliced tart apples
¼ cup/30 g slivered almonds (optional)

Garnish:
whipped cream
cinnamon

Oven Temp: 450°F/230°C
400°F/200°C
Yield: 8 servings

Crust: Cream butter, sugar and vanilla. Blend in flour. Press pastry evenly on the bottom and sides of a 9"/24cm springform pan.

Filling: Beat together cream cheese and sugar. Blend in egg and vanilla. Pour into pastry-lined pan.

Topping: Combine sugar and cinnamon; toss with apples. Arrange apples in concentric circles over cream cheese layer. Sprinkle with slivered almonds if desired.

Bake in a preheated 450°F/230°C oven for 10 minutes. Reduce heat to 400°F/200°C and continue baking for 25 minutes. Cool before removing rim of pan. Serve as is or with whipped cream dusted with cinnamon.

APPLES

In Belgium, the most common cooking apples are Granny Smith and Boskoop, but in general, any tart, firm apple can be used for cooking. Reine des Reinettes, Golden Delicious and Cox are considered good eating and cooking apples. Some of the eating apples available in Belgium are Braeburn, Jonagold, Jonagored, Royal Gala, Elstar and Red Delicious, but many other varieties are available at different times of the year.

> *American recipes reflect the foods from all other countries.*
> Maida Heatter

Tarte au Sucre
Bistrot Du Mail - Pascal Devalkeneer, Chef

Yeast Tart Pastry:
1/3 oz/10 g fresh compressed yeast*
scant 1/2 cup/110 ml milk, slightly warm
2 cups/260 g flour, sifted
2 tbsp granulated sugar
1 tsp salt
1 large egg, lightly beaten
4 tbsp/60 g butter, softened

Sugar Filling:
1/2 cup/100 g fine granulated sugar
1/2 cup/110 g dark brown sugar
1/3 cup/35 g pure almond powder (optional)
3 1/2 oz/100 ml heavy cream
2 large eggs
5 tbsp/75 g butter, softened

Oven Temp: 350°F/175°C
Yield: 8 servings

Pastry: Mix the yeast and half of the milk and let sit until foamy, about 5 minutes. Combine flour, sugar and salt in a large bowl. Make a well in the center and add the egg, yeast mixture and butter. Work into a soft dough with fingertips, adding the rest of the milk a little at a time, until the dough holds together and could be rolled out easily but does not stick to your fingers. Form into a ball and place in a large, lightly oiled bowl. Cover and let rise 2 hours or until doubled in size. Punch down and roll out 1/8"/1/4cm thick. Transfer to a buttered and floured 10"/24cm tart pan and press into place. Trim the edges. Prick holes in the bottom. Cover and let rise 20 to 30 minutes before filling.

Filling: Combine sugars (and almond powder). Beat cream and eggs together. Combine the two mixtures and beat in the butter in small pieces.

Pour the sugar filling into the shell and bake for approximately 20 minutes in a preheated oven or until the filling is set.

* or 1/2 package dry yeast

Fresh compressed yeast must be kept refrigerated since it begins to activate over 50°F/10°C. If it is fresh when purchased, it will keep for about 2 weeks. It may also be frozen for 2 months; however, defrost it overnight in the refrigerator before using. You may dissolve crumbled fresh yeast in warm water (90°F/32°C) for 5 minutes before combining with the other ingredients. One package (1/4 oz/1 tbsp) of dry yeast is the equivalent of 1 (3/5 oz) cake or 1/2 of a (42 gram) cube of yeast.

Strawberry Tart

9"/24cm PÂTE SUCRÉE tart shell, prebaked and cooled

Pastry Cream:
2 cups/475 ml milk
⅓ cup/45 g flour
6 tbsp/75 g granulated or vanilla sugar
6 large egg yolks
1 tbsp/15 g unsalted butter
vanilla extract

4 cups/1 liter whole strawberries
2 - 4 tbsp strawberry or red currant jam
kirsch (optional)

Oven Temp: 375°F/190°C
Yield: 8 - 10 servings

Pastry Cream: Scald the milk. Mix the flour and sugar in a heavy saucepan. Whisk the hot milk into the flour mixture and cook over medium heat, stirring constantly, until it has boiled for 1 to 2 minutes.

Beat egg yolks until thick and lemon colored. Whisk a little of the hot mixture into the egg yolks, then slowly stir them back into saucepan. Stir constantly over medium heat until the pastry cream begins to hold a slight shape. Do not let it boil!

Remove from heat, stir in the butter, and put through a strainer. Let cool, covered with plastic wrap, and then refrigerate until cold. Stir in vanilla to taste. Keep refrigerated. Whisk gently to smooth it just before using. (Pastry cream makes 2½ cups/600 ml and can be kept 5 days in the refrigerator.)

> *...with berries as big as your thumb... and thick with juice, and a crust to endear them that will go to cream in your mouth, and both passing down with such a taste that will make you close your eyes and wish you might live forever in the wideness of that rich moment.*
> Richard Llewellyn

Clean and hull the strawberries. Spread the pastry cream into the shell. Arrange berries closely together on top. Warm the jam until melted (add a few drops of kirsch) and brush the berries to glaze.

Variation: Sliced strawberries may be substituted for a pleasing alternative. Overlap the berries in concentric circles and glaze.

Pumpkin Tart

*A*delicious alternative to the traditional PUMPKIN PIE.

2 recipes COOKIE CRUMB CRUST

Filling:
8 oz/225 g cream cheese, softened
2 large eggs
¾ cup/150 g granulated sugar

Topping:
1 (1 lb/450 g) can pumpkin purée
½ cup/120 ml milk
3 large eggs, separated
¾ cup/150 g granulated sugar
½ tsp salt
1 tbsp cinnamon
1 envelope unflavored gelatin
¼ cup/60 ml cold water

Oven Temp: 350°F/175°C
Yield: 12 servings

Crust: Press cookie crumb crust mixture into a 9"x 13"/24 x 34cm pan.

Filling: Beat cream cheese with eggs and sugar until smooth. Pour into crust and bake in a preheated oven for 20 minutes.

Topping: Mix the pumpkin, milk, egg yolks, ½ cup/100 grams of the sugar, salt and cinnamon and cook in a large saucepan until thickened. Dissolve gelatin in cold water. Stir into hot pumpkin mixture and cool. Beat 3 egg whites, gradually adding remaining ¼ cup/50 grams sugar, until stiff. Gently fold into the pumpkin mixture. Pour over the filling and refrigerate. Serve with whipped cream if desired.

> The Old Wives' Program for Thanksgiving Week:
> MONDAY - Wash
> TUESDAY - Scour
> WEDNESDAY - Bake
> THURSDAY - Devour
>
> Mother Goose

Pumpkin Pie

A traditional American holiday favorite.

9"/24cm pie crust

¾ cup/150 g granulated sugar
1 tbsp packed brown sugar
1 tbsp cornstarch
2 tsp ground cinnamon
¾ tsp ground ginger
¼ tsp salt
1 (1 lb/450 g) can pumpkin purée
3 large eggs, beaten to blend
¾ cup/175 ml heavy cream
½ cup/120 ml sour cream

Garnish:
sweetened whipped cream

Oven Temp: 325°F/165°C
Yield: 8 servings

Using a whisk, mix granulated sugar, brown sugar, cornstarch, cinnamon, ginger and salt into pumpkin purée until no lumps remain. Blend in eggs, heavy cream and sour cream.

Pour into the unbaked pie crust and bake in a preheated oven until filling puffs at the edges and the center is almost set, about 1 hour. Cool on a rack. Serve with sweetened whipped cream.

Raspberry Meringue Torte

Meringue:
4 large egg whites
pinch of salt
¼ tsp cream of tartar
1 cup/200 g granulated sugar
½ tsp vanilla extract

Filling:
2 pt/1 liter raspberry sherbet, softened
2 cups/475 ml heavy cream
6 tbsp crème de cassis
6 tbsp seedless raspberry preserves

Frosting:
3 cups/700 ml heavy cream
3 tbsp crème de cassis

Garnish:
12 whole strawberries
RASPBERRY CASSIS SAUCE

Oven Temp: 250°F/120°C
Yield: 12 - 14 servings

Meringue: Line 2 baking sheets with baking paper or wax paper. Draw three 8"/20cm rounds on the paper. If using wax paper, grease and flour the circles. Beat egg whites until frothy. Add salt and cream of tartar, beating until stiff. Add sugar, one tablespoon at a time, beating well after each addition, until meringue stands in firm, shiny peaks. Beat in vanilla. Divide meringue among circles and spread evenly, making a smooth surface. Bake in a preheated oven on the center rack for 1 hour. (If baking both sheets in one oven, rotate them halfway through baking time). Turn off the oven, and allow meringues to cool in the oven and dry out for 4 hours or overnight.

Filling: Line an 8"/20cm cake pan with foil or plastic wrap. Fill with sherbet, spread top evenly and freeze solid. Whip cream to soft peaks. Add crème de cassis and preserves and beat until stiff. Set aside.

Assemble torte by placing 1 meringue layer on a small baking sheet. Remove sherbet from cake pan and peel off paper or foil. Place sherbet on first meringue layer. Top with second meringue layer. Spread cassis filling over second layer and top with third meringue. Wrap in foil and freeze until firm (up to 1 week).

Frosting: Whip cream until soft peaks form. Add crème de cassis and beat until stiff. Place torte on serving platter. Spread top and sides with frosting. Pipe rosettes on top if desired. (Completed torte may be frozen overnight.)

Garnish: Before serving, dip 12 strawberries in sauce. Drain on paper towels to remove excess sauce and place on top of torte. Pass remaining sauce.

Sauce:
2 cups/½ liter fresh strawberries
10 oz/280 g frozen raspberries in syrup
3 tbsp crème de cassis

Yield: 2 cups/475 ml

Raspberry Cassis Sauce

Hull and halve the strawberries and place in a small bowl. In a small saucepan, heat raspberries and syrup to boiling. Strain to remove seeds. Add raspberries and crème de cassis to strawberries. Refrigerate at least 1 hour before serving but not more than 8 hours.

Red Currant Meringue Pie
American Women's Club of Brussels - Michel Thomasset, Chef

This delicate dessert makes a lovely presentation served in your best decorative shallow tart pan.

Remove fruit from stems. Mix the berries with the sugar and let macerate while preparing the crust.

Crust: Mix the flour, salt and sugar in a bowl. Mix in the softened butter and the egg yolks. Press the dough into the bottom and up the sides of a slightly buttered 11"/27cm tart pan. Prick the crust with a fork, line the shell with heavy aluminum foil and fill with beans or pie weights. Bake in a preheated oven for 15 minutes or until the edges start to turn brown. Remove the weights and foil and bake another 10 to 15 minutes or until the crust is golden brown.

Filling: Drain the currants and discard the juice. Beat the egg whites with a pinch of salt until stiff peaks form. Stir the egg yolk and then stir in a large spoonful of the whites to lighten it; combine this with the currants. Gently fold in the rest of the whites. Pour the mixture into the baked crust, spreading evenly. Bake for 10 to 12 minutes or just until the meringue turns blond. Allow the pie to cool approximately 1 hour, serving it slightly warm directly from the tart pan.

Variation: If currants are not available, try small, tart blueberries.

Crust:
1 ¼ cups/180 g self-rising flour
pinch of salt
generous ⅓ cup/80 g granulated sugar
½ cup/115 g butter, softened
2 egg yolks

Filling:
1 lb/450 g fresh red currants
½ cup/100 g granulated sugar
3 egg whites
pinch of salt
1 egg yolk

Oven Temp: 350°F/175°C
Yield: 8 - 10 servings

Hazelnut Meringue Torte

Line two cookie sheets with baking paper. Grease paper lightly with butter. Draw an 8"/20cm circle on each buttered paper.

Meringue:
4 large egg whites
1 cup/200 g granulated sugar
1 cup/240 ml minced hazelnuts (4 oz)
¼ tsp vanilla extract

Chocolate Glaze:
¼ cup/60 ml heavy cream
4 oz/115 g semi-sweet chocolate

Coffee Filling:
1½ cups/350 ml heavy cream
⅓ cup/65 g granulated sugar
2 tsp instant coffee powder

Garnish:
whole or sliced hazelnuts
chocolate curls

Oven Temp: 250°F/120°C
Yield: 6 - 8 servings

Meringue: Beat egg whites to form soft peaks. Beat in sugar, one tablespoon at a time, and continue beating to stiff, shiny peaks. Carefully fold in nuts and vanilla. Evenly spread half the meringue on each of the circles. Bake in a preheated oven until dry and very lightly browned (1 to 2 hours). Turn off oven and leave meringues inside until completely dry and cool, at least 2 hours or overnight. Remove from oven and lift off paper.

Chocolate Glaze: Combine cream and chocolate in a small bowl and gently melt in microwave or double boiler, stirring frequently. Cool.

Coffee Filling: Whip cream with sugar and coffee powder until stiff.

Spread tops of meringue layers evenly with chocolate glaze. Place in the freezer for a few minutes until chocolate is firm. Place one meringue layer on a flat serving plate and spread with half of the coffee filling. Top with second meringue, chocolate side up. Spread remaining filling over top and sides of meringue. Garnish and chill well before serving.

Meringues can be stored in an airtight container for about a week. Softened meringues can be recrisped in a 200°F/100°C oven.

Chocolate Chestnut Torte

¾ lb/340 g canned or vacuum-packed whole chestnuts (2 cups)
½ cup/115 g unsalted butter, softened
4 tbsp dark rum
10 oz/280 g bittersweet chocolate, melted
6 large eggs, separated
¼ tsp salt
½ cup/50 g granulated sugar

Glaze and Garnish:
6 oz/170 g bittersweet chocolate, finely chopped
½ cup/120 ml heavy cream
1 tbsp dark rum
8 candied chestnuts

Chestnut Rum Cream:
1 cup/240 ml heavy cream
1 tbsp sugar
1 tbsp dark rum
¾ cup/175 ml chopped candied chestnuts

Oven Temp: 350°F/175°C
Yield: 10 - 12 servings

*L*ine the bottom of a greased 9"/24cm springform pan with wax paper or baking paper. Grease the paper and dust the pan with flour.

If using canned chestnuts rinse, drain and pat dry. In a food processor, purée chestnuts with butter and rum until smooth. Add chocolate and blend. With the motor running, add egg yolks, one at a time. Transfer mixture to a large bowl.

In a separate bowl, beat egg whites with salt to soft peaks. Gradually add sugar, beating to stiff peaks. Whisk one-fourth of the whites into the chocolate mixture to lighten it; fold in the rest. Pour batter into prepared pan, smooth top and bake in preheated oven for 45 to 55 minutes or until tester comes out with crumbs and top is cracked. Let the torte cool in the pan on a rack for 5 minutes; remove sides of pan and invert onto another rack. Remove the bottom of the pan, re-invert onto a rack, top side up, and let cool completely. (It will fall as it cools.)

Glaze and Garnish: Put chocolate in a small bowl. Bring cream to a boil and pour over the chocolate. Stir until chocolate is melted and smooth. Stir in rum. Dip half of each candied chestnut in glaze; transfer to foil and let set.

Invert torte, bottom side up, onto rack set over plate or foil. Pour the remaining glaze over the torte, smooth it evenly and let excess drip down the sides. Let glaze set, about 2 hours. Transfer torte to a plate and garnish with chocolate chestnuts.

Chestnut Rum Cream: Just before serving, beat cream to soft peaks. Beat in sugar and rum and continue beating to stiff peaks. Fold in chopped candied chestnuts. Serve torte with the cream.

In Belgium, candied chestnuts are called marrons glacés.

Chocolate Layered Torte

A chocolate lover's dream - this elegant torte is worth the effort and can be prepared well in advance.

Cake:
½ cup/115 butter, softened
¾ cup/150 g granulated sugar
1 tsp vanilla extract
7 large eggs, separated
3 tbsp cornstarch
⅔ cup/90 g all-purpose flour
2 oz/55 g semi-sweet chocolate

Topping:
⅔ cup/160 ml sour cream
3½ tbsp granulated sugar
½ tsp fresh lemon juice

Frosting:
2 oz/55 g semi-sweet chocolate
1½ tbsp/25 g butter, softened
3 tbsp sour cream
½ tsp vanilla extract
1 cup/115 g (or more) confectioners' sugar

Garnish:
fresh strawberries, hulled and halved

Yield: 12 - 16 servings

Cake: Beat butter, ½ cup/100 grams of the sugar and vanilla until fluffy. Add egg yolks, one at a time, beating well after each. Stir cornstarch into flour and add to butter mixture. Divide the batter in half. Melt chocolate over hot water and cool. Mix melted chocolate into one portion of batter. Set aside.

Beat the egg whites to soft peaks. Gradually add the remaining ¼ cup/50 grams sugar, beating to stiff peaks. Fold half into the vanilla batter and the other half into the chocolate batter. (Batter may appear curdled.)

Preheat the broiler. Spread ½ cup/120 ml chocolate batter on the bottom of greased 9"/24cm springform pan. Place pan under broiler 5"/13cm from heat and broil for 1 to 2 minutes or until baked. Spread ½ cup/120 ml vanilla batter over baked chocolate layer and broil for 1 to 2 minutes. Repeat, alternating layers, for a total of 10 layers.

> *Aptly named the 'food of the gods,' chocolate is rich and exotic, and yet as American as old-fashioned apple pie. An ingredient like no other, chocolate travels well, mingles with authority and marries delectably with flavors from every region of the country...*
> Alice Medrich

Topping: Combine ingredients and spread over top layer of cake. Broil 1 minute. Cool cake for 15 minutes, then carefully remove sides of springform pan and cool completely.

Frosting: Melt chocolate over hot water, stirring until smooth. Cool. Stir in butter, sour cream and vanilla. Gradually beat in confectioners' sugar until frosting is of spreading consistency. Frost sides of cake with two-thirds of frosting.

Arrange strawberries around top outside edge of cake and in center. Use remaining frosting to pipe between strawberries in a spoke pattern. Chill at least 2 hours or overnight.

Plum and Almond Cobbler

Cobblers are an American tradition! The crunchy topping is a perfect complement to this early summer fruit.

½ cup/110 g packed light brown sugar
3 tbsp cornstarch
½ tsp cinnamon
2½ lbs/1¼ kg plums, pitted and quartered
2 tbsp fresh lemon juice
2 tbsp/30 g unsalted butter, cut in bits
1 cup/200 g granulated sugar
¾ cup/100 g flour
1 tsp baking powder
½ tsp salt
¾ cup/175 ml sliced almonds (3 oz)
1 large egg, lightly beaten

Oven Temp: 375°F/190°C
Yield: 10 - 12 servings

In a large bowl, mix together the brown sugar, cornstarch, and cinnamon. Add plums, lemon juice, and butter. Toss mixture well and spoon into a shallow 3 quart/liter baking dish or oval gratin dish.

In a food processor pulse together granulated sugar, flour, baking powder, salt and ½ cup/60 grams of the almonds until the almonds are ground fine. Add egg and pulse just until blended. Spoon flour mixture over plum mixture. Sprinkle remaining almonds over cobbler.

Bake the cobbler in the middle of a preheated oven for 45 minutes until it is golden and bubbling. Cool.

> "As a source of satisfaction, joy, discovery, and renewal, few daily rituals have such extraordinary potential as the act of preparing and sharing a good meal."
> Patricia Wells

Clafoutis aux Cerises
(Cherry Clafoutis)

A clafoutis is a traditional dessert in which pancake batter is poured over fruit and baked.

⅓ cup/45 g flour
⅔ cup/130 g granulated sugar
¼ tsp salt
4 large eggs, slightly beaten
2 cups/475 ml milk
1 vanilla bean or 1½ tsp vanilla extract
1 tbsp/15 g butter
⅛ tsp almond extract
1 tsp grated orange peel
2½ cups/600 ml pitted cherries

Oven Temp: 375°F/190°C
Yield: 4 - 6 servings

Butter an earthenware or oval gratin dish. In a bowl, mix flour, sugar and salt. Add eggs and stir well. Heat the milk with the scraped seeds and pod of the vanilla bean (see index) until it boils. (Vanilla extract may be used but vanilla bean gives a stronger flavor. If you choose extract add it later with the almond extract). Remove the milk from the heat and add the butter, extract(s) and orange peel. Remove vanilla bean if used. Slowly add the milk to the flour, beating constantly with an electric mixer.

Spread the cherries over the bottom of the prepared pan. Pour the batter over the cherries. Bake in a preheated oven for 20 to 30 minutes or until the top is golden brown. Serve warm for dessert or at a special brunch.

Variation: For a delicious alternative, pears or apricots may be substituted.

Apple Cranberry Crisp

You may be lucky and have leftovers - delicious for breakfast!

1½ lb/680 g unpeeled apples
8 oz/225 g cranberries (2 cups)
¾ cup/150 g granulated sugar
1 tsp cinnamon
½ cup/60 g chopped nuts
½ cup/110 g packed light brown sugar
⅓ cup/45 g flour
1 cup/100 g oatmeal
½ cup/115 g butter, melted

Oven Temp: 350°F/175°C
Yield: 6 -8 servings

Butter a 9"x13"/24 x 34cm pan. Core and slice the apples (3 cups/700 ml). Put apples and cranberries in prepared pan. Mix together sugar and cinnamon and sprinkle on top. Combine remaining ingredients. Sprinkle on apple-cranberry mixture. Bake in a preheated oven for 40 to 45 minutes.

To have fresh cranberries available all year, buy extra when they are in season, pick them over to remove any soft ones, and simply pack in plastic bags and freeze. They are excellent for any recipe where they will be cooked.

Apricot Soufflé

8 large egg whites, room temperature
1 cup/240 ml dried apricots (36)
1¼ cups/300 ml water
½ tsp almond extract
½ tsp cream of tartar
½ tsp salt
1 cup/200 g granulated sugar
½ cup/120 ml apricot preserves

Oven Temp: 350°F/175°C
Yield: 6 - 8 large servings
or 6 individual soufflés

Lightly butter and sprinkle with sugar the inside of a 3 quart/liter soufflé mold or 6 large ramekins. In a saucepan, combine dried apricots with water. Bring to a boil, remove from heat and let sit, covered, 20 minutes. Purée apricots and liquid. Add almond extract and transfer to a large bowl.

Add cream of tartar and salt to egg whites. Beat at high speed to soft peaks. Gradually beat in sugar, 2 tablespoons at a time. Continue to beat at high speed until very stiff peaks form. Gently, but thoroughly, fold one-third of the egg whites into the apricot purée. Fold in remaining egg whites just until combined. Turn into mold or ramekins. Set in a bain-marie (see note).

Bake in a preheated oven, on lowest shelf, 30 to 50 minutes, depending on the size of the mold. Gently brush soufflés with warmed apricot preserves. Serve immediately.

A bain marie refers to a method of baking where the baking dish is set inside a larger container of barely simmering water, partially up the side of the baking dish. The purpose is to surround and protect delicate foods, such as egg-based dishes, during the cooking process by maintaining an even, low, moist heat.

Cold Lemon Soufflé

Tantalizing on its own or served on a pool of Raspberry Sauce.

1 tbsp gelatin (see page 299)
½ cup/120 ml cold water
3 large eggs, separated
1 large egg white
1 cup/200 g granulated sugar
½ cup/120 ml lemon juice
1 tsp vanilla
grated zest of 2 lemons
2 cups/475 ml heavy cream

Yield: 6 servings

Dissolve gelatin in cold water and then melt over hot water. Beat the 3 egg yolks with sugar until pale and thick. Beat in the melted gelatin. Add lemon juice, vanilla and zest. Beat 4 egg whites until stiff. Beat 1½ cups/350 ml cream to stiff peaks. Stir a large spoonful of whites into the yolks, then fold in the remainder. Fold in whipped cream. Pour into a 1½ quart/liter soufflé dish and chill at least 3 hours. Beat remaining cream and use to decorate the soufflé before serving.

Separate eggs while cold to minimize the chance of the yolk breaking. Let egg whites warm to room temperature before beating to achieve greater volume.

Chocolate Mousse

6 oz/170 g semi-sweet chocolate
¼ cup/60 ml light or heavy cream
1 tsp vanilla extract
dash of salt
4 large eggs, separated
¼ cup/50 g granulated sugar

Garnish:
grated white chocolate
whipped cream
Yield: 6 - 8 servings

Melt chocolate over low heat. Remove from heat and stir in cream, vanilla and salt. Beat egg yolks slightly. Gradually add the chocolate mixture to the egg yolks, beating with a wire whisk until thick. In a separate bowl, beat egg whites until foamy. Gradually beat in sugar and continue beating until mixture forms stiff peaks. Stir in 1 large spoonful of beaten egg whites to lighten chocolate mixture. Gently, but thoroughly, fold in remaining whites. Spoon into individual dessert dishes. Chill at least 2 hours. Decorate with grated white chocolate and/or a little whipped cream just before serving.

Variation: Replace vanilla with 1 tablespoon Kahlúa, brandy or other favorite liqueur.

White Chocolate Mousse with Raspberry Grand Marnier Sauce

9 oz/250 g European white chocolate
3 large egg yolks
⅓ cup/40 g confectioners' sugar
1¼ cups/300 ml heavy cream, chilled

Yield: 6 servings

Melt white chocolate over barely simmering water, stirring occasionally. Remove from heat.

In a bowl set over hot water, whisk together the egg yolks and sugar until well combined. Remove bowl from over water and beat in ¼ cup/60 ml of the cream. Slowly stir in the melted chocolate until well combined.

Whip the remaining cream to stiff peaks. Gently fold together whipped cream and chocolate mixture. Spoon into individual dessert dishes and refrigerate several hours before serving.

Top each bowl of white chocolate mousse with the sauce.

Sauce:
1 (10 oz/280 g) pkg frozen raspberries, defrosted and drained
¼ cup/50 g ultrafine sugar
2 tsp Grand Marnier (orange liqueur)

Yield: 1 cup/240 ml

Raspberry Grand Marnier Sauce

Combine raspberries, sugar and Grand Marnier in a blender or food processor and purée. Chill.

GELATIN
- American and Belgian gelatins range between 7 and 13 grams per envelope. Despite the difference in gram weight, one envelope will gel roughly the same amount of liquid (between 2 to 2½ cups/480 to 600 ml). Between 3 and 5 sheets of gelatin are equivalent to 1 envelope depending on the size of the sheets (read the package).
- Powdered gelatin should be softened in cold liquid (1 envelope gelatin to ¼ cup/60 ml liquid) and then gently warmed to melt it before adding to other ingredients. Gelatin should never be boiled as this interferes with its ability to gel.
- Sheets of gelatin should be soaked in cold water until pliable. Squeeze out excess water and gently dissolve in hot liquid from the recipe.

Crème au Café

A creamy rich dessert - the perfect ending to a light meal!

3 cups/700 ml heavy cream
½ cup/100 g granulated sugar
1 tbsp instant espresso powder
1 tsp vanilla extract
5 large egg yolks

Garnish:
1 cup/240 ml heavy cream
2 tsp granulated sugar
semi-sweet chocolate curls

Oven Temp: 325°F/165°C
Yield: 6 - 8 servings

In a medium saucepan, combine cream, sugar and instant coffee. Over medium low heat, cook until sugar dissolves. Remove from heat and add vanilla extract. Let cool slightly. In medium bowl, beat the egg yolks with a whisk until smooth but not frothy. Gradually add the cooled cream mixture to the beaten egg yolks and stir until well blended. Strain into 8 (5 oz/150 ml) ramekins. Place in a roasting pan in a bain marie (see index). Bake 25 to 30 minutes or until the mixture just begins to set around the edges. Immediately remove from the pan and place ramekins on a rack to cool, 30 minutes. Cover with plastic and refrigerate until cold.

Garnish: Whip heavy cream with 2 teaspoons sugar until stiff and pipe a little mound onto the top of each ramekin. Make chocolate curls with slightly softened chocolate and a vegetable parer. Place chocolate curls on top.

Variation: For CRÈME AU CHOCOLAT, substitute 1 tablespoon of unsweetened Dutch-processed cocoa for the coffee.

> *I am a pudding man. Nothing depresses me more than a meal which doesn't finish with one. 'Just coffee for me, thanks,' is not a phrase in my book. However boring the occasion, I perk up when they wheel in the sweet trolley.*
> Robert Morley

Crème Brûlée

It is proper to gently crack the caramelized sugar crust of this classic dessert with the back of your spoon!

6 large egg yolks
1 large egg
⅔ cup/130 g granulated sugar
1¾ cups/420 ml heavy cream
1¾ cups/420 ml milk
1 vanilla bean, split
¼ cup/65 g packed light brown sugar

Oven Temp: 325°F/165°C
Yield: 8 servings

In a bowl, whisk together yolks, whole egg and granulated sugar. In a heavy saucepan, heat cream and milk with a split and scraped vanilla bean (see index) over moderately high heat until mixture just comes to a boil. Strain milk mixture into egg mixture in a thin stream, whisking. Skim off any froth.

Divide custard among 8 shallow baking dishes set in a bain marie (see index). Bake in the middle of a preheated oven until barely set, but still trembling slightly, about 30 minutes. Remove baking dishes from the bain marie and cool. Chill custards, covered loosely with plastic wrap, at least 4 hours or overnight.

Set the broiler rack so that the custards will be 3"/8cm from heat; preheat broiler. Sift brown sugar evenly over custards and broil until sugar is melted and caramelized, about 2 minutes. Chill custards 20 minutes and serve immediately.

Variations: For CRÈME BRÛLÉE CAFÉ, stir in 1½ tablespoons instant espresso powder and 2 tablespoons of Kahlua after milk comes to a boil. For CRÈME BRÛLÉE À L'ORANGE, add the grated zest of an orange and 2 tablespoons orange-flavored water to the milk before bringing to a boil.

Crème Caramel à la Crème de Marrons

Caramel:
½ cup/100 g fine granulated sugar
2 - 3 tbsp water

Custard:
2 large eggs
4 large egg yolks
6 tbsp granulated sugar
pinch of salt
2¼ cup/530 ml milk
1 vanilla bean

1 can crème de marrons
⅔ cup/160 ml heavy cream
2 tbsp cognac

Oven Temp: 350°F/175°C
Yield: 6 - 8 servings

Butter and sugar a 1 ½ quart/liter oven-proof ring mold.

Caramel: In a saucepan, combine sugar and water and cook over moderate heat until sugar is dissolved. Boil gently, swirling the pan until it is a pale golden caramel color. Be careful not to let it burn. Remove from heat.

Custard: In a heavy saucepan, combine eggs, egg yolks, sugar and salt. In another pan heat the milk with a split vanilla bean until it comes to the boiling point, stirring occasionally. Remove the vanilla bean. Drizzle hot milk into egg mixture stirring vigorously. Stir in caramel (if it has hardened, heat briefly). Caramel may harden into sugar threads if the custard is too cool, but just keep stirring and the caramel will dissolve. Pour mixture into prepared mold and set mold in a bain marie (see index).

Bake in a preheated oven for 35 minutes. Let cool and refrigerate until cold. Unmold and fill the center with crème de marrons topped with sweetened whipped cream flavored with 2 tablespoons cognac.

Choose dark colored, plump, moist, flexible vanilla beans. The best ones come from Tahiti, Madagascar, and Mexico. One inch of scraped seeds is equivalent to 1 teaspoon of vanilla extract. To infuse a vanilla bean, split the bean pod and heat with milk. Alternatively, split the pod, scrape the seeds into milk and drop in the pod. Let stand in warmed milk until flavored. After infusion, the pod may be dried and re-used (see Vanilla Sugar).

CREAM

- ◆ Crème Fraîche refers to fresh cream in Belgium
- ◆ Half & Half - 12% butterfat
- ◆ Light Cream (Single Cream) - 20% butterfat
- ◆ Heavy Cream - Whipping Cream (Crème Fraîche à Fouetter) - 35% - 40% butterfat
- ◆ Double Cream (British) - 48% butterfat
- ◆ For the thickened, slightly soured French cream, look for Crème Fraîche d'Isigny or Crème Fraîche Epaisse (40% butterfat). The French thickened Crème Fraîche can stand higher temperatures than sour cream before it curdles.
- ◆ Sour Cream (Crème Epaisse) - 18% butterfat
- ◆ Fromage Frais (or Fromage Blanc) is a soft, smooth, light, fresh cheese with the consistency of sour cream, but the brief fermentation imparts a very slight tang similar to yogurt. It ranges from zero fat to about 50% butterfat, and comes flavored or plain. Sprinkle plain fromage frais with sugar and serve with fresh fruit.
- ◆ Petit Suisse and Petit Gervais are cow's milk with yogurt culture added; they are denser, milder, and creamier than yogurt.
- ◆ Yogurt comes in many forms, flavors and fat contents; Greek Yogurt is particularly thick and a wonderful substitute for sour cream.
- ◆ The following recipes produce acceptable substitutes if you cannot find the real thing:

    CRÈME FRAÎCHE EPAISSE: Heat 1 cup/240 ml heavy cream over low heat to 100°F/40°C. Add 1 tbsp buttermilk and mix well. Put in covered jar and let stand at room temperature for 6 to 8 hours (ultra-pasteurized cream may take longer) until it thickens. Refrigerate 24 hours before serving. (The cream will continue to thicken.) May be kept covered in the refrigerator for 2 to 3 weeks.

    FROMAGE FRAIS: Heat 2 quarts/2 liters buttermilk gently for about 5 minutes to 110°F/43°C. Set aside to cool to room temperature. Line a colander with 2 or 3 layers of cheesecloth. Drain the buttermilk overnight (8 to 10 hours) and discard the liquid. Transfer the fromage frais to a bowl, cover, and refrigerate. Thin with a little milk if necessary.

Tiramisu

This Italian favorite makes an elegant company dessert.

3 large eggs, separated
5½ tbsp granulated sugar
11 oz/310 g mascarpone cheese
¾ cup/175 ml heavy cream
2 cups/475 ml espresso coffee
1 tbsp cognac
10 oz/300 g dry lady finger biscuits*
1 tbsp unsweetened Dutch-processed cocoa

Yield: 8 - 10 servings

Beat egg yolks with 4½ tablespoons of the sugar until thick and fluffy. Add mascarpone and combine well. Beat the egg whites to soft peaks. Beat cream to peaks. Fold whites and cream into cheese mixture.

Mix coffee, cognac and 1 tablespoon of sugar in a shallow dish with sides. Dip biscuits quickly in liquid, one at a time, and arrange in the bottom of a glass trifle dish. Layer with some of the cream mixture. Repeat three or four times, ending with cream. Sprinkle top with cocoa. Refrigerate until time to serve (at least 4 hours).

* Boudoir biscuits

> " Sometimes the simplest recipe can be a star if it is done properly. "
> Delia Smith

Sour Cream Pound Cake

3 cups/600 g granulated sugar
1 cup/225 g butter
6 large eggs, separated
1 cup/240 ml sour cream
1 tsp vanilla extract
¼ tsp almond extract
3 cups/400 g flour
¼ tsp baking soda
¼ tsp salt

Oven Temp: 300°F/150°F
Yield: 10 - 12 servings

Cream together sugar and butter. Add egg yolks one at a time, beating well after each addition. Add sour cream and continue mixing. Add extracts. Mix in 1 cup/130 grams flour. Beat egg whites until they hold peaks and fold them in. Combine remaining flour, soda and salt and gently add to batter. Turn into greased and floured bundt pan. Bake in a preheated oven for 1 hour. Cool 10 minutes in pan and then turn out onto a rack to cool.

Serve plain, sprinkled with confectioners' sugar, or with whipped cream, fresh fruit or CHOCOLATE SAUCE.

Chocolate Sheet Cake

2 cups/400 g granulated sugar
2 cups/260 g flour
½ cup/115 g butter
½ cup/120 ml vegetable oil
1 cup/240 ml water
4 tbsp unsweetened Dutch-processed cocoa
½ cup/120 ml milk or buttermilk
2 large eggs, slightly beaten
1 tsp cinnamon
1 tsp soda
1 tsp vanilla extract

Frosting:
½ cup/115 g butter
4 tbsp unsweetened Dutch-processed cocoa
6 tbsp/90 ml milk
1 lb/450 g confectioners' sugar
1 tsp vanilla extract
1 cup/120 g nuts, chopped (optional)

Oven Temp: 400°F/200°C
Yield: 24 squares

Grease a 9"x13"/24 x 34cm pan.

Combine sugar and flour in a large bowl. In a saucepan, mix butter, oil, water and cocoa. Bring to a rapid boil. Pour into the dry mixture. Stir well. Add milk, eggs, cinnamon, soda and vanilla. Mix well, pour into pan and bake in a preheated oven for 25 to 30 minutes.

Frosting: Mix butter, cocoa and milk. Bring to a boil and remove from heat. Add confectioners' sugar, vanilla (and nuts). Spread on the cake while still hot.

In early summer, wild strawberries (fraises des bois) always turn a simple dessert into something special. This tiny fruit has a delicate flavor and mild sweetness.

Desserts

Chocolate Birthday Cake

2 cups/260 g flour
1 tsp baking soda
½ tsp salt
½ cup/120 ml boiling water
½ cup/50 g unsweetened Dutch-processed cocoa
1 cup/225 g butter
1½ cups/300 g granulated sugar
2 large eggs, separated
¾ cup/175 ml buttermilk
1 tsp vanilla extract

Frosting:
3½ oz/100 g semi-sweet chocolate
4 tbsp/55 g butter
3¾ cups/450 g confectioners' sugar
pinch of salt
7 tbsp/100 ml evaporated milk
1 tsp vanilla extract

Oven Temp: 375°F/190°C
Yield: 10 servings

*B*utter two 9"/24cm cake pans.

Stir together flour, soda and salt; set aside. Add boiling water to cocoa and let cool. Beat together butter and sugar until fluffy; then add the egg yolks, one at a time, beating after each addition. Add the cocoa mixture and combine well. In a small bowl, combine buttermilk and vanilla. Add the flour mixture to the batter, alternating with the buttermilk mixture, beginning and ending with flour. Mix well. Beat egg whites until they hold soft peaks and gently fold into the mixture. Pour into prepared cake pans. Bake in a preheated oven for 30 minutes. Turn out onto racks. Frost when cool.

Frosting: Melt chocolate and butter in a double boiler over gently simmering water. Mix sugar with salt, milk and vanilla. Add chocolate and beat well. Stir occasionally until spreading consistency.

Gâteau aux Framboises
Les Olivades - Christian Lapicoré, Chef

7 oz/200 g almonds, ground (2 cups)
1 cup/100 g granulated sugar
7 tbsp/140 g seedless raspberry jam
4 large eggs
7 tbsp/100 g butter, melted
3½ oz/100 ml heavy cream

Garnish:
fresh raspberries
confectioners' sugar

Oven Temp: 325°F/165°C
Yield: 8 servings

Grease and flour a large tart pan with a removable bottom and place in the refrigerator until cold. In a large bowl, combine almonds, sugar, 5 tablespoons/100 grams jam, eggs, butter and cream, and stir with a wooden spoon. Pour the mixture into the tart pan and bake in a preheated oven for 35 minutes.

Let the tart cool to room temperature and remove from pan. Brush remaining jam over the top and garnish with the fresh raspberries. Sprinkle confectioners' sugar over the top and serve with vanilla ice cream or sweetened, softly whipped cream.

Cranberry Cake

This is a very simple dessert for the holidays.

Cake: Sift together flour, sugar, baking powder, salt and baking soda. Add buttermilk, butter, cranberries and vanilla. Pour mixture into a greased 9"x13"/24 x 34cm pan and bake in a preheated oven for 20 to 25 minutes or until a toothpick comes out clean.

Sauce: Bring sugar, half & half, butter and vanilla to a boil and let simmer for 5 to 10 minutes or until thick.

When cool, cut cake into squares and serve on a pool of sauce.

2½ cups/325 g flour
1½ cups/300 g granulated sugar
2 tsp baking powder
¼ tsp salt
½ tsp baking soda
1¼ cups/300 ml buttermilk
2 tbsp/30 g butter, melted
12 oz/350 g chopped cranberries (2½ cups)
1½ tsp vanilla extract

Sauce:
1¼ cups/250 g granulated sugar
1¼ cups/300 ml half & half (see index)
5⅓ tbsp/75 g butter
1¼ tsp vanilla extract

Oven Temp: 350°F/175°C
Yield: 12 - 16 squares

FLOUR

- All recipes in this cookbook were converted using the "lightly spooned and swept" method where a level 1 cup (250 ml) dry measure of flour equals 130 grams.
- For an American recipe that specifies all-purpose flour, you may need an extra tablespoon of Belgian flour per cup.
- Farine de Froment or Farine de Blé - plain all-purpose flour suitable for pastry, cookies, cakes, and cooking in general
- Farine pour Pâtisserie - pastry flour suitable for pastry and cakes
- Farine Fermantante - self-rising flour which contains leavening. If you are substituting self-rising for regular flour, read the package to see what you need to leave out of your recipe.
- Farine pour Pain Blanc or Pain de Campagne - suitable for making bread
- If the word tamisée is added, the flour is pre-sifted.
- You will also find special flours for crêpes, pizza, waffles, and blinis.
- Flour specifically for cakes does not exist in Belgium. You can try this substitute if you are not happy with the way your cakes turn out:
    CAKE FLOUR: Spoon 2 tablespoons of cornstarch into a dry 1 cup/250 ml measure. Sift (if the recipe specifies a sifted measurement) or spoon flour into the cup until the measure is full. Tap it gently to settle the flour and fill again if necessary. Sift the flour/cornstarch mixture before using to combine evenly.

Carrot Cake

1 scant cup/225 ml vegetable oil
1½ cups/150 g granulated sugar
3 large eggs, beaten
2 cups/260 g flour
1 tsp cinnamon
1 tsp nutmeg
½ tsp allspice
1 tsp baking soda
1 tsp baking powder
1 tsp salt
3 cups/700 ml shredded carrots
1 cup/80 g shredded coconut (optional)
1 can (8¼ oz/220 g) crushed pineapple, drained
1 tsp vanilla extract
1 scant cup/100 g chopped walnuts

Cream Cheese Frosting:
¾ cup/170 g butter, softened
12 oz/340 g cream cheese, softened
1¾ cups/200 g confectioners' sugar
juice of ½ lemon
1 tsp vanilla extract

Oven Temp: 350°F/175°C
Yield: 10 servings

Grease and flour two 9"/24cm cake pans.

Blend oil and sugar and beat in eggs. Combine all dry ingredients and add to egg mixture. Add carrots, coconut, pineapple, vanilla and nuts and stir until thoroughly combined. Pour into prepared pans. Bake for 30 to 35 minutes in a preheated oven. Cool in pan 10 minutes then turn out on racks to cool completely before frosting.

Frosting: Cream together butter and cream cheese. Add sugar gradually, then lemon juice and vanilla.

Frost the cake and refrigerate at least 1 hour before serving.

> *Cakes are often symbols of love and friendship*
> Delia Smith

La Reina Nobile

Lemon Curd Filling:
- 6 egg yolks
- 1 cup/200 g granulated sugar
- ½ cup/120 ml fresh lemon juice
- ½ cup/115 g cold unsalted butter
- 1½ tbsp minced lemon peel

Cake:
- 5 extra-large eggs, separated
- 1½ cup/300 g granulated sugar
- ½ cup/120 ml fresh orange juice
- 1½ tsp lemon juice
- 1 cup/130 g flour, sifted 4 times
- 1 tsp baking powder
- ½ tsp salt

Garnish:
- confectioners' sugar
- 12 candied violets
- fresh strawberries, raspberries and blueberries
- fresh mint sprigs

Oven Temp: 325°F/165°C
Yield: 8 - 10 servings

Lemon Curd Filling: Place egg yolks in a saucepan and beat slightly with a wire whisk. Whisk in sugar until blended. Gradually stir in lemon juice. Cook over low heat, stirring constantly with a wire whisk until mixture coats the back of a wooden spoon or registers 168°F/75°C on a candy thermometer. Do not boil. Remove from heat and whisk until slightly cooled, about 3 to 5 minutes. Cut butter into small bits and whisk, a few bits at a time, into egg yolk mixture until melted. Stir in lemon peel. Cool completely. (Filling can be made ahead and stored, tightly covered, in the refrigerator for up to 1 week.)

Cake: Beat egg yolks until thick. Add ¾ cup/150 grams sugar and beat slightly. Add orange and lemon juices and blend well. Sift together flour, baking powder and salt. Add to yolk mixture and beat well.

In a separate bowl, beat egg whites until foamy and thick. Beat in remaining sugar until fairly stiff peaks just begin to form. Do not over beat. Stir 1 spoonful of whites into batter to lighten and then gently fold in remaining egg whites. Lightly grease two 9"/24cm springform pans. Fill each pan with half the mixture. Bake in a preheated oven, 25 to 30 minutes or until golden brown.

Place pan on wire rack. Immediately run a thin paring knife gently around sides of cake, using a vertical motion. Carefully remove sides from pans. Let cakes cool 10 minutes. Slice each cake in half horizontally. Place the four layers, cut sides up, on racks to cool completely.

Place one of the cake bottoms on a 12"/30cm round plate, cut side up. Spread a third of the filling evenly over the top of cake layer. Do not spread to the rim of the cake. Place another cake bottom over first cake layer and spread with half the remaining filling. Top with one of the cake tops. Spread with remaining filling. Top with final cake layer, browned side up.

To serve, sift confectioners' sugar over the top of the cake. Place 12 candied violets evenly around the perimeter of the cake. Surround the cake with strawberries, blueberries and raspberries. Garnish with mint sprigs.

Galette des Rois

This puff pastry dessert is filled with either marzipan or a mixture of apple or apricots and marzipan - don't forget to hide the fève before baking.

pâte feuilletée (puff pastry)
9 tbsp/125 g butter, softened
9 oz/240 g almond paste or marzipan
2 tbsp flour
1 large egg
1 tbsp water
vanilla sugar (see index)

Oven Temp: 400°F/200°C
Yield: 10 - 12 servings

Roll out the pastry and cut into two circles, approximately 8"/20cm diameter. Mix butter, almond paste and flour together and spread over one circle, leaving at least a ½"/1¼cm border. Lightly beat the egg with water. Brush the border with the egg wash, cover with the other circle and seal. Brush top with egg wash. Cut shallow slits in the top crust. Place in the freezer for at least one hour. Remove from freezer and sprinkle with vanilla sugar. Place in a preheated oven and bake 20 to 25 minutes until golden brown.

You will find this traditional Epiphany cake in pâtisserie shops around January 6th when it is served as Sunday dessert. According to Belgian custom, one of the younger children is chosen to hide under the table while an adult cuts the cake. The child chooses the person to receive each slice - whoever finds the fève (porcelain charm) hidden in the Galette is king or queen for the day!

Cheesecake Supreme

Delicious plain or served with Rasberry Sauce *or* Summer Fruit Compote.

Crust:
2½ cups/600 ml graham cracker crumbs*
½ cup/115 g butter, melted
¼ cup/50 g granulated sugar
½ tsp cinnamon
1½ cups/175 g coarsely chopped pecans

Filling:
16 oz/450 g cream cheese
3 large eggs
¾ cup/150 g granulated sugar
1 tsp vanilla extract

Topping:
2 cups/475 ml sour cream
1¼ cups/250 g granulated sugar
1 tsp vanilla extract

Oven Temp: 350°F/175°C
400°F/200°C
Yield: 10 - 12 servings

Crust: Combine cookie crumbs with sugar, cinnamon and nuts. Pour in melted butter and stir until combined. Pat evenly onto the bottom of a 10"/26cm springform pan. Chill in the freezer for 10 to 15 minutes or refrigerate for 1 hour.

Filling: Mix together cream cheese, eggs, sugar and vanilla with an electric beater at high speed. Pour into the crust and bake in a preheated 350°F/175°C oven for 40 to 50 minutes or until edges are firm and the center barely shakes. Remove, cool and refrigerate for 3 to 5 hours or overnight.

Topping: Stir together the ingredients for the topping and pour over cheesecake. Bake in a preheated 400°F/200°C oven for 20 minutes until the topping bubbles slightly around the edges. Chill until firm. Serve at room temperature.

* For alternatives to graham crackers see Cookie Crumb Crust.

> " *After you have been a very good person for a very long time and are thin as a bean, you may decide to fall briefly into sin.* "
> Laurie Colwin

Raspberry Sauce

½ lb/225 g ripe raspberries or thawed frozen raspberries
6 tbsp/75 g sugar
1 tsp lemon juice
1 tbsp kirsch (optional)

Yield: 1 cup/240 ml

Mash the raspberries; put through a sieve to remove the seeds.

In a saucepan, combine sugar, lemon juice and 3 tablespoons of water; boil 3 minutes. Add the raspberry pulp and stir. Refrigerate. (When the sauce is cold, add kirsch.)

Summer Fruit Compote

Fruit Coulis (fruits may be frozen):
4 oz/115 g red currants
4 oz/115 g strawberries
2 oz/60 g raspberries
¼ cup/50 g granulated sugar

Fruit Filling (best if fruits are fresh*):
4 oz/115 g red currants
4 oz/115 g black currants
2 tbsp sugar
8 oz/225g raspberries
8 oz/225g strawberries

Yield: 3 cups/700 ml

As a topping for CHEESECAKE SUPREME or ice cream, this fresh fruit combination is divine when berries are in season.

Fruit Coulis: Strip fresh currants from the branch. Let the fruits macerate in the sugar for 30 minutes. Blend in a food processor to make a smooth sauce. Pass the sauce through a sieve to extract the seeds.

Fruit filling: Strip the red currants and black currants into a saucepan, add the sugar and place on medium heat. Let cook for 3 to 4 minutes or until the juice begins to run. Transfer to a bowl and, when cold, gently stir in the raspberries and strawberries.

Just before serving, gently fold the fruit filling into the coulis.

* 4 oz of berries measures approximately ¾ cup/175 ml

Desserts

Embassy Brownies

*T*his makes a chewy and moist brownie. They were served at the American Embassy in Brussels during a 4th of July celebration.

6 oz/175 g semi-sweet chocolate
¼ cup/60 ml chocolate syrup
½ cup/115 g unsalted butter, softened
1 tsp vanilla extract
2 large eggs, lightly beaten
¾ cup/150 g granulated sugar
pinch of salt
½ cup/65 g all-purpose flour

Oven Temp: 350°F/175°C
Yield: 64 tiny brownies

Butter and flour an 8"/20cm square baking pan.

Melt chocolate in a small, heavy saucepan over very low heat, stirring constantly. Stir in the syrup. Remove the pan from the heat and add the butter. Beat until the mixture is smooth. Stir in the vanilla and eggs and mix thoroughly. Sift together the sugar, salt and flour. Add this to the chocolate mixture and blend thoroughly.

Pour the batter into the prepared pan, and bake in a preheated oven just until cooked, 30 minutes. Allow the brownies to cool completely in the pan; cut into squares and transfer to a serving plate.

Ultimate Chocolate Chip Cookies

2½ cups/260 g oatmeal
1 cup/225 g butter
1 cup/220 g packed light brown sugar
1 cup/200 g granulated sugar
2 large eggs
1 tsp vanilla extract
2 cups/260 g flour
½ tsp salt
1 tsp baking powder
1 tsp baking soda
12 oz/340 g chocolate chips (pieces)
1½ cups/180 g chopped nuts (optional)

Oven Temp: 375°F/190°C
Yield: 60 cookies

Blend oatmeal in a blender or food processor to a fine powder. Cream together butter and sugars. Add eggs and vanilla and mix well. Mix together flour, oatmeal, salt, baking powder and baking soda and combine well with creamed mixture. Add chocolate chips (and nuts). Roll into balls and place 2"/5cm apart on a lightly greased cookie sheet.

Bake for 10 minutes in a preheated oven. Cool on a rack.

SUGAR
- Granulated sugar - Sucre crystallisé (available in Belgium in light and dark brown)
- Fine granulated sugar - Sucre semoule fin S2 (Castor sugar)
- Ultrafine granulated sugar - Sucre semoule ultrafine S1 (Bar sugar)
- Sucre granulé gros grains - a large grained sugar used to decorate tops of tarts, pies and cookies
- Confectioners' sugar - Sucre impalpable (10X, powdered sugar, icing sugar)
- Brown sugar - Cassonade
  light brown - blonde (Cassonade Graeffe seems most like American)
  dark brown - brune
  very dark brown - foncé (Muscavado has a strong molasses taste)
- Pearl sugar - Sucre perlé (pebble-like pieces of white sugar)
- White and brown sugar rock candy chunks and cubes are available for coffee/tea.
- Vanilla sugar is sold in small packets; it is also easy to make your own. Fill a large jar with confectioners' or granulated sugar. Bury 1 to 2 split vanilla beans (fresh or previously used are suitable) in the sugar. Cover tightly and let stand at least a few days before using. Replace sugar as it is used. The vanilla beans will continue to flavor the sugar for several months.
- Maple syrup, molasses, and corn syrup, not widely available in Belgium, can be found at stores specializing in American products.
- If you like a stronger brown sugar taste, try mixing half light and half dark brown sugar in place of all light brown sugar.
- If your brown sugar becomes hard, seal it in a container with several slices of apple. It will become soft in a few days.

Sugar Cookies

2½ cups/325 g all-purpose flour
1 tsp cream of tartar
½ tsp baking soda
¼ tsp salt
¼ tsp freshly grated nutmeg
1 cup/225 g unsalted butter, softened
1 tsp vanilla
1¼ cups/250 g granulated sugar
2 large eggs, well beaten

Oven Temp: 375°F/190°C
Yield: 70 cookies

Sift together the flour, cream of tartar, baking soda, salt and nutmeg and set aside. In a large bowl, cream the butter with the vanilla until light and fluffy. Gradually beat in ¾ cups/150 grams of the sugar to make a smooth mixture. Stir in the eggs. Add the dry ingredients gradually, mixing well after each addition. Form the dough into 2 balls. Dust the balls with additional flour, wrap in plastic wrap and chill for 2 hours.

Roll out one ball, ¼"/½cm thick, on a floured surface. Cut out cookies and arrange them 2"/5cm apart on a lightly greased baking sheet. Sprinkle each cookie with some of the remaining sugar and bake in the middle of a preheated oven for 8 to 10 minutes, or until lightly golden. Sprinkle the cookies lightly with sugar again while they are still warm. Transfer the cookies to a rack to cool. Repeat with remaining dough.

> *Over their delicate brown tops was sprinkled white sugar. The sparkling grains lay like tiny drifts of snow.*
> Laura Ingalls Wilder

Chocolate Crackles

½ cup/65 g all-purpose flour
½ cup/100 g granulated sugar
4 tbsp unsweetened Dutch-processed cocoa
½ tsp baking powder
¼ tsp salt
2 tbsp/30 g unsalted butter, softened
1 large egg, beaten lightly
2 tbsp confectioners' sugar

Oven Temp: 400°F/200°C
Yield: 30 cookies

In a bowl, stir together flour, granulated sugar, cocoa, baking powder, and salt. Using fingers, blend in butter. Stir in egg until mixture is blended. Spread dough in a thin layer in a bowl and freeze 10 minutes, or until firm.

Lightly grease 2 baking sheets and set aside. Spoon level teaspoons of dough onto a sheet of wax paper or aluminum foil. Put 2 tablespoons confectioners' sugar in a small bowl and dust hands with additional. Roll each piece of dough into a ball and then roll in confectioners' sugar. Arrange balls 2"/5cm apart on baking sheets and bake in upper and lower thirds of a preheated oven, switching sheets halfway through baking time, for 8 to 10 minutes, or until cookies are just set. Transfer cookies to a rack to cool.

Molasses Spice Cookies

4 cups/525 g all-purpose flour
½ tsp salt
2¼ tsp baking soda
2 tsp ground ginger
1¼ tsp ground cloves
1¼ tsp cinnamon
½ cup/115 g unsalted butter, softened
½ cup/100 g vegetable shortening
3½ cups/700 g granulated sugar
½ cup/120 ml unsulfured molasses
2 large eggs

Oven Temp: 325°F/165°C
Yield: 50 large cookies

In a large bowl, stir together flour, salt, baking soda, ginger, cloves and cinnamon. In another large bowl, beat together butter, shortening, and 3 cups/600 grams sugar until light and fluffy. Beat in molasses. Add eggs, one at a time, beating well after each addition. Gradually beat in flour mixture and combine well.

Put remaining sugar in a small shallow bowl. Form dough into 1½"/4cm balls and roll in sugar. On 2 well-greased baking sheets, arrange balls 4"/10cm apart and flatten slightly with bottom of a glass dipped in sugar.

Vegetable shortening, Crisco in the United States, is called Ozo in Belgium.

Bake cookies in batches in the middle of a preheated oven for 12 minutes, or until puffed and golden. (Cookies should be soft.) Transfer cookies to a rack and cool.

Ginger and Spice Sugar Cookies

An elegant cookie for an afternoon tea.

1¾ cups + 2 tbsp/250 g all-purpose flour
1 tsp baking soda
¼ tsp salt
¾ cup/170 g unsalted butter, softened
½ cup + 2 tbsp/125 g granulated sugar
3 tbsp minced crystallized ginger
1 large egg white
2 tbsp light corn syrup
1¼ tsp ground cinnamon
1 tsp ground ginger
1 tsp ground cloves

granulated sugar
confectioners' sugar

Oven Temp: 350°F/175°C
Yield: 35 cookies

Combine flour, baking soda and salt in a medium bowl. In a separate bowl, using an electric mixer, beat butter, granulated sugar and crystallized ginger until fluffy. At low speed, beat in egg white, corn syrup, cinnamon, ground ginger and cloves. Add dry ingredients and beat just until moist clumps form. Press together to form a smooth dough.

Form level tablespoons of dough into 1"/2½cm balls. Roll in granulated sugar and place on large greased cookie sheets, spacing cookies 2"/5cm apart on sheet. Dip bottom of glass into granulated sugar. Press cookies to 2½"/6cm rounds with a glass, dipping the glass into sugar before each pressing. Bake in a preheated oven until cookies are light brown, about 13 minutes. Let cookies stand on sheets 5 minutes. Transfer to rack and cool completely. Sift confectioners' sugar over each cookie.

Christmas Cookie Exchange

∞

Truffles

∞

Sugar Cookies

∞

Molasses Spice Cookies

∞

Speculoos (St. Nicholas)

∞

Spitzbuben

Speculoos

3¼ cups/425 g flour
1½ tsp cinnamon
¼ tsp baking soda
2¼ cups/500 g packed brown sugar
9 tbsp/125 g butter, softened
scant ¼ cup/50 ml water

Oven Temp: 375°F/190°C
Yield: 20 large cookies

These deliciously crisp spice cookies, whose origins go back for many centuries, are given to the children in Belgium on St. Nicholas' Day, December 6 - a great feast day when the Saint comes to reward the good children and punish the bad!

Mix flour, cinnamon and baking soda. Beat together sugar and butter and add flour mixture and water. Let the dough rest for 30 minutes. Roll the dough to ¼"/½cm thickness and cut with a cookie cutter or shape in wooden molds. Place on a greased cookie sheet and bake in a preheated oven for 10 to 15 minutes.

In Belgium, Speculoos are shaped by pressing the dough into decorative wooden molds (often St. Nicholas) rather than using a cutter. Dust the mold with flour and roll the dough onto the mold, pressing down firmly. Cut off extra dough, turn the mold over onto the cookie sheet and give it a firm rap to loosen the cookie.

Spitzbuben

These jam-filled shortbread cookies are a traditional Austrian Christmas treat.

1 cup/225 g unsalted butter, softened
1 cup/115 g confectioners' sugar, plus additional for dusting cookies
2 large egg yolks
2⅓ cups/300 g all-purpose flour
⅔ cup/160 ml seedless raspberry jam

Oven Temp: 350°F/175°C
325°F/165°C
Yield: 36 cookies

In a bowl, beat butter with an electric mixer until light and fluffy. Add sugar, beating until well combined. Add egg yolks, one at a time, beating thoroughly after each. Sift flour over butter mixture and fold in thoroughly.

Wrap dough in plastic wrap and press into a 10"/25cm square, about ½"/1¼cm thick. Chill dough until firm, about 2 hours. (Dough may be made 4 days ahead and kept chilled.) Divide the dough into 4 pieces. Keeping remaining dough chilled, lightly flour one piece of dough and on a lightly floured surface gently pound with a rolling pin to soften. Roll out dough into an 8"/20cm square, about ¼"/½cm thick. With a 2"/5cm round cutter cut out cookies, chilling scraps, and arrange them about 1"/2½cm apart on 2 large baking sheets lined with baking paper or foil. Make more cookies in the same manner with remaining dough. With a ⅜"/1cm plain pastry tip, cut a hole in the center of half of the cookies (these will be tops). The remaining whole cookies will be bottoms.

Place cookies in a preheated 350°F/175°C oven and immediately reduce the temperature to 325°F/150°C. Bake cookies until pale gold and firm, about 20 minutes, switching position of sheets halfway through baking. Cool sheets on racks. Lightly dust cookie tops with additional confectioners' sugar. Arrange cookie bottoms upside down on work surface.

In a small saucepan heat jam over low heat until slightly melted. Spread about ¼ teaspoon jam onto each cookie bottom and arrange a cookie top over it to form a sandwich. Transfer remaining jam to a small resealable plastic bag and snip a small hole in one corner. Squeeze a drop of jam into each opening in cookie tops and let stand until dry. Cookies may be frozen between layers of wax paper or parchment paper in an airtight container up to 2 weeks.

Variation: Also delicious with apricot jam.

Almond Macaroons

10 oz/285 g sliced blanched almonds (3 cups)
1½ cups/300 g granulated sugar
4 large egg whites
2 tbsp flour

Oven Temp: 325°F/165°C
Yield: 50 macaroons

In a food processor, grind almonds for 10 seconds. Add half of the sugar and blend another 10 seconds. Add egg whites and blend until smooth. Add flour and remaining sugar and blend until well combined.

Transfer batter to a pastry bag fitted with a ½"/1¼cm plain tip and pipe about fifty 1¼"/3cm diameter mounds onto 2 large cookie sheets lined with baking paper; leave 1½"/4cm between mounds. Bake macaroons in a preheated oven in the upper and lower thirds of oven, switching position of pans halfway through baking, until pale gold and firm to touch, 30 to 35 minutes. Transfer macaroons, still on paper, to racks and cool completely. Peel macaroons off paper. (May be made 3 days ahead and kept in an airtight container.)

If you do not own a pastry bag, spoon dough into a strong (freezer weight) plastic storage bag and diagonally clip off one corner to make a ½"/1¼cm hole. You may also spoon the batter into mounds.

Chocolate Truffles

9 oz/250 g dark chocolate
7 tbsp/100 g butter, softened
1 tbsp heavy cream
2 tbsp liqueur (optional)
unsweetened Dutch-processed cocoa
chocolate sprinkles
chopped nuts

Yield: 25 - 30 truffles

Melt chocolate over hot water. Remove from heat and add butter and cream. Mix well. (If desired, add 2 tablespoons of your favorite liqueur.) Place mixture in the refrigerator for no longer than 2 hours. To form balls, scrape surface of chocolate with a spoon and roll mixture between palms. Roll balls in cocoa powder, chopped nuts or chocolate sprinkles. Store in refrigerator.

Variation: Change the flavor by varying the liqueur. Rum, Irish Cream and Grand Marnier are particularly good with chocolate.

Chocolate Sauce

A silky, smooth sauce for dame blanche, or SOUR CREAM POUND CAKE - or use as a dip for fresh fruit.

8 oz/225 g semi-sweet chocolate
2 tbsp/30 g unsalted butter
sugar to taste (optional)
5 tbsp/75 ml boiling water
1 tsp vanilla extract

Yield: 1 cup/240 ml

Melt chocolate in a double boiler over gently simmering water. Add butter (and sugar) and stir until melted. Whisk in hot water and vanilla extract. Serve warm.

May be prepared ahead. Reheat in a double boiler over gently simmering water.

> ## CHOCOLATE
> In Belgium, there seems to be a chocolate shop on every street corner - you have so much to choose from. As a guideline, the higher the percentage of cocoa solids in the chocolate, the more bitter it tends to be, but there are other factors that influence the taste such as the beans, the roasting process, processing differences, and the sugar content. Belgium is truly a chocolate wonderland - taste, test, experiment. You will find Belgian chocolates richer, silkier, and meltingly flavorful. Find your own personal favorites and enjoy!
>
> *When the recipe does not specify a type of chocolate, dark chocolate is intended.*
>
> ◆ **Dark Chocolate:** Unsweetened chocolate, such as the baking chocolate found in the United States, does not exist in Belgium. Bitter chocolate (Noir de Noir, Noir and Amer) generally has a cocoa percentage of 55% or higher. Fondant or Dessert chocolate is slightly sweeter but still has less sugar than American dark chocolate. If you prefer sweeter chocolate, look for low cocoa percentages, somewhere around 45%. If you choose to use a sweeter chocolate than the recipe calls for, eliminate some of the sugar from the recipe. Since sweetness levels vary, it is important to taste the chocolate to determine if you need to make an adjustment. Dark chocolate will keep for 2 years under ideal storage conditions.

" In Chocolate We Trust... "
Alice Medrich

When melting chocolate, never allow it to exceed 120°F/49°C or there will be a loss in flavor. Always melt chocolate uncovered since even a drop of water (even steam) in the chocolate will cause it to seize. If you are adding liquid to melted chocolate, there must be a minimum of 1 tablespoon liquid to 1 ounce/30 grams chocolate to prevent seizing. If the melted chocolate does seize, adding fat (vegetable shortening or clarified butter) will somewhat restore the chocolate to a usable condition.

...more on CHOCOLATE

♦ Milk Chocolate: Milk chocolate contains pure chocolate liquor, milk solids, butter, vanilla (or vanillin) and extra cocoa butter. Milk chocolate is sweeter than dark chocolate. Since the milk solids can become rancid, it keeps only a little over a year under ideal conditions.

♦ White Chocolate: White chocolate contains no cocoa solids, but fine quality European white chocolate is made with real cocoa butter. Real white chocolate contains about 30% fat, 30% milk solids and 30% sugar with vanilla and lecithin added. It sets faster than dark chocolate after being melted, but is softer at room temperature. White chocolate has a shorter shelf life, lasting under ideal conditions less than a year.

♦ Unsweetened Dutch-Processed Cocoa Powder: The cocoa powder used in baking is referred to as unsweetened Dutch-processed cocoa to distinguish it from the sweetened type used to make chocolate drinks. This type of cocoa is treated to mellow the flavor and make it more soluble.

♦ The flavor of the completely unsweetened chocolate available in the United States is not as "chocolaty" as eating chocolate. If you wish to substitute for unsweetened chocolate, you may do one of the following:

For each 1 ounce/30 grams of bitter chocolate, use 2 ounces/60 grams of bittersweet or semi-sweet chocolate. Then, for every 2 ounces/60 grams of chocolate you use, remove 2 tablespoons of sugar and ⅔ teaspoons of butter from the recipe.

Cocoa gives a recipe a richer, stronger chocolate taste than chocolate. If you prefer, for every 1 ounce/30 grams of unsweetened chocolate, substitute 3 tablespoons of Dutch-processed unsweetened cocoa plus 1 tablespoon of unsalted butter. Dissolve the cocoa in 2 tablespoons of the liquid used in the recipe for the richest flavor.

♦ Storage: Chocolate should be stored, well wrapped, in an airtight container, at 60°-75°F/19°-24°C in a place with low humidity.

Gaufres Liègeoises
(Waffles with Pearl Sugar)

2¼ cups/500 g butter
½ cup/100 g granulated sugar
1⅓ oz/42-50 g fresh compressed yeast*
2 tbsp lukewarm milk
4 large eggs, lightly beaten
17 oz/½ liter milk
2⅓ lb/1 kg flour
pinch of salt
pinch of cinnamon
18 oz/500 g pearl sugar

Yield: 36 - 40 waffles

Melt the butter and add the granulated sugar. In a small bowl, proof the yeast (see index) with 2 tablespoons warm milk. Add the eggs and 17 oz/½ liter milk to the butter mixture and then stir in the yeast. Stir in the flour, salt and cinnamon until well combined. Add pearl sugar and stir well. (The batter will be quite thick.)

Warm the waffle iron (one with large holes works best) and brush lightly with oil. Spoon on the waffle batter so that it will not spread all the way to the edges if you prefer rough edges rather than squared. Cook on moderately high heat until brown and glazed. You need to balance the heat so the outside is just caramelized when the inside is cooked through.

There are two types of waffles to enjoy in Belgium. Gaufres Bruxelloises (crisp and dry) are delicious heated and served with a scoop of ice cream or whipped cream. Gaufres Liègeoises (thick and cakey) are heated until the exterior is caramelized and the interior is soft and warm. You will find them available on practically every street corner - the warm smell of caramel is especially enticing on a winter day!

* 2 (¼ oz/7 g) pkg dry yeast, proofed in ½ cup/120 ml warm milk from the recipe

> " There is nothing more wonderful than the sweet scent of waffles... fresh from the iron, the greaseproof paper in the palm of one's hand... strolling past the din of the colorful carousel with one's mouth full. "
> Rosine Dijn

Cookie Crumb Crust

1¼ cups/300 ml crumbs
4 tbsp/55 g butter, melted
2-4 tbsp granulated sugar
dash cinnamon (optional)

Yield: 9"/24cm pie crust

Graham crackers are most commonly used for cookie crumb crusts in the United States, but they are not readily available in Belgium. You may substitute Digestive Biscuits, Petit Beurre, or Bastogne cookies or some combination of these.

Mix crumbs, butter, sugar (and cinnamon). If the cookie has a high butter content, you may need slightly less butter. If the cookie has a high sugar content, use the lesser amount of sugar.

Twenty 1½"/6½cm squares of graham crackers equal 1¼ cups/300 ml of crumbs which will cover the bottom and sides of a 9"/24cm pie plate.

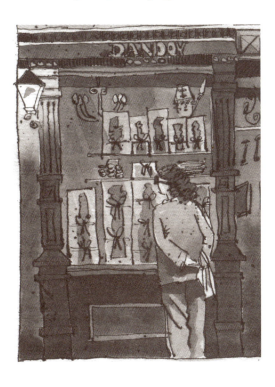

Pâte Brisée

This is a classic short crust pastry for tarts, quiches and pies. The crust is high in butter with a tender, flaky, dry texture.

1 ¼ cup/165 g all-purpose flour
pinch of salt
9 tbsp/125 g unsalted butter
4 tbsp ice water

Oven Temp: 350°F/175°C
Yield: 1 crust

Mix flour and salt. With pastry blender or knives, cut the butter into the flour until pea-sized pieces are formed. Add chilled water, a tablespoon at a time, and mix with a fork until you can work it into a ball with your hands. The dough should not be handled too much. Cut dough into two pieces, place each ball into a plastic bag and chill 3 hours or overnight. (Dough can be frozen up to one week.)

On a well-floured pastry cloth or surface, roll out chilled pastry to about ¼"/½cm thickness. Fit dough into one large or individual pans. Press dough into place and trim excess pastry. If the recipe calls for a runny filling, do not prick the bottom of the pastry in the tart pans.

Prebaking (Blind Baking): If the recipe calls for prebaking (blind baking) the tart shell, line the pastry with foil and use pie weights or beans to prevent bubbling of the pastry. Bake 15 minutes in a preheated oven. Remove beans and foil and continue baking until golden brown.

Pâte Sucrée

Yield: 1 crust

This is a sweetened version of PÂTE BRISÉE. The addition of sugar makes it more appropriate for dessert preparations.

Follow the same method as for PÂTE BRISÉE, mixing 2 teaspoons of fine granulated sugar with the flour and salt.

Pâte Sablée

This is a sugar crust pastry which uses an egg as one of its ingredients. It is rich, dense and sweet, and particularly suitable for fruit and creamy dessert fillings. It tends to stay crisp since it is closer to delicate cookie dough than a flaky pastry.

1 cup/130 g flour
7 tbsp/100 g unsalted butter
⅛ teaspoon salt
½ cup/60 g confectioners' sugar
1 large egg yolk
drop of vanilla extract (optional)

Oven Temp: 375°F/190°C
Yield: 10"/24cm tart shell

Sift flour onto a work surface or into a bowl and make a well in the center. Dice the butter into the well and work in with fingertips until very soft. Sift sugar onto flour mixture, add salt and work in. Make a well in the center, add the egg yolk and mix, gradually drawing in the flour. (If using vanilla, add and rub into dough by smearing it quickly across work surface with the palm of your hand.) Do not overwork the dough. Put on lightly floured wax paper or plastic wrap and flatten into a disk. Dust fingers with flour, transfer dough into a loose-bottomed tart pan and working quickly with fingertips, press into pan and up the sides. Cover with plastic wrap and refrigerate 2 to 3 hours. Remove the plastic wrap, and prick the dough with a fork. Line the shell with heavy foil, pressing well into edges, and fill with pie weights or dried beans. Bake in a preheated oven for 20 minutes.

For a partially baked shell, remove the weights and foil and bake an additional 10 minutes or until lightly browned all over.

For a fully baked shell, remove the weights and foil and bake an additional 10 to 20 minutes, watching carefully to be sure it does not burn. Cool before filling.

To make the dough in a food processor, place flour, butter, salt and sugar in the work bowl. Process just until the mixture resembles coarse crumbs. Add the egg yolk (and vanilla), and pulse just until the pastry begins to hold together. Transfer to lightly floured wax paper or plastic wrap and flatten into a disk. Continue as above.

Acknowledgments

The American Women's Club of Brussels would like to thank and acknowledge those individuals whose dedication, expertise and commitment to quality have made this book possible:

Recipe Category Chairmen:
Nadene Beck - Poultry and Game
Anna Becker - Appetizers
Pam Briggs - Pasta, Rice and Vegetables
Carolyn Demps - Seafood
Karen Di Pasquale - Soups and Salads
Carrie Doyle - Bread and Brunch
Marty Niebel - Desserts
Vicky Ralph - Soups and Salads
Lori Roos - Meat
Cathy Vorwald - Pasta, Rice and Vegetables

Typists:
Sharon Soldenwagner
Inger Tucker

Research:
Catherine Braas
Frances Snyder-Meurgey

Proofing:
Weezie Blanchard
Carol Gerber
Dorothy Gillette
Carolyn Grulich
Marianne Lipman
Barbara McFadden
Linda Tesauro

Accounting:
Diane Walden

Quotes:
Weezie Blanchard

Restaurant Recipes:
Sandy Dumont
Roberta Gaines
Madeline Leone

Special Thanks:
Susan Claypool
Sue Corti
Sharon Crane
Sophie D'Assche
Mary Fay
Celeste Gardiner
Gale Gropp
Roseanne Hahn
Cynthia Hall
Rosalie Hancook
Sue Hawkins
Nancy Kapstein
Christel Letellier
Teri Meyer
Susan O'Leary
Meredith Spangenberg
Candace Strusse
Marjorie Tommer
Fancy Cake

A special thank you is extended to the individuals on the AWCB Board of Directors and the Executive Board. We extend an extra thank you to Clare Swain and Elsie Bose for their encouragement and support.

Apple Pie to Waterzooi

Contributors

Antoinette Alloy-Contratto ◆ Judy Arrieta ◆ Carole Baginski ◆ Mindy Bartholomae ◆ Gwen Basile ◆ Anna Becker ◆ Joanne Berg ◆ Weezie Blanchard ◆ Elsie Bose ◆ Marijean Boueri ◆ Vicki Bridgewater ◆ Pam Briggs ◆ Judy Bronczek ◆ Nancy Brown ◆ Amparo Brunner ◆ Pamela Burkley ◆ Francie Camp ◆ Barbara Carmichael ◆ Teresa Cannon ◆ Debbie Cavillon ◆ Susan Claypool ◆ Denise Crenwelge-DeValck ◆ Marion Cromarty ◆ Jany De Keersmaeker ◆ Karen Di Pasquale ◆ Carrie Doyle ◆ Beth Eley ◆ Fran Falender ◆ Janet Faure ◆ Shirley Feather ◆ Kathleen Fiorenza ◆ Katharine Fodnaess ◆ Pamela Fontainas ◆ Annicq Gaby ◆ Roberta Gaines ◆ Marian Gale-Batten ◆ Celeste Gardiner ◆ Susan Gassner ◆ Michelle Gessner ◆ Lori Gibson ◆ Laurie Gosch ◆ Joan Grady ◆ Karen Graham ◆ Joan Grecchi ◆ Janet Green ◆ Karen Gregg ◆ Gale Gropp ◆ Carolyn Grulich ◆ Roseanne Hahn ◆ Elizabeth Hallerman ◆ Pamela Hamburger ◆ Rosalie Hancook ◆ Marian Harris ◆ Kate Hawk ◆ Nancy Hobby ◆ Brenda Hollingsworth ◆ Lou Ann Holtzleiter ◆ Cheryl Honig ◆ Carol Hull ◆ Judy Jankowski ◆ Sue Jones ◆ Kathy Joshua ◆ Cynthia Kaiser ◆ Cindy Kanwar ◆ Bonnie Kearney ◆ Ann King ◆ Jackie King ◆ Ellen Kirk ◆ Mary Kokot ◆ Cathy Kotanchik ◆ Mary Lae ◆ Sally Larson ◆ Karul Lasher ◆ Angelina Le Moli ◆ Madeline Leone ◆ Marianne Lipman ◆ Kris Loeber ◆ Carolyn Ludwig ◆ Doreen Mackinsie-Wilson ◆ Vicky Mall ◆ Mary Anne Martin ◆ Laurie Mayers ◆ Pam McClure ◆ Barbara McFadden ◆ Maura Mudd McGill ◆ Carol McKie ◆ Caryn Mefford ◆ Catherine Meuris ◆ Julie Miller ◆ Kathryn Morrissey ◆ Dixie Lee Morse ◆ Karen Mosteller ◆ Joyce Mostinckx ◆ Marty Niebel ◆ Eric Novotny ◆ Susan O'Leary ◆ Regina Olmstead ◆ Beverly Orr ◆ Dona Parady ◆ Lorna Peacock Van-Hulle ◆ Hilary Pickles ◆ Karen Ploetz ◆ Denise Radecke ◆ Vicki Ralph ◆ Gigi Ries ◆ Lori Roos ◆ Sandy Roswall ◆ Nancy Savage ◆ Marie Schmude ◆ Cathy Schrock ◆ Glenna Sevage ◆ Esther Shafran ◆ Liz Shoults ◆ Joan Skoog ◆ Linda Smyers ◆ Frances Snyder-Meurgey ◆ Linda Sørensen ◆ Karen Stiros ◆ Jaime Stone ◆ Debra Summers ◆ Clare Swain ◆ Lisa Tedder ◆ Elizabeth Telegdy ◆ Linda Tesauro ◆ Marjorie Tommer ◆ Karen Turner ◆ Susan van Alsenoy ◆ Loveday Van de Wetering de Rooy ◆ Dolly van Dierendonck ◆ Gerry van Gelder ◆ Catherine Vorwald ◆ Liz Wachs ◆ Susan Walsh

Testers

Janice Allan ◆ Antoinette Alloy-Contratto ◆ Susan Aparicio ◆ Judy Arrieta ◆ Carole Baginski ◆ Leslie Balloti ◆ Nancy Barnum ◆ Mindy Bartholomae ◆ Shirley Barton ◆ Gwen Basile ◆ Suzanne Beard ◆ Angela Beck ◆ Mary Jo Biedenharn ◆ Weezie Blanchard ◆ Elsie Bose ◆ Guynoir Bowen ◆ Sheila Brewster ◆ Judy Bronczek ◆ Amparo Brunner ◆ Pamela Burkley ◆ Anne Caprioglio ◆ Sheryl Carlson ◆ Barbara Carmichael ◆ Jacqueline Casse ◆ Debbie Cavillon ◆ Jennifer Conlin ◆ Patty Cordaro ◆ Patricia Costa ◆ Sharon Crane ◆ Diane Cullinan ◆ Sherry Deaton ◆ Heidi de Vries ◆ Shirley Feather ◆ Maggie Flammand ◆ Katharine Fodnaess ◆ Judy Foerster ◆ Marian Gale-Batten ◆ Roberta Gaines ◆ Michelle Gessner ◆ Joan Grady ◆ Janet Green ◆ Lauren Greenberger ◆ Karen Gregg ◆ Carolyn Grulich ◆ Roseanne Hahn ◆ Elizabeth Hallerman ◆ Karen Harris ◆ Diane Henninger ◆ Carol Hull ◆ Jana Lindsey ◆ Jan Linsky ◆ Kris Loeber ◆ Marion Lonn ◆ Loren Malcolm ◆ Vicky Mall ◆ Laurie Mayers ◆ Judy McClung ◆ Jane McFadden ◆ Joy Mimberg ◆ Chris Mirabile ◆ Kitty Moore ◆ Kathryn Morrissey ◆ Nancy Morrissey ◆ Dixie Lee Morse ◆ Karen Mosteller ◆ Carrie Murrin ◆ Susan Narta ◆ Lynette Norris ◆ Erin O'Neill ◆ Hilary Pickles ◆ Lisa Polizzi ◆ Helen Pyne ◆ Robin Rauch ◆ Corrine Sawyer ◆ Nancy Schwartz ◆ Judy Seaman ◆ Liz Shoults ◆ Joan Skoog ◆ Linda Smyers ◆ Frances Snyder-Meurgey ◆ Cindy Stuart ◆ Candice Strusse ◆ Lisa Tedder ◆ Linda Tesauro ◆ Christa Thompson ◆ Marjorie Tommer ◆ Harriet Tritell ◆ Liz Wachs ◆ Susan Walsh ◆ Joyceinne Williams ◆ Deborah Winkelhaus

Recipes have been tested and every attempt has been made to ensure accuracy. Restaurant recipes have been printed as submitted.

Equivalents and Measurements

Whenever possible, dry ingredients have been measured by grams (for accuracy) and by volume (the method more familiar to American cooks). Use the chart below to convert to the measuring system you prefer. Some ingredients, such as vegetables, fruits or nuts are given by volume (liquid measure). Since ounces (oz) may mean either weight or fluid measure, check the metric conversion to avoid confusion. When ounces (oz) are converted into grams (g) it is a weight measure; when ounces (oz) are converted into milliliters (ml) it is a liquid or fluid ounce measurement. Fluid ounce measurements use an American Standard ounce, not an Imperial ounce.

Measuring Butter: Butter measurements have been given in standard 15 ml tablespoons and metric weight. To convert tablespoons to ounces, halve the number of tablespoons given (4 tbsp = 2 oz). There are 8 tablespoons in 1/2 cup of butter.

1 teaspoon (tsp) = 1 cuillère à cafe = 5 ml
1 tablespoon (tbsp) = 1 cuillère à soupe = 15 ml
1 Imperial ounce = 28.4 ml
1 American ounce = 29.56 ml

Conversions are as accurate as possible, but in some cases have been rounded slightly for convenience.

WEIGHT		VOLUME	
American Standard	Metric	American Standard	Metric
1 oz	30 g	1 fluid oz	30 ml
2 oz	55 g	2 fluid oz	60 ml
3 oz	85 g	3 fluid oz	90 ml
4 oz	115 g	4 fluid oz	120 ml
5 oz	140 g	5 fluid oz	150 ml
6 oz	170 g	6 fluid oz	175 ml
7 oz	200 g	7 fluid oz	200 ml
8 oz	225 g	8 fluid oz (1 cup)	240 ml
9 oz	250 g	10 fluid oz (1 1/4 cups)	300 ml
10 oz	280 g	12 fluid oz (1 1/2 cups)	350 ml
11 oz	310 g	16 fluid oz (2 cups/1 pt)	475 ml
12 oz	340 g	32 fluid oz (4 cups/1 qt)	950 ml
13 oz	370 g	34 fluid oz	1000 ml
14 oz	400 g		(1 liter)
15 oz	425 g		
16 oz (1 lb)	450 g		
24 oz (1½ lbs)	680 g		
32 oz (2 lbs)	900 g		
35⅓ oz (2⅕ lbs)	1000 g		
	(1 kilo)		

Oven Temperatures

Fahrenheit	Celsius	Gas Mark	Temperature
250°F	120°C	1/2	Cool
275°F	135°C	1	Very Slow
300°F	150°C	2	Slow
325°F	165°C	2-3	Very Moderate
350°F	175°C	3	
375°F	190°C	4	Moderate
400°F	200°C	5	Moderately Hot
425°F	220°C	6	Hot
450°F	230°C	7	
475°F	245°C	8	Very Hot
500°F	260°C	9	Extremely Hot

Abbreviations

C	celcius
cm	centimeter
env	envelope
F	fahrenheit
g	gram
"	inch
kg	kilogram
ml	milliliter
oz	ounce
pt	pint
lb	pound
pkg	package
qt	quart
tbsp	tablespoon
tsp	teaspoon

Index

A

Abbreviations, 333
Al dente pasta, about, 195, 197
Algerian Brochette, 147
Almond Macaroons, 321
Almond Tart with Pears and Chocolate, 281
Almonds, *see* Nut(s)
Anguilles au Vert, 110
Appetizers:
 see section listing, 8
 Last Minute, 32
Apple(s):
 about, 285
 cake, cinnamon, 254
 compote, 256
 cranberry crisp, 296
 honey mustard vinaigrette, 77
 pie, 277
 salad, curried chicken, pasta and, 92
 tart, Bavarian, 285
 tart with caramel sauce, 283
 tarte tatin, 284
Apple Compote, 256
Apple Cranberry Crisp, 296
Apple Honey Mustard Vinaigrette, 77
Apple Pancakes, 259
Apple Pie, 277
Apple Tart with Caramel Sauce, 283
Apricot and Almond Tart, 280
Apricot Soufflé, 297
Armoricaine Sauce, 189
Artichoke Dip, 41
Arugula, about, 94
Arugula Salad with Avocado, Shiitakes and Prosciutto, 71
Asparagus:
 about, 21
 asperges à la Flamande, 20
 pasta, with shrimp and, 191
 salad vinaigrette, 82
 wrapped in prosciutto, 19
Asparagus Salad Vinaigrette, 82
Asparagus Wrapped in Prosciutto, 19
Asperges à la Flamande (asparagus), 20
Aspic/Gelée, about, 40
Aubergine, *see* Eggplant

Avocado(s):
 salad, orange, 79
 salad, arugula, with shiitake, prosciutto and, 71
 super guacamole, 43

B

Bain marie, about, 297
Baking powder, about, 233
Baking Powder Biscuits, 246
Balsamic Grilled Chicken, 148
Balsamic Vinegar, about, 148
Banana Bread, 231
Bananas, freezing, tip for, 231
Basic Savory Tart Pastry, 272
Basic Vinaigrette, 99
Bavarian Apple Tart, 285
Bean(s), dried:
 cooking, tips for, 73
 soaking, tip for, 66
 black bean soup, 63
 four bean chicken salad, 73
 lentil soup, 61
 lentils, about, 61
 winter vegetable beef soup, 66
Bean(s), green:
 Italian, 215
 with Roquefort and walnuts, 216
 salade Liègeoise, 84
 with walnuts, 216
Béarnaise au Vin Rouge, 184
Béchamel Sauce, 152
Beef:
 about, 180-181
 Burgundy, 179
 carbonnade de boeuf à la gueuze, 177
 carbonnades Flamandes, 178
 chili con carne, 183
 filet mignon avec sauce béarnaise au vin rouge, 184
 filet mignon with green peppercorn sauce, 185
 lasagne, 182
 soup, goulash, 64
 soup, winter vegetable, 66
 and venison stew, rich, 163
Beef Burgundy, 179

Belgian Bread, about, 239
Belgian Customs:
 dining "chez vous," 15
 Epiphany cake, about, 311
 frites, 208
 the pâtisserie, 244
 soup, 47
 speculoos, 319
 waffles, 324
 waterzooi, 105
Belgian Endives, *see* Endive(s), Belgian
Beurre manié, about, 10
Biscuit(s) and Roll(s):
 baking powder biscuits, 246
 cheese pinwheel biscuits, 246
 cinnamon pinwheel biscuits, 246
 cinnamon sticky buns, 247
 crusty yeast rolls, 245
 English cream scones, 248
 orange marmalade pinwheel biscuits, 246
 popovers, 243
 sticky buns, 247
Bisque de Poisson et Fruits de Mer, 49
Black Bean Soup, 63
Blanquette d'Agneau (lamb), 170
Blanquette de Veau (veal), 170
Blue Cheese(s):
 about, 276
 Gorgonzola, in endive spears, smoked chicken with, 26
 Roquefort, and walnuts, with green beans, 216
 Roquefort cheese puffs, 30
 Roquefort, endive, pear and walnut salad, 77
 Roquefort, endive salad with, 77
 Roquefort tartlets, 37
 salad dressing, 101
 Stilton, and pork stroganoff, 167
Blue Cheese Salad Dressing, 101
Blueberry, lemon bread, 235
Blueberry Pancakes, 259
Boursin Soup, 59
Bouquet garni, about, 48
Braised Endives, 226
Braised Veal Shanks with White Beans and Tomatoes, 169
Bran Muffins, 243

Apple Pie to Waterzooi   335

Brazilian Shrimp and Coconut Soup, 56
Bread(s):
see also Biscuit(s) and Roll(s); Bread(s), sweet; Bread(s), yeast; Corn Bread(s) and Cornmeal; Muffins
    Belgian Bread, about, 239
    bruschetta, 27
    croutons, homemade, 53
    sausage and cheese strata, 264
Bread(s), sweet:
    banana, 231
    date nut, 237
    gingerbread, soft, 234
    lemon blueberry, 235
    mango tea, 236
    poppy seed, 238
    pumpkin, 233
    zucchini, 232
Bread(s), yeast:
    English muffin, 241
    oatmeal, 240
    Sally Lunn, 250
Breakfast Corn Muffins, 242
Breakfast Pancakes, 259
Brie:
    en croûte, variations, 36
    mushroom soup, 52
    with sun-dried tomatoes, 36
Brie en Croûte, variations, 36
Brie with Sun-Dried Tomatoes, 36
Broccoli:
    purée, 223
    sesame, oriental, 222
    soup, cream of, 59
Broccoli Purée, 223
Broiled Swordfish with Mustard Sauce, 122
Brown sugar, softening, tip for, 315
Brownies, see Cookies and Brownies
Bruschetta, 27
Brussels Sprouts:
    cooking, tip for, 225
    roasted, 225
    shredded, with prosciutto, 224
Bulgur Wheat, see Rice and Grain(s)
Butter, garlic herb, 143
Butter, measuring, 332
Butter, yeast baking with, tip for, 245
Buttermilk Pancakes, 259
Buttermilk, substituting, tips for, 242, 249

C

Cabbage(s):
    about, 94
    cole slaw, 98

soup, bean and, Tuscan, 62
    white, 228
Caesar Salad, 100
Caesar Salad Dressing, 100
Cake(s) and Torte(s):
see also Cake(s), breakfast; Cake(s), savory
    carrot cake, 309
    cheesecake supreme, 312
    chocolate birthday cake, 306
    chocolate chestnut torte, 293
    chocolate layered torte, 294
    chocolate sheet cake, 305
    cranberry cake, 308
    galette des rois, 311
    gâteau aux framboises, 307
    hazelnut meringue torte, 292
    raspberry meringue torte, 290
    reina nobile, la, 310
    sour cream pound cake, 304
Cake(s), breakfast:
    cinnamon apple, 254
    overnight crunch coffee cake, 252
    pecan and almond coffee cake, 251
    raspberry cream cheese coffee cake, 253
Cake(s), savory:
see also Quiche(s), Strata(s) and Frittata(s)
    curried chicken cheesecake, 265
    hot spinach cheesecake, 266
    gâteau de crêpes à la Florentine, 11
California Pasta Salad, 91
Caramel Sauce, 283
Carbonnade de Boeuf à la Gueuze, 177
Carbonnades Flamandes, 178
Carmelized Onion and Chèvre Canapés, 31
Carrot(s):
    cake, 309
    flans, 217
    spring soup, 47
    sunshine glazed, 219
Carrot Cake, 309
Carrot Flans, 217
Cashew, Shrimp and Pea Salad, 88
Cashews, see Nut(s)
Cassolette de Palourdes au Champagne (clams), 138
Caviar Pie, 44
Celery Root (Celeriac), about, 22
Cheese Pinwheel Biscuits, 246
Cheese Soufflé, 263
Cheese(s):
see also Blue Cheese(s); Brie; Chèvre
    about, 276
    Boursin soup, 59
    chutney cheese spread, 41
    curried chicken cheesecake, 265
    petites gougères (cheese puffs), 30

Romano, about, 200
    and sausage strata, 264
    soufflé, 263
Cheesecake, curried chicken, 265
Cheesecake, spinach, hot, 266
Cheesecake Supreme, 312
Cheeses, blue, see Blue Cheese(s)
Cherry Clafoutis, 296
Chestnut(s):
    candied, about, 293
    chocolate torte, 293
    crème caramel à la crème de marrons, 302
    soup, 58
Chestnut Soup, 58
Chèvre:
    about, 74, 276
    and caramelized onion canapés, 31
    with cod and roasted peppers, 127
    Crottin de Chavignol salade, 74
    eggplant, tomatoes and, 213
    mesclun aux timbales de chèvre, 75
    and smoked salmon canapés, 31
    spread, 237
    warm, with red bell pepper sauce, 12
Chèvre Spread, 237
Chicken:
    balsamic grilled, 148
    breasts in phyllo, 155
    breasts on wild mushroom ragoût, 154
    brochette, Algerian, 147
    with cashews, 145
    cheesecake, curried, 265
    garlic herb, roast, 143
    and leek lasagne, 152
    and lemon grass soup, 55
    mousse de foie de volaille, 40
    Niçoise, 142
    piccata, 146
    pizza, Malaysian, 149
    raspberry, 147
    salad, curried, pasta and apple, 92
    salad, four bean and, 73
    salad, golden, and spiced wheat, 93
    salad, oriental, 72
    saté, 144
    smoked, and Gorgonzola in endive spears, 26
    waterzooi de volaille à la Gantoise, 141
    in white wine, 153
Chicken and Leek Lasagne, 152
Chicken and Lemon Grass Soup, 55
Chicken Breasts in Phyllo, 155
Chicken Breasts on Wild Mushroom Ragoût, 154
Chicken in White Wine, 153
Chicken Niçoise, 142
Chicken Piccata, 146
Chicken Saté, 144

Chicken with Cashews, 145
Chicon, about, 94
Chicon, see Endive(s), Belgian
Chili Con Carne, 183
Chilled Cucumber Soup, 47
Chocolate:
  birthday cake, 306
  chestnut torte, 293
  crackles, 317
  crème au chocolat, 300
  embassy brownies, 314
  frosting, 305, 306
  melting, tips for, 323
  mousse, 298
  mousse, white chocolate, with
    raspberry Grand Marnier sauce, 299
  muffins, 244
  sauce, 322
  sheet cake, 305
  tart, almond, with pears and, 281
  tart gourmandise, 282
  torte, layered, 294
  truffles, 321
  types of, about, 322-323
  ultimate chocolate chip cookies, 315
Chocolate Birthday Cake, 306
Chocolate Chestnut Torte, 293
Chocolate Crackles, 316
Chocolate Layered Torte, 294
Chocolate Mousse, 298
Chocolate Muffins, 244
Chocolate Sauce, 322
Chocolate Sheet Cake, 305
Chocolate Tart Gourmandise, 282
Chocolate Truffles, 321
Chutney Cheese Spread, 41
Cider, French, about, 172
Cilantro, about, 164
Cinnamon Apple Cake, 254
Cinnamon Pancakes, 259
Cinnamon Pinwheel Biscuits, 246
Cinnamon Sticky Buns, 247
Clafoutis aux Cerises, 296
Clams, see Shellfish
Classic Mussels, 137
Cobbler(s) and Crisp(s):
  apple cranberry crisp, 296
  cherry clafoutis, 296
  plum and almond cobbler, 295
Cocoa, unsweetened Dutch-processed,
  about, 323
Coconut, and shrimp soup, Brazilian, 56
Cod with Chèvre and Roasted
  Peppers, 127
Coffee:
  crème au café, 300
  tiramisu, 304
Coffee Cakes, see Cake(s), breakfast
Cold Cucumber Sauce, 117

Cold Lemon Soufflé, 298
Cole Slaw, 98
Compote, apple, 256
Compote, summer fruit, 313
Cookie Crumb Crust, 325
Cookie crumbs, about, 325
Cookies and Brownies:
  almond macaroons, 321
  chocolate crackles, 317
  embassy brownies, 314
  ginger and spice sugar cookies, 318
  molasses spice cookies, 317
  speculoos, 319
  spitzbuben, 320
  sugar cookies, 316
  ultimate chocolate chip cookies, 315
Coquilles Saint-Jacques à l'Effilochée
  d'Endives, 135
Coriander, about, 164
Corn Bread(s) and Cornmeal:
  breakfast corn muffins, 242
  cornmeal pancakes, 260
  roast breast of turkey with corn bread,
    spinach and pecans, 156
  Texas corn bread, 249
Cornmeal Pancakes, 260
Country Sausage, 264
Court-bouillon, homemade, 128
Court-bouillon, instant, about, 111
Couscous salad, Greek, 94
Couscous, see Rice and Grain(s)
Crab Quiche, 271
Crab Squares, 29
Cranberries, freezing, tip for, 296
Cranberry, apple crisp, 296
Cranberry Cake, 308
Cream, about, 303
Cream Cheese Frosting, 309
Cream of Broccoli Soup, 59
Cream of Fennel Soup, 50
Cream of Potato and Leek Soup, 57
Cream puff dough, about, 30
Creamy Dill Dressing, 88
Creamy Seafood Sauce, 115
Crème au Café, 300
Crème au Chocolat, 300
Crème Brûlée, 301
Crème Brûlée à l'Orange, 301
Crème Brûlée Café, 301
Crème Caramel à la Crème
  de Marrons, 302
Crème Fraîche Epaisse, about, 303
Crêpes, 258
Crêpes aux Fruits de Mer, 125
Crisps, see Cobbler(s) and Crisp(s)
Croquettes aux Crevettes Grises, 24
Croquettes, salmon, 117
Crottin de Chavignol Salade, 74
Croutons, homemade, 53

Crudités, about, 42
Crusts, see Pastry and Crust(s)
Crusty Yeast Rolls, 245
Cucumber(s):
  chilled soup, 47
  mold, fresh, 97
  sauce, cold, 117
Currant(s), fresh:
  about, 256
  red, jelly, 255
  red, meringue pie, 291
Curried Chicken Cheesecake, 265
Curried Chicken, Pasta and Apple
  Salad, 92
Curry Dip, 42
Custard(s):
  crème au café, 300
  crème au chocolat, 300
  crème brûlée, 301
  crème brûlée à l'orange, 301
  crème brûlée café, 301
  crème caramel à la crème
    marrons, 302
  lemon curd, 310

D

Date Nut Bread, 237
Demi-glace, about, 51
Desserts:
  see section listing, 274-275
Dining "Chez Vous," 15
Dip(s) and Spread(s):
  artichoke dip, 41
  caviar pie, 44
  chèvre spread, 237
  chutney cheese spread, 41
  curry dip, 42
  egg spread, 19
  green goddess dip, 42
  mousse de foie de volaille, 40
  shrimp spread, 39
  smoked trout pâté, 38
  tapenade of sun-dried tomatoes, 44
Dough, sweet roll, 248
Dressing, for poultry, see Stuffing
Dressings, salad, see Salad Dressing(s)
Duck, see Poultry
Duck breasts, about, 161
Dutch-processed cocoa, unsweetened,
  about, 323

E

Echalotes, see Shallot(s)
Echalotes au Vin Rouge, 228
Eel with Spinach and Sorrel, 110

Eels, about, 110
Egg spread, 19
Eggplant:
   about, 198
   pappardelle melanzane, 198
   and roasted pepper terrine,
     with parsley sauce, 16
   spaghetti with aubergine sauce, 199
   tomatoes and chèvre, 213
Eggplant and Roasted Pepper Terrine
   with Parsley Sauce, 16
Eggplant, Tomatoes and Chèvre, 213
Eggs, shirred, 262
Eggs, whites, tips for, 298
Embassy Brownies, 314
Endive Boats with Marinated Smoked
   Salmon, 27
Endive, Pear, Roquefort and Walnut
   Salad, 77
Endive Salad with Roquefort, 77
Endive(s), Belgian:
   about, 94, 226
   boats, with marinated smoked
     salmon, 27
   braised, 226
   coquilles Saint-Jacques à l'effilochée
     d'endives, 135
   et jambon au gratin, 227
   salad, pear, Roquefort and walnut, 77
   salad with Roquefort, 77
   spears, smoked chicken and
     Gorgonzola in, 26
Endives et Jambon au Gratin, 227
English Cream Scones, 248
English Muffin Bread, 241
Escalope de Veau Normande, 172
Equivalents and Measurements, 332

F

Fennel, about, 94
Fennel, pears and Parmesan, with
   mixed greens, 78
Fennel, soup, cream of, 50
Filet Mignon avec Sauce Béarnaise
   au Vin Rouge, 184
Filet Mignon with Green Peppercorn
   Sauce, 185
Fish:
   see also Salmon; Seafood; Shellfish
     and names of individual fish and
     shellfish
   about, 108-109
   anguille au vert (eel), 110
   bisque de poisson et fruits de mer, 49
   cod, spicy, with snow peas, 126
   cod with chèvre and roasted
     peppers, 127

   crêpes aux fruits de mer, 125
   goujonnettes de filets de sole
     aux jeunes pousses d'épinards, 107
   halibut with mango sauce, 124
   poached ray with brunoise of potatoes
     and tomatoes (skate), 10
   raie au beurre noisette (skate), 111
   removing odor, tip for, 121
   smoked terrine, 9
   smoked trout pâté, 38
   sole meunière, 106
   stock, about, 51
   swordfish brochette, 123
   swordfish, broiled, with mustard
     sauce, 122
   truite de l'abbé gourmand (trout), 112
   waterzooi de lotte (monkfish), 105
Flans, carrot, 217
Flavored Oil, 101
Flour, see note, 275
Flour, types of, about, 308
Foie gras, about, 22
Foie Gras Poêlé au Vinaigre
   Balsamique, 22
Four Bean Chicken Salad, 73
Fraises des bois, about, 305
French Cider, 172
French fries (Frites), 208
French Onion Soup, 60
French Potato Salad, 85
Fresh compressed yeast, see Yeast
Fresh Cucumber Mold, 97
Fresh Currants, 256
Frisée, about, 94
Frites, 208
Frittata, vegetable, 267
Fromage Frais, about, 303
Frosting(s):
   chocolate, 305, 306
   cream cheese, 309
Fruit(s):
   see also Apple(s); Avocado(s);
     Currant(s), fresh; Lemon(s); Pear(s);
     Raspberry(ies); and names of other
     individual fruits
   compote, summer, 313
Fusilli Rustica, 200

G

Galette des Rois, 311
Game:
   see section listing, 140
   about, 158
Garlic:
   about, 99
   chopping, tip for, 166
   herb butter, 143

   roasting with salt, 123
   salt, 127
   shrimp, 17
   storing, tip for, 183
Garlic Herb Butter, 143
Garlic Salt, 127
Garlic Shrimp, 17
Gâteau aux Framboises, 307
Gâteau de Crêpes à la Florentine, 11
Gâteau de Langoustines au Parfum
   de Curry Léger, 13
Gaufres Liègeoises, 324
Gelatin, tips for, 299
Gelée, about, 40
Gigot d'Agneau Farci en Croûte, 176
Ginger:
   ground, about, 234
   prawn tarts, 25
   salmon, 120
   soft gingerbread, 234
   and spice sugar cookies, 318
   storing, fresh, tip for, 220
Ginger and Spice Sugar Cookies, 318
Ginger Prawn Tarts, 25
Ginger Salmon, 120
Gingerbread, soft, 234
Glace de viande, about, 51
Goat Cheese:
   see also Chèvre
   about, 74, 276
Golden Chicken and Spiced Wheat
   Salad, 93
Gorgonzola, see Blue Cheese(s)
Goujonettes de Filets de Sole aux
   Jeunes Pousses d'Epinards, 107
Goulash Soup, 64
Graham cracker crust, see Cookie
   Crumb Crust, 325
Graham crackers, substituting for, 325
Grain(s), see Rice and Grain(s)
Greek Couscous Salad, 94
Green Beans, see Bean(s), green
Green Beans with Roquefort and
   Walnuts, 216
Green Beans with Walnuts, 216
Green Goddess Dip, 42
Green onions, about, 86
Grilled Salmon Steaks, 121
Guacamole, super, 43
Guinea Hen, see Poultry

H, I, J, K

Half & half (cream), about, 303
Halibut with Mango Sauce, 124
Hazelnut Meringue Torte, 292
Hazelnuts, see Nut(s)
Herb and Garlic Roast Pork, 166

Herbed Pork Loin with Bourbon Gravy, 168
Herbed Rack of Lamb, 174
Herbed Tomato Tart, 28
Herbed Vinaigrette, 99
Herbed Vinegar, 101
Herbes de Provence, homemade, 176
Herbs, fresh, cooking with, 169
Herbs, fresh, preserving, 213
Herbs, substituting dried for fresh, 58
Homard Braisé et Mousseline de Tomates, 128
Horseradish Mashed Potatoes, 212
Hot Spinach Cheesecake, 266
Icing, see Frosting(s)
Italian Green Beans, 215
Italian Mushroom Soup, 53
Jelly, red currant, 255

L

Lamb:
  about, 181
  with almonds, 175
  blanquette d'agneau, 170
  brochette, 174
  gigot d'agneau farci en croûte, 176
  rack of, herbed, 174
Lamb Brochette, 174
Lamb with Almonds, 175
Langoustine Stock, 13
Langoustines, about, 18
Langoustines au Curry, 18
Langoustines, gâteau de, au parfum de curry léger, 13
Lapin à la Moutarde, 162
Lardons, about, 100
Lasagne, 182
Lasagne, chicken and leek, 152
Last Minute Appetizers, 32
Leek(s):
  cleaning, about, 14
  and cream of potato soup, 57
  lasagne, chicken and, 152
  and lemon salad dressing, 78
  with mussels, saffron and cream, 136
  with orange ginger sauce, 220
  and truffles, scallops with, 133
Leeks with Orange Ginger Sauce, 220
Lemon(s):
  blueberry bread, 235
  cold soufflé, 298
  curd, 310
  and garlic pasta, 193
  leek salad dressing, 78
  rice, 207
  sauce, 234
  veal chops, braised, 173

Lemon and Garlic Pasta, 193
Lemon balm, about, 9
Lemon Blueberry Bread, 235
Lemon Braised Veal Chops, 173
Lemon Curd, 310
Lemon grass, about, 55
Lemon grass, soup, chicken and, 55
Lemon Leek Salad Dressing, 78
Lemon Rice, 207
Lemon Sauce, 234
Lentil Soup, 61
Lentils, about, 61
Lettuces, about, 94-95
Linguine with White Clam Sauce, 192
Lotte, waterzooi de, 105
Lobster, see Shellfish

M

Madeira Sauce, 155
Magret de canard, about, 161
Magret de Canard à la Crème, 161
Magret de Canard à l'Orange, 161
Malaysian Chicken Pizza, 149
Mango sauce, halibut with, 124
Mango Tea Bread, 236
Marrons, see Chestnut(s)
Mayonnaise, 102
Meat(s):
  see also Beef; Lamb; Pork; Veal
  about, 180-181
  lapin à la moutarde, 162
  rich venison and beef stew, 163
  stock, about, 50-51
Menus:
  After the Hunt, 162
  Afternoon Tea, 280
  An Evening in Venice, 215
  Autumn at the Market, 200
  Autumn Dinner, 52
  Belgian Coast Casual Dining, 126
  Belgian Evening, 179
  Belgian Restaurant Fare, 120
  Bistro Fare, 142
  Christmas Cookie Exchange, 318
  Cocktails on the Terrace, 26
  Entertaining Weekend Guests, 236
  Late Spring Dinner, 175
  Light Summer Luncheon, 88
  Neighborhood Coffee, 252
  Pasta Sampler, 194
  Puttin' on the Ritz, 31
  Ringing in the New Year, 184
  Seafood Mixed Grill, 132
  South of the Border Supper, 63
  Summer Barbecue, 90
  Sunday Brunch Buffet, 269
Meringue(s):

pie, red currant, 291
storing, tips for, 292
torte, hazelnut, 292
torte, raspberry, 290
Mesclun, about, 95
Mesclun aux Lardons, 76
Mesclun aux Timbales de Chèvre, 75
Milk, to scald, 240
Miniature Quiches, 37
Mirin, about, 120
Mixed Greens with Fennel, Pears and Parmesan, 78
Molasses Spice Cookies, 317
Monkfish, see Lotte
Moules, see also Mussels
Moules à la Crème, 137
Moules à l'Ail et aux Fines Herbes, 137
Moules Marinière, 137
Moules Marinière à la Gueuze, 137
Moules Provençale, 137
Mousse, chocolate, 298
Mousse de Foie de Volaille, 40
Mousse, white chocolate with raspberry Grand Marnier sauce, 299
Mousseline Sauce, 21
Muffin(s):
  baking, tips for, 243
  bran, 243
  breakfast corn, 242
  chocolate, 244
Mushroom(s):
  about, 150-151
  arugula salad with avocado, shiitakes and prosciutto, 71
  croustades, 33
  dried, about, 151
  dried wild, risotto with, 203
  and prosciutto tortellini, 195
  soup, Brie, 52
  soup, Italian, 53
  wild, on croutons, 23
  wild, ragoût, chicken breasts on, 154
Mushroom Brie Soup, 52
Mushroom Croustades, 33
Mushroom and Prosciutto Tortellini, 195
Mussels:
  about, 136
  with leeks, saffron and cream, 136
  leftover, uses for, 137
  moules à la crème, 137
  moules à l'ail et aux fines herbes, 137
  moules marinière (classic mussels), 137
  moules marinière à la gueuze, 137
  moules Provençale, 137
  sauces, tip for, 137
Mussels with Leeks, Saffron, and Cream, 136
Mustard sauce, broiled swordfish with, 122

Apple Pie to Waterzooi

N

Nut(s):
  see also Chestnut(s)
  almond, and plum cobbler, 295
  almond macaroons, 321
  almond tart, apricot and, 280
  almonds, lamb with, 175
  cashew, shrimp and pea salad, 88
  cashews, chicken with, 145
  date nut bread, 237
  hazelnut meringue torte, 292
  pecan and almond coffee cake, 251
  pecan toffee sauce, with sticky toffee puddings, 257
  pecans, corn bread and spinach, roast breast of turkey with, 156
  tarte amandine aux poires et au chocolat, 281
  walnuts, green beans with, 216
  walnuts, green beans with Roquefort and, 216
  walnuts, wild rice with, 204

O

Oak leaf lettuce, about, 95
Oatmeal Bread, 240
Oil, flavored, 101
Oil, olive, about, 75
Oil, oriental sesame, about, 222
Onion soup, French, 60
Onions, about, 218
Orange Avocado Salad, 79
Orange ginger sauce, leeks with, 220
Orange Marmalade Biscuits, 246
Oriental Chicken Salad, 72
Oriental Dressing, 72
Osso Buco, about, 169
Oven Temperatures, 333
Overnight Crunch Coffee Cake, 252

P

Pancakes and Waffles:
  apple pancakes, 259
  blueberry pancakes, 259
  breakfast pancakes, 259
  buttermilk pancakes, 259
  cinnamon pancakes, 259
  cornmeal pancakes, 260
  crêpes, 258
  raised waffles, 261
  waffles with pearl sugar, 324
  whole-wheat pancakes, 259

Papaya, and scampi, with hot sweet and sour sauce, 131
Pappardelle Melanzane (eggplant), 198
Parsley, about, 16
Parsley, fried, 24
Parsley Sauce, 16
Pasta:
  about, 196-197
  al dente, about, 195
  cooking, about, 197
  fusilli rustica, 200
  lemon and garlic, 193
  linguine with white clam sauce, 192
  mushroom and prosciutto tortellini, 195
  pappardelle melanzane (eggplant), 198
  with prawns and tomato fondue, 190
  salad, California, 91
  salad, curried, chicken and apple, 92
  salad with roasted peppers, basil and cheese, 90
  with scallops and bacon, 193
  scampi and tagliolini with armoricaine sauce, 189
  sesame noodle salad, 89
  with shrimp and asparagus, 191
  southwest, 201
  spaghetti with aubergine sauce (eggplant), 199
  spaghettini with fresh basil and tomato sauce, 194
  spinach stuffed shells Alfredo, 197
  tortellini pesto vegetable soup, 65
  warming, tip for, 191
Pasta Salad with Roasted Peppers, Basil and Cheese, 90
Pasta with Prawns and Tomato Fondue, 190
Pasta with Scallops and Bacon, 193
Pasta with Shrimp and Asparagus, 191
Pastry and Crust(s):
  see also Phyllo
  basic savory tart pastry, 272
  browning, tip for, 277
  cookie crumb crust, 325
  pâte brisée, 326
  pâte brisée au fromage, 268
  pâte sablée, 327
  pâte sucrée, 326
  pizza crust, 149
  prebaking (blind baking), 326
  pricking, tip for, 272
  yeast tart pastry, 286
Pâté:
  mousse de foie de volaille, 40
  smoked trout, 38
Pâte Brisée, 326
Pâte Brisée au Fromage, 268
Pâte Sablée, 327
Pâte Sucrée, 326

Pea salad, cashew and shrimp, 88
Peach Crumb Pie, 278
Pear(s):
  about, 281
  mixed greens with fennel, Parmesan and, 78
  salad, endive, Roquefort, walnut and, 77
  tart, almond, with chocolate and, 281
Pearl sugar, 315
Pecan and Almond Coffee Cake, 251
Pecan Toffee Sauce, 257
Pecans, see Nut(s)
Pepper, about, 185
Pepper(s), bell:
  eggplant and roasted pepper terrine with parsley sauce, 16
  pasta salad with roasted peppers, basil and cheese, 90
  roasted, with cod and chèvre, 127
  roasting, tips for, 71
  warm chèvre with red bell pepper sauce, 12
  yellow, roasted, and tomato soup, 54
Pesto, 201
Pesto, tortellini, vegetable soup, 65
Petite Salade du Sud-Ouest, 69
Petite Tarte aux Herbes Potagères, 14
Petites Gougères (cheese puffs), 30
Phyllo:
  chicken breasts in, 155
  flowers, 35
  freezing, about, 155
  spanakopeta, 34
  tiropita, 34
Phyllo Flowers, 35
Pie Crusts, see Pastry and Crust(s)
Pie(s) and Tart(s):
  see also, Tart(s), savory
  almond tart with pears and chocolate, 281
  apple pie, 277
  apple tart with caramel sauce, 283
  apricot and almond tart, 280
  Bavarian apple tart, 285
  chocolate tart gourmandise, 282
  peach crumb pie, 278
  pumpkin pie, 289
  pumpkin tart, 288
  red currant meringue pie, 291
  strawberry rhubarb pie, 279
  strawberry tart, 287
  tarte au sucre, 286
  tarte tatin, 284
Pink Peppercorn Raspberry Sauce, 118
Pintadeau à la Bière de Framboise, 160
Pintadeau à la Moutarde, 159
Pizza Crust, 149
Plum and Almond Cobbler, 295

Poached Ray with Brunoise of Potatoes and Tomatoes, 10
Popovers, 243
Poppy Seed Bread, 238
Poppy Seed Dressing, 79
Pork:
  about, 181
  country sausage, 264
  fajitas, San Jacinto, 164
  herb and garlic roast, 166
  loin, herbed, with bourbon gravy, 168
  sausage and cheese strata, 264
  and Stilton stroganoff, 167
  tenderloin with mustard sauce, 165
Pork and Stilton Stroganoff, 167
Pork Tenderloin with Mustard Sauce, 165
Potato(es):
  about, 211
  Anna, 210
  au gratin, 209
  with Dijon mustard, 209
  frites, 208
  and leek soup, cream of, 57
  mashed, horseradish, 212
  roasted, rosemary, 212
  salad, French, 85
  salad with caraway, 86
  salade Liègeoise, 84
Potato Salad with Caraway, 86
Potatoes Anna, 210
Potatoes au Gratin, 209
Potatoes with Dijon Mustard, 209
Poultry:
  see also Chicken
  magret de canard à la crème (duck breasts), 161
  magret de canard à l'orange (duck breasts), 161
  petite salade du sud-ouest, 69
  pintadeau à la bière de framboise (guinea hen), 160
  pintadeau à la moutarde (guinea hen), 159
  turkey, and wild rice casserole, 158
  turkey, roast breast of, with corn bread, spinach and pecans, 156
  stock, about, 51
Pound cake, sour cream, 304
Prawns, see Shrimp and Scampi
Proofing Yeast, tips for, 245
Prosciutto:
  about, 19
  arugula salad with avocado, shiitakes and, 71
  asparagus wrapped in, 19
  and mushroom tortellini, 195
  saltimbocca, 171
  shredded Brussels sprouts with, 224
Pumpkin Bread, 233
Pumpkin Pie, 289
Pumpkin Tart, 288

Q

Quiche au Saumon, 270
Quiche(s), Strata(s) and Frittata(s):
  see also Cake(s), savory
  crab quiche, 271
  crab squares, 29
  miniature quiches, variations, 37
  quiche au saumon, 270
  sausage and cheese strata, 264
  tarte Provençale, 268
  tomato and onion quiche, 269
  vegetable frittata, 267

R

Rabbit:
  lapin à la moutarde, 162
Radicchio, about, 95
Raie au Beurre Noisette (skate), 111
Raised Waffles, 261
Raspberry(ies):
  cassis sauce, 290
  chicken, 147
  cream cheese coffee cake, 253
  gâteau aux framboises, 307
  Grand Marnier sauce, 299
  meringue torte, 290
  pink peppercorn sauce, 118
  sauce, 313
Raspberry Cassis Sauce, 290
Raspberry Chicken, 147
Raspberry Cream Cheese Coffee Cake, 253
Raspberry Grand Marnier Sauce, 299
Raspberry Meringue Torte, 290
Raspberry Sauce, 313
Ray, poached, with brunoise of potatoes and tomatoes (skate), 10
Red Currant Jelly, 255
Red Currant Meringue Pie, 291
Red Wine Béarnaise Sauce, 184
Reina Nobile, La, 310
Restaurant Recipes:
  American Women's Club of Brussels (Four Bean Chicken Salad), 73
  American Women's Club of Brussels (Red Currant Meringue Pie), 291
  American Women's Club of Brussels (Salade Liègeoise), 84
  Aux Armes de Bruxelles (Carbonnade de Boeuf à la Gueuze), 177
  Bistrot Du Mail (Foie Gras Poêlé au Vinaigre Balsamique), 22
  Bistrot Du Mail (Tarte au Sucre), 286
  Brasseries Georges, Les (Croquettes aux Crevettes Grises), 24
  Brasseries Georges, Les (Goujonnettes de Filets de Sole aux Jeune Pousses d'Epinards), 107
  Café Camille, Le (Mesclun aux Lardons), 76
  Café Restaurant de l'Ogenblik (Cassolette de Palourdes au Champagne), 138
  Castello Banfi (Pasta with Prawns and Tomato Fondue), 190
  Castello Banfi (Warm Scampi Salad), 70
  Il Carpaccio (Pappardelle Melanzane), 198
  In't Spinnekopke (Pintadeau à la Bière de Framboise), 160
  Jaco's (Scampi and Papaya with Hot Sweet and Sour Sauce), 131
  Maison du Boeuf, La - Hilton Hotel (Vegetable Terrine with Tomato Coulis), 214
  Maison du Cygne, La (Waterzooi de Volaille à la Gantoise), 141
  Olivades, Les (Gâteau aux Framboises), 307
  Patrick Devos Restaurant (Poached Ray with Brunoise of Potatoes and Tomatoes), 10
  Quatre Saisons, Les - Royal Windsor Hotel (Truite de l'Abbé Gourmand), 112
  Restaurant 't Pandreitje (Scallops with Leeks and Truffles), 133
  Restaurant De Pottekijker (Bisque de Poisson et Fruits de Mer), 49
  SaliCorne, La (Gâteau de Langoustines au Parfum de Curry Léger), 13
  Scholteshof (Langoustines au Curry), 18
  Truite d'Argent, La (Homard Braisé et Mousseline de Tomates), 128
  Vallauris (Quiche au Saumon), 270
Rhubarb, strawberry pie, 279
Rhubarb, tip for, 279
Rice and Grain(s):
  golden chicken and spiced wheat salad, 93
  Greek couscous salad, 94
  lemon rice, 207
  rice pilaf, 204
  risotto with dried wild mushrooms, 203
  risotto with Parmesan cheese, 202
  saffron rice, 205
  spiced rice, 206
  wild rice and turkey casserole, 158
  wild rice with walnuts, 204
Rice Pilaf, 204

Apple Pie to Waterzooi   **341**

Rich Venison and Beef Stew, 163
Risotto with Dried Wild Mushrooms, 203
Risotto with Parmesan Cheese, 202
Roast Breast of Turkey with Corn Bread, Spinach and Pecans, 156
Roast Garlic Herb Chicken, 143
Roast Guinea Hen with Mustard, 159
Roasted Brussels Sprouts, 225
Roasted Yellow Bell Pepper and Tomato Soup, 54
Rolls, see Biscuit(s) and Roll(s); Muffin(s)
Romano, about, 200
Roquefort, see also Blue Cheese(s)
Roquefort Cheese Puffs, 30
Roquefort Tartlets, 37
Rosemary Roasted Potatoes, 212
Rouille, 49

S

Saffron:
  about, 205
  and mussels with leeks and cream, 136
  rice, 205
  sauce, salmon braids with, 113
  sauce, scallops in, 134
Saffron Rice, 205
Salad(s):
  see section listing, 68
Salad Dressing(s):
  apple honey mustard vinaigrette, 77
  basic vinaigrette, 99
  blue cheese, 101
  Caesar, 100
  creamy dill, 88
  herbed vinaigrette, 99
  lemon leek, 78
  mayonnaise, 102
  oriental, 72
  poppy seed, 79
  sweet and sour, 100
Salad Greens, about, 94-95
Salade de blé, about, 95
Salade Liègeoise, 84
Salade Niçoise, 96
Sally Lunn, 250
Salmon:
  braids with saffron sauce, 113
  croquettes, 117
  ginger, 120
  marinated smoked, endive boats with, 27
  phyllo flowers, 35
  with pink peppercorn raspberry sauce, 118
  quiche au saumon, 270
  scallops, about, 119
  smoked, and chèvre canapés, 31

with sorrel sauce, 119
steaks, grilled, 121
Wellington, 114
whole poached, 116
Salmon Braids with Saffron Sauce, 113
Salmon Croquettes, 117
Salmon, scallops, about, 119
Salmon Wellington, 114
Salmon with Pink Peppercorn Raspberry Sauce, 118
Salmon with Sorrel Sauce, 119
Saltimbocca, 171
San Jacinto Pork Fajitas, 164
Sandwiches, tea, ideas for, 39
Sauce(s):
  see also, Sauce(s), sweet
  armoricaine, 189
  aubergine (eggplant), 199
  BBQ, spicy, 186
  béarnaise au vin rouge, 184
  béchamel, 152
  cold cucumber, 117
  creamy seafood, 115
  Madeira, 155
  mango, 124
  mousseline, 21
  mousseline de tomates, 128
  mustard, 122
  parsley, 16
  pesto, 201
  pink peppercorn raspberry, 118
  rouille, 49
  saffron, 113
  shashlik, 186
  sorrel, 119
  tomato coulis, 214
  tomato fondue, 190
Sauce(s), sweet:
  caramel, 283
  chocolate, 322
  lemon, 234
  pecan toffee, with sticky toffee puddings, 257
  raspberry, 313
  raspberry cassis, 290
  raspberry Grand Marnier, 299
Sausage and Cheese Strata, 264
Sausage, country, 264
Sautéed Sea Scallops with Creamed Endives, 135
Scallion brushes, how to make, 89
Scallops:
  about, 193
  coquilles Saint-Jacques à l'effilochée d'endives, 135
  in saffron sauce, 134
  pasta, with bacon and, 193
  with leeks and truffles, 133
Scallops in Saffron Sauce, 134

Scallops with Leeks and Truffles, 133
Scampi, see Shrimp and Scampi
Scampi and Papaya with Hot Sweet and Sour Sauce, 131
Scampi and Tagliolini with Armoricaine Sauce, 189
Scampi, warm, salad, 70
Scones, English cream, 248
Seafood:
  see section listing, 104
  see also Fish; Shellfish; and names of individual fish and shellfish
Seafood, creamy sauce, 115
Seafood Crêpes, 125
Sesame Broccoli Oriental, 222
Sesame Noodle Salad, 89
Shallot(s):
  about, 228
  échalotes au vin rouge, 228
Shashlik Sauce, 186
Shellfish:
  see also Fish; Mussels; Scallops; Shrimp and Scampi; and names of individual shellfish
  about, 130
  bisque de poisson et fruits de mer, 49
  cassolette de palourdes au champagne (clams), 138
  crab quiche, 271
  crab squares, 29
  crêpes aux fruits de mer, 125
  gâteau de langoustines au parfum de curry léger, 13
  homard braisé et mousseline de tomates (lobster), 128
  langoustines au curry, 18
  linguine with white clam sauce, 192
  scallops in saffron sauce, 134
  scallops with leeks and truffles, 133
Shirred Eggs, 262
Shredded Brussels Sprouts with Prosciutto, 224
Shrimp and Scampi:
  Brazilian shrimp and coconut soup, 56
  cashew, shrimp and pea salad, 88
  croquettes aux crevettes grises, 24
  garlic shrimp, 17
  ginger prawn tarts, 25
  pasta with prawns and tomato fondue, 190
  pasta with shrimp and asparagus, 191
  scampi and papaya with hot sweet and sour sauce, 131
  scampi and tagliolini with armoricaine sauce, 189
  shells, uses for, 132
  shrimp, buying, tip for, 39
  shrimp, cleaning, tips for, 17
  shrimp étouffée, 129

shrimp on the bar-b, 132
shrimp spread, 39
warm scampi salad, 70
Shrimp Etouffée, 129
Shrimp on the Bar-B, 132
Shrimp Spread, 39
Skate, *see* Fish
Smoked Chicken and Gorgonzola in
  Endive Spears, 26
Smoked Fish Terrine, 9
Smoked Salmon and Chèvre Canapés, 31
Smoked Trout Pâté, 38
Snow Pea Salad, 83
Snow peas, spicy cod with, 126
Soft Gingerbread, 234
Sole, cleaning, tip for, 106
Sole, goujonnettes de filet de,
  aux jeunes pousses d'épinards, 107
Sole Meunière, 106
Sorrel, about, 95, 119
Sorrel sauce, salmon with, 119
Sorrel, with eel and spinach, 110
Soufflé(s):
  apricot, 297
  cheese, 263
  cold lemon, 298
  making ahead, tip for, 263
Soupe à l'Oignon Gratinée, 60
Soup(s):
  see section listing, 46
Sour cream, about, 303
Sour Cream Pound Cake, 304
Soured milk, about, 249
Southwest Pasta, 201
Spaghetti with Aubergine Sauce
  (eggplant), 199
Spaghettini with Fresh Basil and
  Tomato Sauce, 194
Spanakopeta, 34
Speculoos, 319
Spiced Rice, 206
Spicy BBQ Sauce, 186
Spicy Cod with Snow Peas, 126
Spinach:
  about, 95
  gâteau de crêpes à la Florentine, 11
  goujonettes de filets de sole aux
    jeunes pousses d'épinards, 107
  hot, cheesecake, 266
  salad with chutney dressing, 80
  salad with warm dressing, 81
  spanakopeta, 34
  stuffed pasta shells Alfredo, 197
  turkey, roast breast of, with corn
    bread, pecans and, 156
Spinach Salad with Chutney Dressing, 80
Spinach Salad with Warm Dressing, 81
Spinach Stuffed Pasta Shells Alfredo, 197
Spitzbuben, 320

Spreads, *see* Dip(s) and Spread(s)
Spring Carrot Soup, 47
Stew(s):
  beef Burgundy, 179
  blanquette d'agneau (lamb), 170
  blanquette de veau (veal), 170
  carbonnade de boeuf à la gueuze
    (beef), 177
  carbonnades Flamandes (beef), 178
  rich venison and beef, 163
  stroganoff, pork and Stilton, 167
  waterzooi de lotte (monkfish), 105
  waterzooi de volaille à la Gantoise
    (chicken), 141
Sticky Buns, 247
Sticky Toffee Puddings with Pecan
  Toffee Sauce, 257
Stock(s) and Broth(s):
  about, 50-51
  clarifying, tip for, 40
  fish stock, 51
  langoustine stock, 13
  meat stock, 50
  poultry stock, 51
  shrimp shells, broth from, 132
  vegetable broth, 51
Stratas, *see* Quiche(s), Strata(s)
  and Frittata(s)
Strawberry Rhubarb Pie, 279
Strawberry Tart, 287
Stuffed Leg of Lamb in Puff Pastry, 176
Stuffing:
  corn bread, spinach and pecans, 156
Sugar, about, 315
Sugar Cookies, 316
Summer Fruit Compote, 313
Summer Tomato Soup Mozzarella, 48
Sunshine Glazed Carrots, 219
Super Guacamole, 43
Sweet and Sour Dressing, 100
Sweet Roll Dough, 248
Swordfish Brochette, 123

T

Tapenade of Sun-Dried Tomatoes, 44
Tart shells, *see* Pastry and Crust(s)
Tarte Amandine aux Poires et au
  Chocolat, 281
Tarte au Sucre, 286
Tarte Provençale, 268
Tarte Tatin, 284
Tart(s), savory:
  ginger prawn, 25
  herbed tomato, 28
  petite tarte aux herbes potagères, 14
  Roquefort tartlets, 37
Tarts, sweet, *see* Pie(s) and Tart(s)

Tea sandwiches, ideas for, 39
Terrine de Poissons Fumés, 9
Terrine, eggplant and roasted pepper,
  with parsley sauce, 16
Terrine, vegetable, with tomato coulis, 214
Texas Corn Bread, 249
Tiramisu, 304
Tiropita, 34
Tomato(es):
  about, 87
  bruschetta, 27
  coulis, vegetable terrine with, 214
  eggplant and chèvre, 213
  fondue, pasta with prawns and, 190
  herbed tart, 28
  mousseline de tomates,
    homard braisé et, 128
  and onion quiche, 269
  peeling and seeding, about, 48
  Provençal, 87
  and roasted yellow bell pepper, soup, 54
  sauce, spaghettini with fresh basil
    and, 194
  summer mozzarella, soup, 48
  sun-dried, tapenade of, 44
  sun-dried, with Brie, 36
  veal shanks, braised, with white beans
    and, 169
Tomato and Onion Quiche, 269
Tomato fondue, pasta with prawns and, 190
Tomatoes Provençal, 87
Tortellini Pesto Vegetable Soup, 65
Tortes, *see* Cake(s) and Torte(s)
Trout, *see* Fish
Truffles, about, 151
Truffles, and leeks, with scallops, 133
Truffles, chocolate, 321
Truite de l'Abbé Gourmand, 112
Turkey, *see* Poultry
Tuscan Bean and Cabbage Soup, 62

U, V

Ultimate Chocolate Chip Cookies, 315
Vanilla beans, about, 302
Vanilla Sugar, 315
Veal:
  about, 181
  blanquette de veau, 170
  braised shanks, with white beans and
    tomatoes, 169
  chops, lemon braised, 173
  escalope de veau Normande, 172
  Marsala, 173
  piccata, 146
  saltimbocca, 171
  scallops, about, 171
Veal Marsala, 173

Veal Piccata, 146
Vegetable(s):
    see also Asparagus; Bean(s), dried; Bean(s), green; Broccoli; Brussels Sprouts; Cabbage(s); Carrot(s); Cucumber(s); Eggplant; Endive(s), Belgian; Leek(s); Mushroom(s); Pepper(s), bell; Potato(es); Shallot(s); Spinach; Tomato(es); and names of other individual vegetables
    beef soup, winter, 66
    broth, about, 51
    crudités, about, 42
    frittata, 267
    soup, tortellini pesto, 65
    tarte provençale, 268
    terrine with tomato coulis, 214
    zucchini au gratin, 221
Vegetable Frittata, 267
Vegetable shortening, about, 317
Vegetable shortening, yeast baking, tip for, 245
Vegetable Terrine with Tomato Coulis, 214
Venison, about, 158
Venison, beef stew, rich, 163

Vinaigrettes, see Salad Dressing(s)
Vinegar, herbed, 101

W, X, Y, Z

Waffles, see Pancakes and Waffles
Waffles with Pearl Sugar, 324
Walnuts, see Nut(s)
Warm Chèvre with Red Bell Pepper Sauce, 12
Warm Scampi Salad, 70
Waterzooi de Lotte, 105
Waterzooi de Volaille à la Gantoise, 141
White Cabbage, 228
White Chocolate Mousse with Raspberry Grand Marnier Sauce, 299
Whole Poached Salmon, 116
Whole-Wheat Pancakes, 259
Wild Mushrooms on Croutons, 23

Wild Rice and Turkey Casserole, 158
Wild Rice with Walnuts, 204
Winter Vegetable Beef Soup, 66
Yeast, fresh compressed, about, 286
Yeast, proofing, tips for, 245
Zest, tip for, 159
Zucchini au Gratin, 221
Zucchini Bread, 232